How Human Rights Can Build Haiti

How Human Rights Can Build Haiti

*Activists, Lawyers, and
the Grassroots Campaign*

Fran Quigley

Vanderbilt University Press
Nashville

This book is printed on acid-free paper.
Manufactured in the United States of America

Library of Congress Cataloging-in-Publication Data on file
LC control number 2014008050
LC classification number KGS3003.Q85 2014
Dewey class number 342.729408'5—dc23

ISBN 978-0-8265-1993-1 (cloth)
ISBN 978-0-8265-1995-5 (ebook)

For Ellen

Contents

How Human Rights Can Build Haiti

Introduction

We will fight for the rights of poor people;
fight to change this unjust system.
I am not afraid. We say in Haiti,
Viktwa se pou pep la—*the victory*
is for the people. We believe in that.

—MARIO JOSEPH

I t is a hot morning in Port-au-Prince in June 2011, and the temperature has already climbed over ninety degrees Fahrenheit. Behind the office of Bureau des Avocats Internationaux, a human rights law firm known as BAI, two men and one woman sit at a folding table facing a half-dozen cameras and reporters. Just behind the media, a hundred people gather in a tightly packed, sweaty group, watching the press conference.

The three people facing the reporters, and the hundred people watching them, all live in an internally displaced persons (IDP) camp they call Django. Django is in fact just a dusty lot the size of a small city block, packed with shacks, tents, broken-down cars, and all manner of scavenged materials—all serving as improvised shelters. Later that same day, residents will show touring human rights lawyers the temporary toilets that for several months have been "full," as one camp resident says. This is an understatement, as feces have piled up high above the rim of the pits. As the visitors move between shelters, they interrupt a woman squatting between two tents to relieve herself. Another woman sitting outside a tent has an open wound the size of a baseball on her left foot. She swats the air intermittently, trying in vain to keep flies from alighting on the wound's shiny crimson surface. A wide-eyed baby stares out from inside a dark hovel that has as its eastern wall a dirty blanket featuring Disney's Aladdin cartoon character. The structure's ceiling is a sheet of gray plastic marked "USAID." In the narrow passageway between tents, insects swarm over the fetid mix of cloudy water and raw sewage running through shallow ditches.

At the press conference, the camp leaders begin by reading from written statements, describing the camp's problems in formal, almost stilted, language. But eventually they push their scripts aside, and the pace and tone of the delivery ramp up. People in the crowd stir in their seats. Then Gerda Coles, the president of the residents' committee for the Django camp, who has been addressing the reporters, stops in mid-sentence. She tilts her chin upward, raises her head to look past the cameras and microphones, and points to the crowd gathered behind the media. "We women . . . ," she begins loudly in Creole. The crowd instantly replies, "Demand justice!"[1]

A full year and a half after the earthquake that devastated Haiti on January 12, 2010, the residents of Django are still homeless. Worse, they now face eviction from their squalid, cramped quarters in the Delmas district of Port-au-Prince. The mayor of Delmas recently sent armed men through Django marking tents and shacks with red spray-paint, designating them for demolition. Soon, he promised, he would be following up with bulldozers. One of the mayor's men had knocked down a pregnant woman living in the camp, and the injured woman became a rallying point for the camp residents resisting eviction. The mayor said that he was acting at the behest of Haiti's newly elected president, Michel "Sweet Mickey" Martelly, who had vowed to clear such camps. Much of the press conference rhetoric is directed toward Haiti's leader. "We are waiting for the government to produce the housing they have promised so we can relocate," says Coles. "When President Martelly was a candidate and said he was going to move us from the tents, we thought it was going to be to new housing, not to put us out by force."[2]

The residents of Camp Django are not the only Haitians still suffering the effects of the earthquake. Throughout Port-au-Prince, huge piles of chalky-white broken concrete remain in the places where buildings once stood. Nearly every inch of available space in the city is covered with the makeshift shelters of plastic tarp and scraps of wood that serve as uncertain housing for more than half a million people whose homes were destroyed by the quake. Some of the shelters are built on rock and dirt hillsides, where on rainy nights the residents in torn tents try to sleep standing up while the rain pours water and mud over the ground beneath them. Most of those left homeless have squeezed into camps like Django. When it rains on one of these camps, mud oozes into the shelters and water pours down from gaps in the ceilings. A survey taken seven months after the earthquake showed that as many as a third of these camps had not a single toilet, and 40 percent had no access to water.[3] Many of the camp residents are going hungry, and many are sick.

Even so, Haitians living in the camps consider themselves lucky compared to the tens of thousands who were crushed under buildings that collapsed in the quake, including schools, hospitals, and many government headquarters. At many sites throughout the city, it took weeks to extricate the bodies from under the tons of broken concrete. Once the remains were retrieved, workers would sometimes douse the corpses with gasoline and set them on fire in piles next to the street. Many of these small mounds would smolder for days, giving off thin wisps of smoke as pedestrians and cars maneuvered around them.

The tragedy that is Haiti was not caused by an act of God, insists Mario Joseph, a Haitian human rights lawyer and the director of BAI. "We had an earthquake, yes, but far too many people died in this earthquake. And that is because we in Haiti have no respect for the rule of law," he says. Most of those killed in the disaster, Joseph explains, died in the collapse of poorly constructed homes that had been perched on steep, overcrowded hillsides. Haitian building and zoning codes prohibit such development, but the laws were never enforced when Port-au-Prince swelled with people leaving the countryside looking for work in the city.[4] A truism often repeated by seismologists is that earthquakes don't kill people, buildings do—and the buildings crudely thrown together to house Port-au-Prince's poor claimed lives by the thousands. Now, rebuilding is stymied because investors are reluctant to finance construction on land in a country where it is next to impossible to prove legal title. A post-earthquake cholera outbreak fulfilled the worst fears of public health observers who saw the poorest Haitians being unable to exercise their rights to basic social services, including the rights to decent housing, food, and health care. Those rights can be found in article 22 of the Haitian Constitution ("The State recognizes the right of every citizen to decent housing, education, food and social security") as well as article 23 ("The State has the obligation to ensure for all citizens . . . appropriate means to ensure protection, maintenance and restoration of their health"), clearly stated and completely ignored.

The international community responded to the tragedy of the 2010 Haitian earthquake with record-breaking levels of generosity. Foreign governments and other public sector organizations pledged $5.35 billion in aid for Haiti relief and development, joined by private donations estimated at another $4 billion. Half of all US households gave money to Haiti relief efforts. But, even at the time of this writing, more than four years after the earthquake, nearly half of what was pledged for earthquake relief has not been delivered. Of the money that has been delivered, the United Nations (UN) estimates that less than 1 percent of the funding has been delivered through the Haitian government, where the money could help build the state's long-term capacity to provide services. Instead, most of the funds have been delivered to a disjointed and inefficient jumble of non-Haitian non-governmental organizations, too many of which have wasted the money meant to help those in need.[5]

Now, as before the earthquake, Haiti is an epicenter of suffering. Four out of five Haitians are not formally employed, and most children are not in school. The per capita income is less than $2 per day. Two-thirds of Haitians face regular bouts of hunger, and most Haitians do not have access to a clean source of drinking water. Not coincidentally, a late 2010 outbreak of cholera killed eight-thousand-plus people, sickened more than a half-million, and continues to claim victims.

I was a member of the human rights lawyer delegation watching the Django residents' press conference in the summer of 2011, and I tagged along on the camp visit. Afterward, I asked one of the human rights lawyers connected with BAI what he expected the outcome to be in Django. "I don't think this is going to end well," he said.

Six weeks later, Haitian police burst into the camp, forcibly pulled out the residents, and leveled the shelters. The residents scattered, some to the streets, some to other camps, some to sleep in damaged buildings. A US Agency for International Development (USAID) survey conducted at about the same time as the Django eviction estimated that almost a half-million Haitians were living in "red" buildings, so marked because they were at imminent risk of collapse.[6]

The pervasive state of poverty and the gruesome and enduring extent of earthquake damage all could have been avoided, Mario Joseph says, if only Haiti were a nation that followed its laws and required accountability from its leaders. "But we have this problem of impunity," he says.

———

Joseph's observation echoes a Haitian Creole proverb: *Konstitisyon se papye, bayonet se fè*—the Constitution is paper, the bayonet is steel. The saying accurately summarizes Haiti's troubled history of impunity for the powerful and suffering for the poor. But the Haitian and American lawyers and activists profiled in this book are determined to write a new legacy for Haiti. They are confronting the might-makes-right bayonet with dramatic legal claims, daring community-based advocacy, and sweeping international calls for justice.

The leader of this effort is Mario Joseph. Joseph grew up poor and fatherless in rural Haiti before he worked his way through school to become the most respected human rights lawyer in the country. He has earned a string of courtroom victories along with a reputation for passionate arguments and deep identification with Haiti's poor. A companion US effort is led by Brian Concannon, who directs the Boston-based Institute for Justice and Democracy in Haiti (IJDH). As an idealistic young American lawyer, Concannon left a job with the UN to partner with Joseph in grassroots efforts to empower Haiti's disenfranchised poor and bring their oppressors to justice. Together, in 2000, Joseph and Concannon won for their clients the most significant human rights court verdict in Haitian history. Fifty-three military and paramilitary soldiers and officers were convicted of human rights violations in connection with the brutal 1994 massacre in the coastal community of Raboteau, and the court ordered them to pay the victims the equivalent of US$140 million.

Joseph and Concannon did not stop there. Now working from Port-au-Prince (Joseph) and Boston (Concannon), these lawyers have created a unique model of global South–global North partnership that pursues justice for victims of human rights abuses in Haiti. Chapter 1 of this book tells the story of the genesis and development of their unprecedented multi-billion-dollar class-action lawsuit against the UN for triggering the deadly 2010 cholera outbreak in Haiti. It is an ambitious and historic claim that holds the potential to create a landmark precedent of the world's poorest citizens successfully asserting their rights against the world's most powerful institutions. The case could change the way the UN does its work around the globe, as well as bring justice to the half-million-plus cholera victims and trigger the construction of a desperately needed modern water treatment system in Haiti. Chapter 2 describes the lawsuits that Joseph, Concannon, and others are using to spur the prosecution of former Haitian "President for Life" Jean-Claude Duvalier for political repression and financial crimes committed during the stunningly brutal and greedy Duvalier reign. Duvalier's Haitian victims and international human rights activists agree that this prosecution is necessary if Haiti is to reverse its two-century legacy of impunity for the country's wealthy and political elite.

Chapter 3 takes a broad view of the centuries-old argument, steeped in both philosophy and social science, that the rule of law is an essential precursor to economic development and a stable government. The historical record suggests the only way to transform Haiti's legal and political system is through a bottom-up social movement supported by local and international challenges to the status quo. Fortunately, that recipe for reform mirrors the strategy followed by Joseph, Concannon, and their clients and colleagues profiled in this book. Together, these activists represent Haiti's best hope of escaping the cycle of disaster, corruption, and violence that has characterized the country's two-hundred-year history. At the same time, their efforts are creating a template for a new and more effective human rights–focused strategy to turn around failed states and end global poverty.

The subject of Chapter 4 is the historic 2000 Raboteau trial that launched the modern Haitian human rights movement and cemented the partnership between Joseph and Concannon. Chapter 5 tells the tragic story of the lost opportunities in the global response to the devastating 2010 earthquake centered in Port-au-Prince. At the time of this writing, 2014, hundreds of thousands of Haitians remain homeless, much of the donated money has not been spent—especially not in Haiti—and the dollars used have had a fraction of the hoped-for impact. The post-earthquake relief and recovery effort is destined to be seen as an object lesson in the limitations imposed by shortsighted and self-interested approaches to international aid. But this high-profile failure also has the potential to spur the adoption of a different model, one that follows a rights-based approach to aid and development. Such a model can be a vehicle for getting much-needed assistance to the world's poor in a manner that respects their dignity and autonomy, while at the same time building the capacity of their government to provide the services and human rights protection the poor so desperately need.

Chapter 6, entitled "Beyond the Courtroom," outlines how the advocacy of Mario Joseph, Brian Concannon, and their colleagues travels far beyond the traditional human rights lawyer's path of filing lawsuits. A significant portion of this chapter is devoted to BAI's and IJDH's work, along with that of partner organizations, to respond to the epidemic of rapes that occurred in the IDP camps in the post-earthquake chaos. One study shows that a startling 14 percent of families in the camps had a member sexually assaulted in the months after the earthquake.[7] Initially, the police and the prosecutors and the judges in the Haitian justice system responded to this crisis with indifference and even hostility. But Joseph and fellow advocates intervened to help empower victims and their families, badgered police and court officials, created security patrols and know-your-rights training in the camps, pursued prosecutions, and launched an international advocacy campaign through media and official channels. Now, the number of attacks has sharply diminished, and women are more willing to make official complaints. Once-hostile police and court officials are even referring victims to lawyers and other partners for help in pursuing their claims. "Where the rule of law does not exist, you have to build it," Joseph says.

Chapter 7 provides an overview of Haiti's troubled history, with a focus on the significant role that foreign nations, especially the United States, have played in Haiti's struggles. Most Americans believe the United States is a benevolent source of aid and relief flowing to a dysfunctional Haiti. Most Haitians believe the US government, fearful of the example provided by Haiti's birth as a successful slave rebellion and its later development as a collectivist democracy close to US shores, and simultaneously covetous of the natural resources and unregulated labor market in Haiti, has oppressed and sabotaged their country since its inception. Sadly, the Haitian perspective is closer to the truth, as the overview in Chapter 7 explains.

Finally, Chapter 8 makes the case that the efforts of Joseph, Concannon, and other Haitian human rights activists have the potential to transform not just Haiti but the global human rights movement. It is a movement in undeniable need of a boost. The human rights revolution launched in the mid-twentieth century has stalled out, bogged down in a morass of treaties and declarations and constitutions that fail to deliver on their promises of justice and equality. For most people on the planet, including Haitians, the grand assurances of the Universal Declaration of Human Rights of 1948, and the many international agreements and domestic laws created in its wake, have never been fulfilled.

Modern analysts of social movements say that there is a tipping point where political will for the enforcement of human rights is launched—a time and place and event when long-pent-up energy bursts forth to create lasting reform. Joseph and Concannon and a growing number of supporters, including human rights experts interviewed for this book, believe that the tipping point for Haiti can be the grassroots/transnational movement pushing forward the claims of the thousands of Haitian cholera victims. The cholera claims could force the world's most influential organization, the UN, to embrace the rule of law in deed as well as in name. By recognizing the poorest of Haitians as individuals with enforceable rights, the UN can create a global precedent that will have an impact for generations to come.

If successful, Joseph, Concannon, and their colleagues will push Haiti toward recovery from its many natural and unnatural disasters. They are poised to achieve a historic human rights triumph that will serve as a shining example for struggling people across the globe.

1

Kolera and the United Nations

Heading northeast by car from the center of Port-au-Prince, it takes more than an hour to escape the capital's sweaty, traffic-choked streets. I am traveling with a BAI lawyer and an interpreter. We pass piles of smoldering, rotting garbage flanked by vendors selling toilet paper, cooked meals, and secondhand clothes. The vendors have set up in front of concrete buildings whose walls are painted with colorful advertisements for lottery tickets, cell phones, and private elementary schools. Small motorcycles cut in and out of traffic. In front of us, an ancient truck belches clouds of blue-gray exhaust while a half-dozen young men cling to its rear door. Women balancing impossible loads of bottles and food on their heads step around the gray water flowing through the gutter. Checkpoint police carry automatic rifles and wear bulletproof vests under their beige uniforms.

It is a relief when we finally turn left, away from the chaotic main streets outside Croix-des-Bouquets, and are suddenly in the countryside on our way to Mirebalais. We pass a vast brown field that has been cleared for post-earthquake housing, though there are still no signs of actual buildings. Then our car begins climbing *Mon Kabrit*—Goat Mountain.

Our destination is the village of Rivye Kano, where we plan to see several BAI clients. We soon make another turn and are now off the paved road. Our car lurches up and down a pitted dirt and rock path. Sugar cane lines the left side of our route; corn is planted on the right. We pass skinny goats, children in sun-yellow school uniforms, and a younger boy jumping rope. The rope jumper is wearing a blue-and-white checkered shirt and no pants. Harvested corn hangs in enormous bunches from the trees, up high enough so that the rats can't get to it at night. We steer to the right to give room to an older woman riding a donkey. We pass a young man, casually swinging a machete as he walks. Our car fords a stream where another young man, his clothes piled on the bank, fully immerses himself, holding a bar of soap.

The village center of Rivye Kano turns out to be a crossroads where we are directed to pull off and park between a mango tree and a banana tree. The initial greeting party of a half-dozen people quickly swells to fifty or more. Two young men—one wearing a green and white shirt with the printed message "You looked better on MySpace"—each bring out two wooden chairs and place them in the shade of the mango tree. The lawyer, the interpreter, and I are directed to sit in three of the chairs, with the fourth chair facing us. Everyone else stands silently. Then, one at a time, the people of Rivye Kano sit down and tell us about the horror that descended on their community in the fall of 2010.

Andre Paul Joseph goes first. He describes how, in the middle of the night, he was suddenly seized by violent diarrhea followed by vomiting. Then Semans Pierre shares a similar story. One after another the residents of Rivye Kano come forward, and we hear about desperate family members rushing fathers and mothers and children down the mountain to the closest hospital. There, they found a panicky staff already tending to dozens of others in similar distress. It was a massive outbreak of cholera.

The World Health Organization labels cholera "an easily treatable disease." The main remedy is rehydration, often with oral salt solutions and sometimes with intravenous fluids and a course of antibiotics.[1] But treatment works only if it is provided soon after infection, and many here in Rivye Kano did not reach care in time. Saint Claire Vincent watched her mother die at the hospital in Mirebalais. Her body was quickly placed in a bag and taken away to be thrown into a pit with other *kolera* victims. Maudena Zalys and her brother survived cholera infection, but their father did not. "I can't explain the feeling I got when they announced he had died," she tells us. Cholera is not gone from Rivye Kano or the rest of Haiti. The community leader scheduled to welcome us at this meeting had to send his regrets. He was burying his father today, another victim of cholera.[2]

In both its origins and its effects, cholera is a decidedly foul disease. The process starts when feces-contaminated water carries the bacterium *Vibrio cholera*. The resulting infection causes acute watery diarrhea in the afflicted, thereby spreading its pathogen with ruthless, disgusting proficiency. Left untreated, the diarrhea caused by cholera quickly drains the body and can cause death within hours. Extremely virulent, and with a short incubation period of two hours to five days, cholera moves quickly. In scholarly articles and white papers describing the course of cholera in Haiti, academic and scientific terminology invariably gives way to the adjective "explosive." The term is used to describe both the disease outbreak and the debilitating diarrhea suffered by its victims.[3]

Before mid-October 2010, hospital admission records along the valley of the Artibonite River, Haiti's longest river, show a pattern of only occasional treatment of a patient for diarrhea, and those treated were mostly children. Then, on October

18, an agricultural worker fell ill with diarrhea and was dead on arrival at Albert Schweitzer Hospital in Deschapelle. The same night, an adult died of acute diarrhea in Mirebalais Hospital. St. Nicholas Hospital in St. Marc went from zero cases of diarrhea on October 18 to eighteen cases on October 19. The hospital then saw 404 cases on the 20th, with 44 deaths.[4] One witness described the facility as a "horror scene": "I had to fight my way through the gate as a huge crowd of worried relatives stood outside, while others screamed for access as they carried dying relatives into the compound. The courtyard was lined with patients hooked up to intravenous (IV) drips. It had just rained and there were people lying on the ground on soggy sheets, half-soaked with feces."[5]

As one physician put it later, cholera had hit central Haiti "like a bomb."[6] Within the span of a few days, cholera went from a disease that had been off Haiti's radar screen for generations to an infection that killed two thousand people in a month. Hospitals unprepared for the onslaught did not have adequate supplies of rehydration salts and were without "cholera cots"—beds with holes in the middle to allow the volumes of diarrhea to exit from patients unable to control their bowels. Instead, patients defecated in the beds or on the way to toilets, and the floors were often covered in human waste. By October 2013, cholera had killed over 8,600 Haitians and infected over 684,000, a figure that represents nearly one in every fifteen people in the country. To put that into context, that same rate of nearly 7 percent infection in the United States would cause twenty-two million people to be sickened, more than the population of the New York metropolitan area.[7]

Paul Farmer, the physician founder of Haiti-based Partners In Health, describes the country's heightened vulnerability to catastrophe with the medical term "acute on chronic." Farmer refers to the ongoing ("chronic") poverty and infrastructure deficiencies that leave Haitians vulnerable to devastation when struck by sudden ("acute") phenomena like earthquakes, hurricanes, and, in this case, an infectious disease outbreak.[8] A waterborne disease like cholera could hardly have found a more welcoming community than Haiti, where river water is used for bathing, drinking, and washing, and sewage and wastewater treatment facilities simply do not exist. "The Artibonite is not only Haiti's largest river, it is the country's breadbasket, where most people are living off the land farming," said Cate Oswald, Haiti country director for Partners In Health. "They are not just drinking the water, they are using it for their crops, they are bathing in it. And so it is this vicious cycle."[9]

Haiti is home to so many charitable non-governmental organizations that Haitians sometimes wryly refer to their country as the "Republic of NGOs." But it takes government-scale efforts to cover the breadth of systemic water, health, and sanitation reform. It's not as if the government of Haiti hasn't tried: in 2001, Haiti secured a commitment for $146 million in loans for water and sanitation infrastructure from the Inter-American Development Bank (IDB). But the George W. Bush administration expressed its displeasure at the left-leaning policies of Haiti's then-president, Jean-Bertrand Aristide, by blocking the loans. All told, the political maneuvering cost Haiti access to $500 million in loans, and the European Union withheld aid as well, choking off the Aristide government's ability to provide services and stunting the water and sanitation improvement plans.[10] The consensus among public health experts is that, now that cholera has reared its ugly head in Haiti, it is destined to become endemic there.[11]

To the casual observer of this troubled country, an infectious disease outbreak was sad but unsurprising news. Haiti certainly has endured more than its share of public health crises in the past century, from the HIV pandemic that hit Haiti hard in the 1980s to the massive 7.0 earthquake that rocked Port-au-Prince in January 2010. But cholera was not among Haiti's many problems. The country had not reported a single instance of cholera in over a century. What triggered this sudden, deadly onset?

It was not hard to track the path of the infections. The first hospitalized cholera patients lived in Meille (also spelled Meye), a small village near the Rivye Kano community and a few kilometers south of Mirebalais. The villagers consumed water from the Meille Tributary, which flows into the Artibonite. The cholera outbreak then traveled down the Lower Artibonite and spread out into the valley surrounding it. Just a few hundred meters upstream from the homes of those first sickened in Meille sits a UN camp that houses troops serving as part of the UN mission in Haiti, known by its French acronym, MINUSTAH.

Within hours of the outbreak, accusations were directed toward the UN camp. The mayor of Mirebalais, Lochard Laguerre, said that, even before the outbreak, he had complained to the camp commander about the dumping of sewage near the river.[12] Days after cholera-stricken Haitians began flooding into hospitals, Associated Press reporter Jonathan Katz visited the UN camp and observed an overflowing sewage tank, a smell "like a toilet had exploded," and dark, foul-smelling liquid pouring out of a broken pipe toward the river. Katz also saw uncovered waste pits of feces sitting uphill from the river and observed waste from the UN base being transported to the pits by a private contractor. A reporter from Al Jazeera News observed the same fetid scenario that Katz did. Area residents said that, during rainfall, the sewage pits routinely overflowed into the Artibonite tributary below. "Frankly, the place was a sanitation clusterfuck," Katz wrote in a blog later. "The cholera could have come from anywhere there."[13]

Although MINUSTAH had issued a statement the previous day saying there was no reason for concern, Katz saw UN military police at the base testing for cholera. The camp was populated with troops from Nepal, and new contingents of peace-keepers had arrived from Nepal at the Mirebalais camp in three groups between October 9 and October 16. The troops had come from the Katmandu valley, which in the previous two months had reported a surge in cholera.[14]

The UN presence in Haiti is both enduring and vast. MINUSTAH was created by the UN Security Council in April 2004. As of late 2013, over eight thousand uniformed UN personnel were in Haiti. The fiscal year 2014 budget for the mission was nearly $577 million.[15] The UN's global peacekeeping operations received the Nobel Peace Prize in 1988, but its Haitian activities have been mired in a steady flow of controversy. MINUSTAH's 2004 arrival in Haiti came on the heels of the forced exit of President Aristide, still a cause of resentment among the many Haitians who saw the event as a US-supported coup d'état. After arrival, MINUSTAH provided little or no protection to the civilians targeted by the coup government, as evidenced by one Doctors Without Borders hospital alone reporting the treatment of over 2,500 victims of Port-au-Prince gun violence in just sixteen months over 2005 and early 2006.[16]

In fact, MINUSTAH troops were implicated as facilitators to several incidents of political violence. (See the discussion of the Jimmy Charles murder in Chapter 3.) In July 2005, MINUSTAH launched a raid in the poverty-stricken Port-au-Prince community of Cité Soleil, an operation that MINUSTAH claimed targeted armed gangs but critics say actually targeted political opponents of the ruling government. MINUSTAH troops shot over twenty thousand bullets and killed at least five civilians in that raid, while suffering no troop casualties.[17]

Beyond incidents of political violence connected to MINUSTAH, the troops have been implicated in multiple allegations of sexual assault against Haitians. Sexual misconduct with underage girls caused more than one hundred Sri Lankan troops to be sent home in December 2007. In the summer of 2011, a cell phone video was circulated that appeared to show Uruguayan MINUSTAH troops raping an eighteen-year-old Haitian youth. Uruguayan MINUSTAH troops in Port-Salut were also accused of trading their food rations for sexual favors from Haitians. In March 2012, two Pakistani peacekeepers with MINUSTAH were convicted by a Pakistani military court of raping a fourteen-year-old Haitian boy, and sentenced to one year in prison.

Even beyond the sexual scandals and incidents of violence, it is galling to many Haitians that the international community has devoted as much as $800 million per year to a UN presence marked by soldiers with seemingly little to do. The ubiquitous phrase heard in Haiti is "MINUSTAH *se an vakans*"—MINUSTAH is on vacation. With so many unmet needs in their country, most Haitians believe the UN could put its resources to better use. In an August 2011 survey of Port-au-Prince residents, less than a quarter of the respondents agreed with the statement "MINUSTAH's presence is a good thing."[18] In his farewell address to the UN Security Council, then-president René Préval said that MINUSTAH's presence was no longer necessary. "Tanks, armed vehicles and soldiers should have given way to bulldozers, engineers, more police instructors and experts on reforming the judicial and prison systems," Préval said.[19] His successor, Michel Martelly, echoed the sentiments in March 2013, asking the UN to divert some of its billions spent on security to development. "Real insecurity will prevail when you have people who are looking for jobs, people who are looking for food," Martelly said. "Contrary to what is being said Haiti is not insecure. We need to think more about sustainable development than security."[20]

The international community outside Haiti feels differently about MINUSTAH's presence, but apparently the well-being of Haitians is not at the forefront of that analysis. Cables from then-US ambassador to Haiti Janet Sanderson obtained by WikiLeaks contained repeated references to how MINUSTAH's presence protects US interests and the interests of global capital, including a frank admission in a 2008 cable that "a premature departure of MINUSTAH would leave the [Haitian] government . . . vulnerable to . . . resurgent populist and anti-market economy political forces—reversing gains of the last two years."[21]

Mark Weisbrot, the codirector of the Center for Economic and Policy Research, wrote a 2011 column for the UK's *Guardian* labeling the cell phone video of the rape by Uruguayan troops MINUSTAH's "Abu Ghraib moment."[22] Weisbrot echoed Haitians who questioned the purpose of the ongoing UN presence, where troops have played virtually no role in protecting internally displaced persons from unlawful evictions from their camps and have not helped to deter the spike in post-earthquake rapes. In fact, a 2011 report by the HealthRoots student organization at the Harvard School of Public Health documented that most of the unrest the MINUSTAH troops have responded to within Haiti was triggered by acts attributed to the UN troops themselves.[23] "There is no legitimate reason for a military mission of the United Nations in Haiti," Weisbrot wrote. "The country has no civil war, and is not the subject of a peace-keeping or post-conflict agreement. And the fact that UN troops are immune from prosecution or legal action in Haiti encourages abuses."[24]

That immunity from prosecution is guaranteed in Haiti by the Status of Forces Agreement, executed between the UN and the post-Aristide government of Haiti when MINUSTAH was launched in 2004. Similar immunity guarantees are standard operating procedure for UN peacekeepers around the world, but they have fueled resentment and charges of hypocrisy. Allegations of sexual assaults involving UN troops have occurred across the globe, including in Cambodia, Bosnia, and the Democratic Republic of Congo.[25] International human rights experts have long called for the UN to practice what it preaches in terms of accountability for rights abuses. They point out the irony of the world's leading proponent of the rule of law meticulously drafting and enforcing contracts that place it beyond the reach of legal sanctions. Marek Nowicki, the ombudsman for the UN's mission in Kosovo until 2006, called out the organization on this contrast between its rhetoric and its actions. "From a legal point of view Kosovo is the black hole of Europe or like a novel by Kafka. The UN arrives to defend human rights and at the same time deprives people of all legal means to claim these rights."[26]

With so many Haitians already frustrated by MINUSTAH's presence and angry at the UN's seeming indifference to the rights of the Haitian people, it was not hard for them to believe the UN was responsible for the cholera outbreak. Within weeks of the first wave of illness, anti-UN demonstrations broke out in several Haitian towns. Protests near Cap-Haïtien, Haiti's second-largest city, turned violent. Rocks and bottles were thrown, and one demonstrator was shot and killed by a UN peacekeeper. In the town of Hinche, a half-dozen peacekeepers were injured in a clash with protesters.[27] Graffiti referencing Edmond Mulet, the UN's special representative in Haiti, appeared on walls in Port-au-Prince: *Mulet = Kolera*. Meanwhile, the UN continued to deny responsibility. Worse, in the eyes of many Haitians and health-care providers, the organization failed to fully engage in the response to the hundreds of thousands of Haitians falling ill. "Is the UN doing everything they could to stop the epidemic now that it's started?" asked Dr. Evan Lyon of Partners in Health in a 2012 video produced by the New Media Advocacy Project. "They are not. The response has not been up to the problem. If it was, people would not be dying at the rate they are dying."[28] In an interview after the cholera outbreak, IJDH's Brian Concannon pointed out the dissonance created by the UN sending in peacekeepers most Haitians don't want while at the same time not providing the assistance Haitians desperately need: "There's been slow funding for housing. There's been slow funding for cholera treatment. There has not been slow funding for peacekeeping. One-tenth of all UN [global] peacekeepers are in Haiti. Their budget for this year is $800 million. And that's for a country that has not had a war in my lifetime, but does have a cholera epidemic."[29]

Within a few weeks, the angry consensus of the Haitian populace was confirmed by several scientific studies on the origin of the epidemic. The US-based Centers for Disease Control and the Harvard Cholera Group both analyzed the genetic material of the Haitian strains of the *Vibrio cholera* bacterium, and found that all the strains were identical, pointing to a common source. The Haitian strains were a perfect match for the cholera strains previously isolated in Nepal.[30] The Nepalese army's chief medical officer admitted that the screening of the Nepalese troops for cholera before they were deployed to Haiti was conducted only on troops who presented active signs of infection. This practice conformed to UN medical protocols, but those protocols were shockingly deficient, given that cholera is well known to be carried by asymptomatic humans. Also, the screening was last conducted ten days before the troops' departure, even though they were exposed to cholera-endemic areas of Nepal after the screening.[31]

Epidemiologist Renaud Piarroux led a joint French-Haitian investigation team that began researching the origins of the cholera epidemic within weeks of its onset. Writing in the July 2011 issue of the British medical journal *Lancet Infectious Diseases*, Piarroux and colleagues delivered an unequivocal verdict: "There was an exact correlation in time and place between the arrival of a Nepalese battalion from an area experiencing cholera outbreak and the appearance of the first case in Meille a few days after. The remoteness of Meille in central Haiti and the absence of report of other incomers make it unlikely the cholera strain might have been brought any other way. DNA fingerprinting of *V. cholera* isolates in Haiti and genotyping confirm our findings."[32]

UN secretary-general Ban Ki-moon formed an independent panel of four international experts to conduct their own investigation into the source of the outbreak.

The report issued in May 2011 largely echoed the findings of the other investigations. The UN-commissioned report acknowledged that sanitation at the Mirebalais MINUSTAH camp was "haphazard" and created a risk of fecal contamination of the Meille tributary system of the Artibonite and thus the river downstream. It confirmed that the Haitian strain of cholera did not originate in Haiti and was genetically similar to the South Asian strain of cholera. The report also noted the deficiencies in the screening of the Nepalese headed to Haiti and issued strong recommendations that future peacekeepers be better screened or provided a prophylactic dose of antibiotics, and that sanitation systems in peacekeeper camps be significantly upgraded. In conclusion, the UN experts stated, "The evidence overwhelmingly supports the conclusion that the source of the Haiti cholera outbreak was due to contamination of the Meye Tributary of the Artibonite River with a pathogenic strain of the current South Asian type *Vibrio cholera* as a result of human activity."[33]

Case closed? Not according to the UN. The panel also took pains to note that the catastrophic effects of the feces contamination could not have occurred without "simultaneous water and sanitation and health care deficiencies," and that the source of the cholera was no longer relevant to controlling the outbreak. Fair enough, perhaps, but the experts continued to edge away from the logical conclusion of their findings. Saying that the precise country of origin of the Haitian cholera strain is "debatable," the report states, "The Independent Panel concludes that the Haiti cholera outbreak was caused by the confluence of circumstances . . . and was not the fault of, or deliberate action of, a group or individual."[34]

It was as if the UN had carefully laid out the details of an equation, and then argued that it was irresponsible to conclude that the answer to 2 + 2 was 4. The world's great hope for peace, justice, and the rule of law had adopted the character of a 1960s tobacco company executive denying the link between cigarettes and cancer. An anonymous UN official would later admit to the BBC that it was well known that the sanitation conditions at the Mirebalais camp were "deplorable."[35] But the agency's official position dared the cholera victims to prove it. A few months later, the secretary-general's spokesperson, Martin Nesirsky, hid behind the careful language of the panel's report, telling reporters that the evidence is inconclusive as to who bears responsibility.[36] "The scientists say it can't be determined for certainty [*sic*] where it came from," UN assistant secretary-general Anthony Banbury told ABC News. "So we don't know if it was the UN troops or not. That's the bottom line."[37] The UN's head of humanitarian affairs in Haiti told the BBC that it was a waste of time to point fingers of blame.[38]

The brutally apt metaphor was inescapable for Haitians: the international community had just defecated all over them, and was getting a bit annoyed that the Haitians would not shut up about it.

For more than a year after cholera detonated in Haiti, the status quo endured: all the signs pointed toward UN culpability, the UN denied and deflected responsibility for its actions, and Haitians continued to fall ill and die. All the while, Haiti's most formidable human rights lawyers debated whether there was anything they could do about it. For Mario Joseph, the epidemic was personal. His home village of Borel is located in the Artibonite Valley, with the river serving as the Joseph family's source of drinking water, irrigation for rice fields, and countless other daily uses. "When I was a little kid, everyone used to drink that water, use it to water their garden, wash their clothes, and it still is used like that today," he says. "This is why I say that river is our life. It is like our soul." Joseph's seventy-seven-year-old mother still lives in the area, and he makes no effort to hide his anger toward the UN. "It gave me heartbreak to hear that the river is contaminated when my family is living close by and could have caught this sickness. It is an injustice they [the UN] have made to everyone who is living in Artibonite and also to all of Haiti."[39]

Many Haitians agreed. In concert with the many street demonstrations against the UN, a Haitian attorney, performance artist, and blogger pushed forward the argument that the UN should be held accountable. The former Marguerite Laurent, who renamed herself Ezili Dantò after the Haitian warrior goddess whom many credit with inspiring Haiti's first slave revolt in 1791, used her website (*www.ezilidanto.com*) and media interviews to express unfiltered rage about the UN's negligence. Dantò was a longtime critic of the organization's presence in Haiti, having described the UN and NGOs as "poverty pimps living off the blood, gore and suffering. . . . These insects invading Haiti are reprobates, racist and narcissistic."[40] (Dantò has also referred to IJDH and BAI as "carpetbaggers and scalawags" in a critique that argued the organizations did not push the UN hard enough on cholera.)[41] Dantò pointed the finger at the UN within days of the first cholera outbreak and kept up the impassioned criticism. "She is considered to be strident by a lot of people, but in her blog she was very, very persistent about the problem and the lack of accountability," says Ira Kurzban, a Miami immigration attorney who served as Haiti's counsel in the United States during the Aristide administrations, helped form BAI, and now serves as the board president of IJDH. "She kept writing and speaking about it, and I think she reflected the feeling of a lot of people on the ground in Haiti."

While Haitians in the streets demanded justice, Dantò urged Kurzban to pursue a direct lawsuit against the UN. Kurzban tried to recruit law firms to contribute pro bono research about possible legal responses to the epidemic. But he was turned down, even by lawyers who had helped Haitian human rights causes in the past. "Probably because it would have meant taking on the UN," he says. So Kurzban worked with young lawyers in his law firm and with Joseph and Brian Concannon to draft internal memos exploring how to frame an argument that the UN should take responsibility for the deaths and illnesses.

Joseph and Kurzban were ready to plunge ahead, but Concannon resisted the idea. Although he has been known to call the Haitian human rights battle "the mother of all social justice struggles," Concannon also had more prosaic duties. He was responsible for the IJDH budget and staff, both of which were depleted after running a gantlet of post-earthquake litigation and the return of Jean-Claude Duvalier to Haiti. An organization with an annual budget of $750,000 (two-thirds of which goes to support BAI) could not take on a case with the massive scope of the cholera epidemic, Concannon argued. Every day at the BAI offices, more post-earthquake rape victims, Duvalier victims, and internally displaced camp dwellers at risk of eviction were presenting themselves, and Joseph kept agreeing to help them. Concannon admitted to being both admiring of and exasperated by this. "Mario can't say no to people who need help, and with so many opportunities to help people in Haiti, we are chronically overstressed," he said. For months, Concannon held fast to his position that the organizations did not have the time or money to take on cholera litigation, despite Kurzban and Joseph's growing enthusiasm. "I was the one dragging my feet the whole time we talked about it," Concannon admitted. He also thought litigation was unnecessary, as he could not imagine that the UN would not assume responsibility and make things right. It took the May 2011 UN-commissioned report on the outbreak, ducking that responsibility even after acknowledging that all evidence pointed toward UN accountability, to convince Concannon he was wrong.

At a congressional briefing in April 2012, Concannon explained the process of questioning whether lawyers had any business inserting themselves into the middle of a global health crisis:

> When the epidemic first hit, we thought we would sit out. We did not think this was a place for lawyers. We thought this was a place for people to provide medical treatment, to do the public education needed, to do the well-drilling, to stop the immediate harm. We also assumed that in a case where the damage was so great, and the liability so clear, that the UN would take responsibility. I started out in Haiti as a volunteer with the UN, and I understand how a big organization can struggle with accountability issues. But it never occurred to me that the UN would fail to take responsibility for this. . . . Eventually, though, we got tired of looking at our feet when Haitians said, "Who is going to do something about this?"[42]

Kurzban donated $20,000 so BAI and IJDH could start work on the case, a sum they hoped would cover several months of investigation and preparation. Instead, it was drained in a matter of weeks. BAI was deluged with thousands of cholera victims presenting distinct factual claims, medical evidence, and next-of-kin documentation. But now, depleted funds or not, IJDH and BAI were all in. In November 2011, lawyers with BAI delivered over five thousand separate individual claims, plus a summary thirty-seven-page document called "Petition for Relief," to the MINUSTAH base in Tabarre, Haiti. Lawyers with IJDH delivered identical documents to the office of the UN secretary-general in New York. The petitions were filed on behalf of Haitian victims of cholera, some of them the people we spoke to in Rivye Kano. Many of the petitioners did not survive and were represented in the document by their next of kin. One of the dead was the father of twelve children who on October 22, 2010, drank from the canal that irrigates the rice field where he worked each day. Soon after, he felt a sensation in his stomach he described to his family as being "like boiling water." He began to vomit and was in excruciating pain. By the next day, he was dead.

The petition laid the blame for deaths and sicknesses like these on the UN, citing "gross institutional failures," including faulty screening of the Nepalese troops for cholera, the deficient water and sanitation facilities at the Mirebalais camp, and the delay of investigation and corrective action.[43] "UN actions and the UN's failure to act—malfeasance and nonfeasance—are the direct and proximate cause of the cholera-related deaths and serious illnesses in Haiti to date, and of those certain to come," the petition stated.[44] The request was for compensation for the victims—$100,000 for each victim who died and $50,000 for each sickened; the establishment of a countrywide program for clean water, sanitation, and medical treatment; and a public apology. Calling for quick action, the petition noted the UN's need for "moral force" to allow peacekeepers to carry out their mission.[45] It exhorted the UN to honor its legacy and its rhetoric:

> The UN is a unique global leader. It leads in setting human rights standards, in reaffirming the dignity and worth of all people, and in ensuring justice. Today, Petitioners simply ask the UN to live up to the noble ideals it promotes. They ask the UN to be accountable to the Haitian people. In doing so, the UN will encourage other actors to hold themselves accountable to those they have harmed, whether intentionally or accidentally. As the visionary for a just world, the UN must address the claims the Petitioners state herein.[46]

The emotional and factual claims that the cholera victims asserted against the UN were clear enough, but the process by which they would be reviewed was not. The UN's 2004 status of forces agreement with the Haitian government was designed to provide peacekeepers with civil and criminal immunity from claims filed in the Haitian courts. In return, the UN pledged to establish a standing claims commission to receive and review any claims for injury, illness, or death attributable to peacekeepers' actions.[47] No such commission has ever been established in Haiti (or for any other UN mission, despite similar agreements), so the cholera victims had to essentially shove their claims under the noses of the UN officials who had no process to receive them.[48] "Even though the UN promise to create a claims commission had never been fulfilled, we felt that trying to follow the process set out in the agreement put us in the strongest position legally and politically," Kurzban says.

That status of forces agreement calls for the UN to respect the local laws and regulations of Haiti, says Concannon, noting that Haitian law creates a cause of action and remedy for injuries resulting from negligence, including negligent transmission of disease. If the UN fails to establish a commission to hear the cholera victims' claims, Concannon says, it has forfeited its immunity from lawsuits and the petitioners should be allowed to head to court in Haiti or perhaps the United States. "It is actually a very easy case in terms of proof," Concannon says. "We are simply relying on UN facts and UN law to ask the UN to live up to their own ideals. Immunity does not equal impunity."

In its reports and comments on cholera in Haiti, the UN suggests it cannot be held accountable for the outbreak, no matter its origin. The UN argument is that Haiti's deficient water and sanitation system was the true culprit for the epidemic, not the introduction of the cholera bacterium. If a case ever gets to court, it is an argument that is unlikely to hold up well. Most courts follow the iconic tort law "but for" test to determine liability: but for the action of the defendant, the event would not have happened. Clearly, the UN's actions were a necessary precursor for the grievous harm of the cholera epidemic, no matter the problems with Haiti's water system. And the UN was well aware of the risk. Long before the peacekeepers from a region with a cholera outbreak arrived at a UN base with shoddy waste treatment practices, the UN had issued its own reports highlighting the risk of waterborne illnesses in post-earthquake Haiti.[49] "It was like throwing a lighted match into a gasoline-filled room," Dr. Paul S. Keim, a microbial geneticist whose laboratory connected the Haitian and Nepalese cholera strains, told the *New York Times*.[50]

Citing decisions by the International Court of Justice, the European Court of Human Rights, and a Belgian appellate court, the cholera victims' petition filed by BAI and IJDH argues that the victims of UN conduct are entitled to a remedy for the harm caused to them. A 2010 ruling from the Court of Appeal at The Hague also suggests some sort of recourse should be available, as does the Convention on Privileges and Immunities of the United Nations.[51] Yet no tribunal in history has ever heard a case quite like this. "The system [of immunity for peacekeepers] is designed for cases of personal misconduct, but seems ill-suited to respond to a claim at an organization level," says Nicolas LeMay-Hebert, a researcher at the University of Birmingham in the UK who studies UN peacekeeping operations. "The cholera victims' claim is a precedent, both in terms of its size and its scope, which presents a particularly difficult challenge for the UN," LeMay-Hebert wrote in an e-mail response to questions about the case:

> MINUSTAH often refers to the cholera outbreak as the product of a "perfect
> storm"—meaning all the conditions had to be there for such an outbreak
> (temperature of the water, insalubrity of the Nepalese camp, sanitary conditions
> in Haiti, so on). Now, this cholera victims' claim is also a massive storm for the
> United Nations itself. Some people realize the scope and nature of the issue and
> would like to address the root causes of the problems, while others would like to
> avoid taking any measures and "let the storm roll by." This is not solely a legal
> issue, as it goes directly to the heart of the mission, its nature, legitimization,
> relation with the local population, and accountability system.[52]

Indeed, critics of the UN presence in Haiti have already pointed out that MINUSTAH's budget is many times larger than the UN expenditures in response to the cholera epidemic.

Mario Joseph agrees with LeMay-Hebert that the UN's reaction will affect the organization's legitimacy in Haiti and beyond. "This case is important because it calls for the United Nations to uphold the principles they promote, especially the most basic human rights of life, health, and justice," he says. "There is a lot of hypocrisy going on. People with the UN talk a lot about human rights, but then they turn around and don't respect the rights of Haitians. The UN needs to stop denying its crime." On the sixty-third anniversary of the signing of the Universal Declaration of Human Rights in early December 2011, Joseph joined some of the cholera victims who staged a demonstration in front of MINUSTAH headquarters in the St. Marc region, which was particularly hard-hit by the epidemic. Their signs read, "'Universal' Means Haitians, Too."

At least one legal observer opined that the UN was unlikely to voluntarily recognize that principle, at least within the context of the cholera victims' complaints. "A finding in favor of the petitioners in the BAI/IJDH complaint would require the U.N. to commit to paying billions of dollars in victim payouts and public health infrastructure costs," wrote J. P. Shuster of the Georgetown University Law Center's O'Neill Institute for Global Health Law. "Moreover, it would require the U.N. to immeasurably tarnish its own image as a leader for the protection of global health by admitting to criminal negligence and causing the deaths of more than 7,000 citizens of an impoverished country it was entrusted to protect. An expectation that the U.N. will generate such a finding by its own volition borders on the illogical."[53]

In February 2013, the UN proved Shuster prophetic. Secretary-General Ban Ki-moon issued a statement saying that the claims filed by IJDH and BAI were "not receivable." The statement did not reference the failure of the UN to abide by its agreement to set up a mechanism for receiving claims for damages, but did claim that "consideration of these claims would necessarily include a review of political and policy matters."[54]

IJDH and BAI quickly responded, saying the UN refusal to hear the claims contradicts its own formalized promises. The secretary-general cited section 29 of the UN immunities convention in its rejection, but that very section states that the UN "shall make provisions for appropriate modes of settlement" of claims against it. "This means that the UN commits to providing justice through internal mechanisms," Concannon said. He continued:

> In rejecting the cholera claims, the UN did not invoke diplomatic immunity, but rather refused to uphold its commitment to provide alternative justice.
>   The UN claims that this case is an exception because it requires examination of UN policies. How can the wrongful acts alleged—for example, pumping

untreated sewage into Haiti's largest river system for days, probably weeks—be a matter of UN policy? Defining this as policy creates an exception so broad that section 29 becomes meaningless. In doing so, the UN is putting itself above its own laws and the very principles that it was created to promote.[55]

The ruling triggered criticism from others as well. The *Economist* wrote that the UN was engaged in a double standard, calling for justice for Jean-Claude Duvalier in Haiti while ducking its own responsibility for thousands of deaths.[56] Former Jamaican prime minister P. J. Patterson called the claim of immunity "simply appalling, a most reprehensible behaviour."[57] Louise Ivers, a senior policy advisor for Partners in Health, wrote a column in the *New York Times*, saying, "Regardless of the merits of this argument, the United Nations has a moral, if not legal, obligation to help solve a crisis it inadvertently helped start."[58] A statement issued by the Haitian Kolektif Mobililizasyon Pou Dedomaje Viktim Kolera Yo (The Collective to Mobilise for Reparations for Cholera Victims) after the ruling said, in part, "What moral right does the UN now have to speak about human rights or democracy in Haiti or anywhere else?"[59]

IJDH and BAI said that the ruling left them with no choice but to prepare for litigation. In May 2013, the groups announced they were making a last request for a mediated settlement. If no agreement could be reached, they planned to file claims against the UN on behalf of all the cholera victims, and include in that lawsuit a request for damages that could total more than $30 billion. They braced themselves for a fight over whether a court can hear such claims against the UN. "The case itself is easy; their liability is so obvious if we just can get it into a courtroom," Concannon says. The UN did not respond to these final pre-litigation entreaties, so the class action lawsuit was filed against the UN in the US District Court for the Southern District of New York in October 2013. The complaint asks the court to order the UN to provide the water and sanitation infrastructure necessary to stop cholera, compensate the victims, and issue an apology to the Haitian people.[60]

———

As they push for a settlement or court ruling, IJDH and BAI continue to try their case in the court of public opinion. On an April afternoon after the original petition had been filed with the UN, Concannon jumped off a train in Penn Station in New York City. Concannon's day had started in Washington, where he had spoken at the congressional briefing on Haiti the afternoon before. It was an audience of earnest government aides, NGO staffers, and a handful of members of Congress, and the Georgetown-educated and Boston-raised Concannon is at his best with crowds like these. He leaned forward and talked rapidly and forcefully, explaining complex legal terms in direct language. He distributed copies of media coverage of the cholera claims. His marquee exhibit was a recent Sunday *New York Times* page 1 article describing in great detail the horrors of the Haitian cholera epidemic, including a reference to the pending legal claims against the UN.[61] Concannon told the Capitol Hill crowd about being asked if a lawsuit would have been filed if a private company was responsible for the outbreak instead of the UN. "There would never be any claim needing to be filed in the first place," Concannon said. "Only an organization that has no fear of the consequences would have been as reckless as the UN was in Haiti. A private company, regardless of their conscience, would have been concerned enough about being sued that they never would have sent cholera-infected people to a place they knew was a big risk for cholera, and they would have made sure their waste was disposed of in a way that did not create such huge harm."

By the time I caught up with him the day after his Washington appearance, Concannon had already made a morning stop in Philadelphia, where he delivered a speech to students at the University of Pennsylvania Law School. He then took another train to New York, rushing to meet with an international lawyer on the staff of a member state's mission to the UN. Concannon wheeled his suitcase into a hotel lobby, and he and the international lawyer found facing chairs. Concannon began his pitch. The case once thought quixotic was gaining momentum, he insisted.

He described how the cholera claims and the evidence of UN culpability had generated international media coverage, and how IJDH provided reporters with background information and widely posted and tweeted every article and broadcast. "We thought we may get a spike of media interest in the case after we filed, but it has been steady coverage ever since," Concannon told the lawyer. There is some momentum building, he said. France issued a statement at a UN Security Council meeting about the cholera outbreak and the resulting damage to the UN's reputation, saying, "We can regret it, but we cannot ignore it." Pakistan's representative to the Security Council called for a UN apology, adding that the UN must do "whatever is necessary to making this situation right."[62] Bill Clinton, former US president and now the UN special envoy to Haiti, had admitted to reporters that UN peacekeepers were the "proximate cause" of the cholera epidemic, echoing the same legal responsibility language as the IJDH petition.[63] After a visit to Haiti by the UN Security Council was dogged by Haitians protesting on behalf of cholera victims, US ambassador to the UN Susan Rice publicly called for accountability for the cholera epidemic.[64] Members of the US House of Representatives have demanded that the UN take responsibility for the introduction of cholera and the creation of a safe water system for Haiti.[65] Michel Forst, the UN independent expert on human rights in Haiti, included in a formal April 2012 report a denunciation of his organization's response to the outbreak and investigations into its cause. "The Independent Expert has neither the authority nor the mandate to offer an opinion on the origin of the disease," Forst wrote. "However, he wishes to point out that silence or denial will do nothing to promote a good understanding of the activities of MINUSTAH in a context marked by several distressing episodes of sexual assault in which MINUSTAH military personnel have allegedly been implicated."[66]

"There is no doubt that Clinton's admission and Rice's admonition owe as much to public as to political pressure," wrote the Haiti Support Group in their April 2012 newsletter, dissecting the details of the multinational movement on behalf of the cholera victims. "Every tool in the box has been applied, from mass demonstrations to lawsuits, from email deluges to conferences. Similarly, every possible agent has been recruited, from lawyers to epidemiologists, microbiologists to health promoters, diplomats to grassroots activists."[67] A few weeks after Concannon's New York visit, an article in the *Economist* and an editorial in the *New York Times* referred to the claims filed by IJDH and strongly condemned the UN's response.[68] The *Times* editorial concluded, "The UN and the international community have a responsibility to meet the crisis head-on. There are pledges to fulfill, dollars to deliver and lives to save."[69]

In the hotel lobby, the lawyer agreed with Concannon when he asserted that the UN is embarrassed by the continuing discussion of its failures. Concannon relayed some back-channel rumblings that the UN may be willing to settle the cholera claims, probably by committing to a large safe water and sanitation program in Haiti. Two months after the cholera claims were filed, several UN agencies, including the World Health Organization and UNICEF, announced an ambitious plan to address cholera through investments in water and sanitation.[70] In late 2012, UN secretary-general Ban Ki-moon said that the plan would cost $2.2 billion, but that most of the funding was not in place.[71] Providing clean drinking water to all of Haiti, Concannon pointed out, could be done at the cost of just a couple of years of MINUSTAH's annual budget in Haiti, most recently set at just under $600 million. "This [dumping of sewage and failure to screen peacekeepers] is the kind of thing the UN would only do if they think no one is watching them," Concannon told the lawyer. "We keep hearing from people around Haiti saying the UN dumped untreated waste into their streams, too."

The lobby was crowded and loud, but the lawyer leaned in to hear Concannon's briefing. She nodded regularly and was clearly in sympathy with the cause. But she was also well aware of the daunting legal hurdles standing between the cholera victims and any reparations from the UN. She asked if any court in the world has ever found the UN liable for peacekeeper actions before. She and Concannon both knew the answer. "No, and we realize this is a long shot," Concannon said. He quickly added to his pitch, however, that "if there was ever a case where the court should extend the law, this would be it, because of the massive harm caused by some very obvious negligence on the UN's part." The lawyer did not look convinced. But she agreed to call a few contacts with connections at the UN to see if they could press the case within the organization.

The lawyer left, and Concannon exhaled and let himself sink back into the lobby chair. When he completed his business in New York, he would head back to his home south of Boston. He was anxious to give his wife, Marcy, some relief in caring for their two-year-old daughter and four-year-old son. Then he would turn around and return to New York two days later to meet with a member of the US delegation to the UN. Concannon's younger child was born on January 25, 2010, two weeks after the Haitian earthquake, and a hectic work-home schedule has been the norm ever since. Sitting in the lobby chair, Concannon rubbed his face in exhaustion and ruefully admitted to gaining thirty pounds after having barely exercised since that eventful first month of 2010. E-mails from Concannon sometimes come in during the wee hours of the morning, and he acknowledges that he usually gets far too little sleep.

He did not mention it to the international lawyer in their conversation, but his biggest concern that day was not the cholera case. Mario Joseph's safety appeared to be in jeopardy. Although it has always been precarious for Joseph to be making the case for human rights in Haiti, particularly ominous storm clouds appeared to be gathering. Two Haitian friends of Joseph's, both critics of the current government, were recently killed in unsolved murders. Former Haitian soldiers had taken over abandoned military camps, armed themselves, and that week stormed Parliament, insisting on being heard. (Former president Aristide, citing the military's history of political violence and a lack of external threat to Haiti, dissolved the country's army in 1994. Current president Martelly has promised to revive it.)[72] Joseph had been advising members of the Haitian Senate who were investigating charges that Martelly has held US citizenship, which could have disqualified him from serving as president. In Haiti, this was risky business. "People have killed to keep the presidency of Haiti before," Concannon said, shaking his head.

Joseph was showing the strain as much as Concannon. Both men were in their late forties, but footage of the Raboteau trial from a dozen years earlier suggests that they had aged more rapidly than one might normally expect.[73] Joseph had been diagnosed with diabetes and high blood pressure. The demands of processing and filing thousands of cholera claims had taxed the BAI staff, and ten thousand more claims were stacked up, waiting to be filed. The stress and poor health sometimes made Joseph testy, and there had been a lot of staff turnover in Haiti lately. In a recent interview, Joseph had acknowledged the toll. "This work is very stressful, and I recognize this because it has affected my health. . . . I do not want to die but I know that the cause I am defending is a good cause. I do not have a problem with this. What I would really like to see is for the situation in Haiti to change. This is what I will regret if I do not have a chance to see this."

Concannon was also worried about money. He talked about reading a treatise on fundraising on his train rides and said that the IJDH and BAI organizations have been operating on the edge financially since the earthquake. One of the significant challenges for BAI and IJDH is that their commitment to honest scrutiny of the US government and the international community cuts them off from most USAID and UN funding that sustains so many international non-governmental organizations. In a later interview, Kurzban, the IJDH board president, agrees that money is tight:

> Given the work we have to do, IJDH is grossly underfunded. It is a huge
> struggle when you rely on private donations and foundation grants, and there is

absolutely no consistency in receiving funds. Then you add in the cholera case. It would be a big undertaking even for a US firm, let alone in Haiti, where you have other obstacles like people spread all over the country and medical records are not very easily accessible.

The sad thing is that, if we had the funds, there is so much more we could do to pursue justice in Haiti. We could hire more Haitian lawyers, we could respond to the problem of the army coming back, we could respond to the crises of human rights and health—remember that the government of Haiti has a legal obligation to provide its people with food, health care, education, and infrastructure. And we can't get to so many of those problems. The goal is to have a hundred Marios doing this work. As it is, it is a tribute to Brian's and Mario's skills that we get as much done as we do now.

The chief reason for Concannon's trip to New York was, of all things, a movie premiere. Two American aid workers in Haiti, David Darg and Bryn Mooser, codirected a documentary called *Baseball in the Time of Cholera*, which was to be screened at the Tribeca Film Festival. Darg and Mooser had befriended several boys in post-earthquake Port-au-Prince and decided to teach them the game of baseball. (Ironically, Haiti was once the largest manufacturer of baseballs, but they were solely assembly-line products for richer countries, not toys for Haitian children. The game never caught on in Haiti as it did in other countries, such as the Dominican Republic, which endured similar periods of US military occupation. Some researchers have speculated that Haitians actively resisted playing baseball as a conscious rejection of their occupiers' culture.)[74]

Darg and Mooser purchased some bats and balls and gloves, and the boys formed Haiti's first little league team, the Tabarre Tigers. The two men began filming what they thought would be a sweet story about the fledgling ballplayers. The team's young captain, Joseph Alvyns, one of many Haitians whose family home was destroyed in the earthquake, was an engaging personality who spoke excellent English. After Alvyns gave some TV interviews about the new team, he was invited to travel to Toronto, Canada, and throw out the first pitch for a Toronto Blue Jays major league baseball game. "Seeing him take the field was the proudest moment of our lives," Darg and Mooser wrote later. "From a tent camp to the top of the world."[75] But three weeks after Alvyns returned from Toronto, his mother suddenly fell ill with cholera and died. The boy was devastated. For Darg and Mooser, their day jobs responding to the cholera epidemic had spilled over into their lighthearted film project. Mirroring life in Haiti, their moviemaking took a dark turn, and the documentary now involved the cholera victim cases pressed by IJDH and BAI.

To IJDH, the movie premiere presented an excellent opportunity to reach a crowd that would include delegates to the UN and current and potential donors to the human rights work in Haiti. Two hours before the film was to be shown, Concannon gathered a half-dozen IJDH staffers and volunteers to prepare stacks of cholera case material for distribution. The handouts included an article about the film by Darg and Mooser, published on the *Wall Street Journal* website, and a similar *Huffington Post* column by actress Olivia Wilde, who coproduced the movie with Elon Musk, founder of PayPal and Tesla Motors. The pieces were blunt and powerful. Wilde wrote about watching a little Haitian girl wail in fear and pain as she lay dying from cholera. The actress compared the UN's actions in Haiti to tossing a lit cigarette while pumping gas. "To put it simply, they [the UN] allegedly let their contaminated shit run into the water source for the entire nation," she wrote.[76]

Darg and Mooser were just as accusatory, concluding that "only the United Nations has the power and resources to finally put an end to the crisis."[77] (Darg would later say that the legal claim against the UN was a long shot, "but it is such an important shot!") As the IJDH staff stuffed the articles into blue and yellow folders, Concannon cautioned them about mimicking the tone of the filmmakers' rhetoric. "David and Bryn are angry, and understandably so—their friend's mother died for no good reason," he says. "But a lot of the people there tonight are going to be sympathetic to the UN. So we need to emphasize that we are not interested in attacking the UN; we are just asking it to live up to its values."

The theater had an actual red carpet in front, and multiple photographers lined up celebrities for shots. Wilde attended the premiere, as did actor Ben Stiller. Several IJDH staffers were given invitations to an exclusive after-party at a Manhattan nightclub, complete with champagne, temple-throbbing music, and plenty of models and actors. It was a fleeting taste of the high life, followed quickly by a return to the reality of travel on the budget of human rights advocates. After the party, the staff walked past Manhattan hotels to catch a subway heading to the home of Concannon's sister in Brooklyn. The glut of human rights boarders there left Concannon demoted both from the spare bedroom and his sister's extra futon. He would sleep that night on a couch about five feet long.

In the half-hour-long movie, Joseph Alvyns charms the camera in the early scenes. He joyfully plays baseball with his friends, introduces his family, and even writes "I love my life" on the plywood exterior of their temporary post-earthquake home. Ominously, though, footage of the deadly chaos after the cholera outbreak is interspersed with the scenes of the smiling Alvyns. We see dead bodies and panicky scrambles for small pouches of water being handed out from the back of a pickup truck. Concannon is shown talking on a TV news show, saying, "We hope this is the case that is too big to fail—that the evidence against the United Nations is so overwhelming that the UN would have no choice but to finally take responsibility for its malfeasance." Mario Joseph is shown walking over the bridge of the infected Artibonite River. He crosses paths with a man whose father died from cholera—the man would like to add his father's name to the pending complaints against the UN. Joseph's voice plays over a still photo of a UN truck dumping foul-looking liquid into a stream. "They call them peacekeepers, but they do not bring peace to Haiti. They only bring cholera," Joseph says. "They need to say it is our fault, and let's help the Haitian government to eradicate the cholera. But they continue to deny, and the disease continues to spread."

The film shows a touching phone conversation between Joseph Alvyns and his mother during his Toronto visit. She urges the boy to put on a jacket to ward off the very non-Haitian fall chill of Canada. But that scene is quickly followed by the revelation to the audience that, soon after the boy's return home, his mother fell ill and died. A family video of the funeral is shown, and Alvyns is filmed at the gravesite a few weeks later, shedding tears. "She worked very hard for us," he says. "She will stay in our hearts forever."

The film closes with an audio of Mario Joseph delivering a stirring speech while walking across a field. Slowly, it becomes clear that Joseph is walking toward where the boys play baseball. Joseph Alvyns, transformed from a baseball-playing boy into a saddened young man on the verge of adulthood, walks over to Mario Joseph and the two shake hands. "I am walking around the country in the poor areas and looking for people who have been infected or killed, or who have the disease of cholera," Joseph says over the video. "I'll keep walking until I find the last victims of cholera."

At the Tribeca premiere, the sniffles of crying people could be heard throughout the final ten minutes of the film. The crowd loudly applauded the credits, and later gave a separate ovation for Joseph and Concannon. For the team trying to bring justice for the Alvyns family and thousands of other cholera victims, the night could not have gone better. Except for one thing. Concannon admitted that when he saw the scene of Joseph welcoming the man by the Artibonite to join in the cholera case, he could not help but think, "God no, we already have ten thousand complaints waiting to get filed!"

Given the scope of the tragic loss, and the advocates' insistence on keeping the UN's culpability in the public eye, IJDH and BAI see reason to hope for a voluntary assumption of responsibility by the UN, even if litigation has to spur it to happen. After all, the agency is the world's chief source of rhetoric about the rule of law, and its leaders know well Haiti's notorious and ongoing history of impunity for the powerful. A brutal former dictator walks the streets of Port-au-Prince without yet facing trial or imprisonment, a state of affairs the UN has criticized. The current president was elected only after the most popular political party was blocked from the polls. The country's legacy of violent military coups and political assassinations is well documented.

To the advocates and the victims, it seems the UN has a choice to make: Will it become the latest *gwo neg*—Creole for "big man"—to hold itself above the law in Haiti? Or will it acknowledge a duty to remedy this latest disaster in a country whose people have already suffered so much? If the UN is seeking an exit strategy for its rocky fourteen-year presence in Haiti, it could do worse than establishing a precedent of accountability to the rule of law, clearing the path to the peace and transparency that was always MINUSTAH's stated goal.

2

"Judge Him"

Pursuing Duvalier

Myrtha Jean-Baptiste was thirteen years old the first time Jean-Claude Duvalier's army arrested her. In August 1979, members of a civilian secret police force called the Service Detectif burst into Jean-Baptiste's family home in the Port-au-Prince neighborhood of Fort National. The men seized her, along with her mother, her sister, her three brothers, and a brother-in-law.

The family crime was membership in the Haitian Christian Democrat Party opposing Jean-Claude Duvalier, then the president of Haiti. The Service Detectif, based in the Casernes Dessalines barracks on the grounds of Haiti's presidential palace, was responsible for enforcing Haiti's expansive laws against political offenses—laws that carried penalties up to and including execution. The Christian Democrats' leader, Silvio Claude, was arrested the same year as Jean-Baptiste's family. Duvalier's men kept Claude in prison and incommunicado for two years, torturing him by administering electric shocks to his feet.[1]

After her 1979 arrest, the teenage Jean-Baptiste was interrogated and released, but the rest of her family stayed behind bars. Her older brothers were held for over two years without ever going to court, and they were beaten and tortured by army jailers until the young men bled from their ears. "When they came back, their bodies were broken," Jean-Baptiste says. The brothers both died within a few months after their release from prison. Jean-Baptiste herself was arrested again two years later and brought to the National Penitentiary, where she was held—also without trial—for one year and twenty-one days.

Today, over thirty years after her first arrest, Jean-Baptiste sits in an office at BAI, recounting her painful memories from the era. Now a striking woman of forty-five, she has high cheekbones and wears a white lace blouse, but she is unsmiling and declines to be photographed. On January 16, 2011, when Jean-Claude Duvalier suddenly returned to Haiti after a quarter century in exile, Jean-Baptiste's story gained renewed relevance.

The Haitian government responded to Duvalier's return by reopening investigations into the many allegations of financial crimes and human rights violations committed during his tenure. But Duvalier, who was sixty years old when he returned to Haiti, was not put in jail. He was periodically called in for questioning by a Haitian investigating judge, and in February 2013 Duvalier was compelled to testify during an appeals court hearing. In February of 2014, that three-judge appellate court panel ruled that the human rights charges against Duvalier could proceed. The interim decision only set the stage for future investigations and hearings, but it was a tangible display of the notion that international law governing crimes against humanity should apply in Haiti. The decision also generated an unexpected acknowledgement from the opposition that IJDH's and other groups' international advocacy may be having the desired effect on the rule of law in Haiti. Duvalier attorney Fritzo Canton complained to Reuters that the appellate judges' ruling was influenced by "extreme left-wing" international human rights groups.[2]

Yet, during these proceedings, Duvalier continued to visibly enjoy his freedom. He has met with political leaders, been acknowledged on the dais at public events, and dined at expensive Port-au-Prince restaurants. At the Quartier Latin, his favorite meal is reportedly *poulet creole*.[3] Eventually, even the house arrest order was lifted. Most Haitians are too young to remember Duvalier's presidency, but Jean-Baptiste is among many Duvalier-era victims who were stunned to learn that the ousted former "President for Life" had dared to return to Haiti. She is even more shocked to see that he remains a free man, with no trial set as of this writing. "There is only one way to stop him," she says in Creole. "*Jije li.*"

Translation: Judge him.[4]

Stories like Jean-Baptiste's were common during the three decades the Duvalier family ruled Haiti. François "Papa Doc" Duvalier, a physician and an outspoken critic of Haiti's mulatto elite, assumed the presidency in 1957 after an election victory that was boosted by the exile of his chief opponent, the endorsement of the US embassy, and strong-armed military support. Thanks in large part to the Haitian army's exertions, Duvalier achieved vote totals that in some districts exceeded the actual population of the electorate. Well aware that the military that helped him attain office was the same institution that had forced quick removal of previous Haiti presidents who fell out of the military's favor, Duvalier quickly consolidated power by creating his own personal militia, the Volunteers for National Security. This secret police force was better known as the *tontons makouts*, a Creole name that evoked evil bogeymen with sacks to stuff children in.[5]

Duvalier was not just a physician, he was a former newspaper columnist who attributed his political success to having "a pen in one hand and a gun in the other."[6] He assiduously crafted a Vodou- and Christianity-tinged cult of personality, complete with designation from the Haitian Parliament as President for Life. His self-assigned titles included "Uncontestable Leader of the Revolution" and "Apostle of National Unity," and Duvalier promoted the image of himself as the Vodou spirit Baron Samedi. A government newspaper printed a picture of Jesus Christ laying his hand on Duvalier's shoulder, with the caption "I have chosen him." Duvalier created a corresponding national catechism to be taught in Haitian schools. That curriculum appropriated the Lord's Prayer, with a vengeful twist: "Our Doc, who art in the National Palace for life, hallowed be Thy name by present and future generations. Thy will be done in Port-au-Prince as it is in the provinces. Give us this day our new Haiti and forgive not the trespasses of those antipatriots who daily spit on our country, lead them into temptation and, poisoned by their own venom, deliver them from no evil."[7]

Under Duvalier, the number of *tontons makouts* grew to twice the size of the Haitian military. Duvalier employed the *makouts* on the front lines of a campaign of brutal repression, intent on crushing any dissent from total presidential control. In 1959, a senator who criticized Duvalier was arrested and "disappeared," while five other anti-Duvalier senators fled into exile. In 1961, Haitian citizens were ordered to stone to death five activists hoping to overthrow Duvalier. Later challengers to Duvalier's power were executed on live television or had photographs of their severed heads published in the government newspaper.

The legal veneer for broad-based crackdowns was provided by changes to the Haitian constitution that allowed Duvalier to declare a state of siege, and to suspend civil and political rights, whenever he determined "civil disturbances" warranted such a response. Newspapers criticizing Duvalier were shut down, as were unions and civil society organizations—including the Haitian Boy Scouts. Tens of thousands of Haitians were killed by Duvalier forces. In January 1971, a referendum was reported to have passed, with the surreal margin of 2,391,916–0, approving Duvalier's nineteen-year-old son, Jean-Claude, as the successor *president à vie* upon the elder Duvalier's death.[8] Papa Doc died three months later, and "Baby Doc" assumed the presidency.

As the nickname suggests, Jean-Claude Duvalier's youth, his somewhat pudgy visage (his other nickname was "Baskethead"), and his unsophisticated reputation projected neither the intelligence nor the malevolence that characterized his father. So the transition to Baby Doc's rule in Haiti was greeted with international optimism for an improved human rights environment. The younger Duvalier seized the opportunity, seeking to bolster Haiti's image with international aid donors by hiring a US public relations firm. Baby Doc publicly claimed to have dissolved the notorious *tontons makouts*. But the violent reality of dictatorship in Haiti remained much the same. Jean-Claude Duvalier maintained presidential control of the army and the police and retained the *tontons makouts* under a new name, the Militia of National Security Volunteers. Duvalier later praised the militia as "the first line of defense" and "the linchpin of my government, the major force on which I base myself."[9]

Myrtha Jean-Baptiste and her family discovered that Baby Doc was willing to use that force against anyone who dared challenge his control over Haiti. Broadly worded anticommunist legislation enacted in 1969 had the effect of both criminalizing dissent and currying the favor of the United States, all while providing legal cover for pursuing and punishing Duvalier's political opponents. The law prohibited "communist activities, no matter what their form," and perpetrators and accomplices alike were subject to the death penalty for its violation. This legislation was followed by bans on political parties, advance censorship of all publications, and criminal penalties for members of the press who offended the chief of state or the first lady. A campaign of arrest and imprisonment of any Duvalier critics was thus enabled, although it was rare for the Haitian government to bother to formally charge political prisoners with an actual crime.[10]

Several human rights organizations, most notably Human Rights Watch and Amnesty International, have chronicled the wide swath of repression under Jean-Claude Duvalier.[11] Political prisoners by the hundreds were arrested and held incommunicado, many in the notorious three prisons known collectively as the "Triangle of Death"—Casernes Dessalines, Fort Dimanche, and the National Penitentiary. One political prisoner held in the Casernes Dessalines recalls being placed underground in the detention area on the grounds of the National Palace, where Duvalier lived. The prisoner was led to an area so dark he could not see, but a guard's torchlight revealed the man was sitting amid the skeletons of former prisoners. "It was like living a nightmare inside a mass grave under the Palais National," he said.[12]

In Fort Dimanche, cells measuring ten feet square held as many as thirty-three prisoners each, with such limited space that the prisoners had to sleep in shifts. Food and water for the inmates were severely limited. The sanitation conditions were horrific: the bodies of dead prisoners were left in the crowded cells for hours, and dozens of prisoners were forced to share the same plates and drinking cups.[13] During a court hearing on the charges against Jean-Claude Duvalier in early 2013, Haitian agronomist Alix Fils-Aime, who was a Fort Dimanche prisoner in the 1970s, said that most of his fellow prisoners were tortured and killed. "I was able to hear people being beaten, dragged in the hallway, and I could hear women screaming as they were being forced to have sexual relations with the guard," Fils-Aime testified.[14]

These conditions led to a huge prisoner death toll caused not just by physical injuries but also by tuberculosis, dysentery, and other diseases. Many prisoners, like Jean-Baptiste's brothers, were released in such bad shape that they died soon after. Patrick Lemoine, a political prisoner held from 1971 to 1977, told Human Rights Watch that none of this was accidental: "It is important to understand that prisoners did not just die of bad conditions at Fort Dimanche. Rather, prisoners were condemned to Fort Dimanche to slowly die of starvation, disease, or diarrhea."[15] Some prisoner deaths were caused by more explicit action, including summary executions of multiple political prisoners. The Inter-American Commission on Human Rights (IACHR) reported the names of seventeen prisoners summarily executed in Fort Dimanche on two dates in 1974 and 1976, and most of the evidence points to many more such killings. The contrast between Jean-Claude Duvalier's cultivated international persona as a kinder and gentler Haitian leader and the in-country reality was starkly demonstrated on September 21, 1977. On that date, Duvalier grandly announced the release of 104 political prisoners and signed the American Convention on Human Rights. Yet, on the same day, eight other Haitian prisoners reportedly were executed.[16] In 1978, the IACHR informed Jean-Claude Duvalier that the organization had received reports of 151 deaths in Haiti prisons from 1971 to 1974 due to executions or lack of medical care.[17]

Many casualties of the Duvalier era were never accounted for, as political opponents regularly "disappeared," often courtesy of the Duvalier-appointed section chiefs who governed the rural areas of Haiti where the majority of the country's population lived. (BAI lawyer Mario Joseph distinctly remembers the fear and awe inspired by the section chief in the village of Borel, where Joseph grew up.) Most of the violence was directed at would-be political opponents of Duvalier, but the media was also subject to tight control and reprisals for publishing or broadcasting criticism of the government. Independent newspapers and radio stations were regularly shut down, and journalists opposing Duvalier were expelled from the country. The 1980 election of Ronald Reagan as president of the United States triggered raucous and lavish celebrations by Haitian leaders who cheered the end to the Carter administration and its disapproval of Duvalier human rights abuses. Within days, over one hundred Haitian journalists and activists were arrested. The pro-government newspaper later reported that the arrests were a "dismantling of communist agitators."[18] After the newspaper *L'Information* dared to publish an account of 1984 food riots and to describe injustices in the Haitian system, its editor, Pierre Robert Auguste, was arrested, interrogated, and beaten by police, all in the presence of Duvalier's interior minister. A delegation from Americas Watch and the Committee to Protect Journalists visited Haiti later in 1984 and questioned the arrest of Auguste and other journalists. Jacques Noel, Duvalier's state secretary for political affairs, told the visiting journalists that the arrests were justified "because of the need for stability for economic development."[19]

Financial corruption under Jean-Claude Duvalier was breathtaking in its audacity and breadth. In stark contrast to the penurious lives of the majority of Haitians under his rule, the younger Duvalier flaunted his sports cars, his yacht, and his multiple Manhattan residences. His $3 million wedding to Michèle Bennett in 1980 earned Guinness World Records recognition as the most expensive wedding in history. The new Mrs. Duvalier took friends to Paris for multi-million-dollar shopping expeditions.[20] Even while Duvalier was still in power, his finance minister, former World Bank official Marc Bazin, revealed that $15 million per month in public funds was being directed to "extra-budgetary expenses," including regular deposits into Duvalier's private Swiss bank account.[21] Shortly after Duvalier fled into exile, the governor of the Bank of the Republic of Haiti reported that Duvalier had stolen over $120 million from the Haitian treasury, and that his family and government officials had stolen an even larger sum.[22] In 1988, a Miami court issued a $500 million judgment against Duvalier and his wife in a class action lawsuit alleging the Duvaliers plundered the national treasury.[23]

Arguably, it was this greed that proved Jean-Claude Duvalier's undoing. With the steady flow of US and multilateral aid being diverted in significant portions to Duvalier's personal use, desperate poverty among the Haitian people grew, and food riots broke out in the mid-1980s. Duvalier's crackdowns on journalists could not prevent word of widespread hunger in Haiti from leaking out to the international community, where growing disenchantment with the Duvalier kleptocracy jeopardized the flow of aid. In November 1985, Haitian soldiers reacted to an anti-Duvalier student demonstration by killing three youths, triggering massive protests across Haiti. By early 1986, popular uprisings in Haiti were followed by a formal statement of no confidence from the Reagan administration, which until then had been a particularly forgiving Duvalier supporter. The last underpinnings of the two-generation regime had finally been pulled out. Duvalier and his family fled the country in a US cargo plane on February 7, 1986. Joyous and sometimes unruly street celebrations followed, including the destruction of the Duvalier family tomb in Port-au-Prince. The coastal village of Duvalierville quickly restored its original name of Cabaret. The Port-au-Prince neighborhood of Cité Simone, originally named after Jean-Claude Duvalier's mother, was renamed Cité Soleil. It seemed that Haiti had put the Duvalier era in its rear-view mirror.[24]

But almost twenty-five years later, Jean-Claude Duvalier returned to Haiti, reportedly hoping for the backing of President Martelly in the effort to access millions of dollars in those now-frozen Swiss bank accounts.[25] So far, Duvalier's calculations appear to be on the mark. Martelly is on record supporting amnesty for Duvalier, has met publicly and privately with Duvalier, and invited the former president to appear at high-profile events.[26] (For example, Duvalier's internationally condemned record on human rights did not prevent him from being asked to deliver the speech at a late 2011 Haitian law school commencement. Jorge Heine wrote in the *Toronto Star* that the irony of Duvalier congratulating future defenders of the rule of law was "the equivalent of Robert Mugabe [the Zimbabwean dictator known for crushing independent media and arresting journalists] giving the keynote address at a Freedom of the Press Day event.")[27]

Martelly has several former "Duvalierists" in his administration and circle of aides, including the former president's thirty-year-old son, François Nicolas Duvalier. The third-generation Duvalier flavor of the current administration is apparent to Haitians like Myrtha Jean-Baptiste, who points out that Martelly's first prime minister was the son of a Duvalier minister, and that Martelly is even advised by the son of the Duvalier official who was in charge of the police station where Jean-Baptiste was arrested. "It is part of the past," Martelly told the *Washington Post* about prospects for Duvalier's prosecution. "It is time to unite the country, show tolerance, show compassion, show love for everyone."[28]

It is quite understandable that Myrtha Jean-Baptiste wishes to see Duvalier judged for his crimes. But is it legally possible to prosecute Jean-Claude Duvalier? While Duvalier's personal benefits from the financial crimes of his administration are readily demonstrated, his connections to the brutal human rights abuses of his era are not as clear. When "Baby Doc" was in power, his popular image was that of a playboy who enjoyed fancy cars and good times, and left the continuation of his father's legacy of political violence to more experienced hands. As Amy Wilentz wrote in *The Rainy Season*: *Haiti—Then and Now*, "When [Papa Doc] died in 1971, the Makouts remained, and it was never quite clear whether they and their military and political allies were leading Duvalier's son, the new President-for-Life, or whether Jean-Claude was at least partially in charge."[29] The younger Duvalier did not personally arrest Myrtha Jean-Baptiste or torture her brothers. There is no evidence he was present at any of the thousands of other arrests, beatings, and executions that occurred during his presidency.

But the younger Duvalier was the de jure leader of the forces carrying out Haiti's reign of terror—the Constitution named him commander in chief of the armed forces and police—and he exercised significant actual control as well. Following US senator Edward Brooke's 1977 visit to Haiti, during which he met with Duvalier and several other Haitian officials, Brooke reported that Duvalier and a small palace guard held concentrated power over the country.[30] Many of the most heinous acts of imprisonment and torture took place in the Casernes Dessalines, literally under Duvalier's nose on the grounds of the presidential palace. Haitian chief of police Jean Valmé said that Duvalier gave explicit approval for the roundup of journalists in November 1980 after the defeat of US president Jimmy Carter promised less human rights criticism. Duvalier is reported to have personally ordered the arrest and imprisonment of Haitian businessman Lucien Rigaud. Duvalier quite publicly announced his decisions when releasing some political prisoners.[31]

Senator Brooke, US ambassador to the UN Andrew Young, and the IACHR all repeatedly put Duvalier on notice of the atrocities that occurred on his watch.[32] Duvalier told Brooke in 1977 that, with respect to human rights in Haiti, he was aware of "serious problems in this area."[33] More publicly, in an open rally and in an interview with the *New York Times*, Duvalier took responsibility for the November 1980 crackdown on political dissent and independent media. "We were obliged to act for the simple reason most of these people were implicated in a conspiracy against the security of the Government," Duvalier told *Times* reporter Jo Thomas. "Politics is not a matter for children. Sometimes you have to act even if it is against your own feelings."[34] Compounding the evidence of Duvalier's tacit knowledge and approval of repression during his fifteen-year reign, there is no record of commander in chief Jean-Claude Duvalier ever punishing a police officer, soldier, or paramilitary member for committing abuses, much less trying to prevent any of his subordinates from committing the crimes in the first place.

Publicly known facts like these provide a strong foundation for an indictment and trial of Duvalier, and likely would be buttressed by the evidence that a thorough criminal investigation should uncover. When there is evidence that a superior knowingly participated in, verbally encouraged, or failed to punish criminal behavior by subordinates, Haitian law recognizes him or her as an accomplice to the crimes committed. Customary international law has long supported assigning criminal responsibility to commanders who had reason to know of their subordinates' crimes, recognizing that the commanders' failure to punish or prosecute those subordinates creates an environment for further lawless acts.[35] The law of commander responsibility has Haitian precedent as well. Commander responsibility formed the basis of the prosecution of the Haitian leaders responsible for a 1994 massacre in the coastal community of Raboteau in the city of Gonaïves. The Raboteau court convicted fifty-three soldiers and paramilitary members, including multiple commanders, in proceedings that were praised by international monitors for their fairness. The attorneys for the Raboteau victims were BAI's Mario Joseph and Brian Concannon, who now serve as the lawyers for Jean-Baptiste and several other Duvalier victims. "A Duvalier prosecution in Haiti would be difficult," says Reed Brody of Human Rights Watch. "But Raboteau proved it can be done."

Before dawn on the morning of April 22, 1994, in the Haitian coastal community of Raboteau, Haitian soldiers and paramilitary launched the most deadly of several attacks against the community's pro-democracy movement that was resisting the military dictatorship ruling Haiti at the time. Soldiers broke into homes, shot at civilians, and plunged people into sewers. Some residents fled to the sea, only to be ambushed there by waiting soldiers. When the wounded sought refuge in a nearby hospital, the soldiers hunted them down there, too. Bodies were quickly disposed of, but at least eight people were killed, and dozens of others were arrested and tortured in the attacks. There was little faith in the Haitian government's ability to bring the attackers to justice, even after the military dictatorship was replaced six months later by the return of democratically elected president Jean-Bertrand Aristide.

The barrier between the Haitian courts and the majority of the Haitian people is revealed by the use of French in legal proceedings, despite the fact that only one in ten Haitians speaks the language. Confused by the opaque judicial process and discouraged by the courts' reputation for delay and corruption, ordinary Haitians sometimes take their grievances to Roman Catholic or Vodou priests. When Duvalier was ousted, Haitians dealt with the *tontons makouts* not through formal indictments but with deadly mob violence launched under the slogan of *dechoukaj*, Creole for "uprooting."[36]

Yet the Haitian judicial system does provide one opening for civilians to be closely involved in court proceedings. Under the French procedure adopted in Haiti generations ago, crime victims have legal standing to participate as a civil party, *partie civile*, in the prosecution of those accused of harming them. In the English common law system, followed in the United States, victims can file separate civil suits claiming money damages. But those victims have no formal role in criminal prosecution, which is solely the province of the government. By contrast, crime victims in Haiti can present evidence, question witnesses, and argue to the judge and jury in the same trial where the defendants are being criminally prosecuted.[37]

Ten months after what came to be called the Raboteau Massacre, the restored Aristide government created BAI with the mission of advocating for justice from outside the formal system of criminal prosecution. Joseph and Concannon joined BAI in 1996, and they seized on the *partie civile* avenue to prod a reluctant justice system into action against the Raboteau killers. (The Raboteau prosecution is more fully described in Chapter 4.)

Born in 1963 in the Haitian village of Borel, forty kilometers north of Port-au-Prince, Joseph cannot identify any role model who inspired his passion for human rights. Instead, he points to an almost subconscious sense of injustice that began to gnaw at him in childhood. Joseph's father was usually absent and did not support the family, but there were and are no child support laws in Haiti. The children in Joseph's village struggled to get access to education—his mother was illiterate—but there was no government system of primary schooling in Haiti. A neighbor of the Joseph family was a feared section chief for the Duvalier regime, but there was no law to hold him accountable. Joseph's family was among many who did not always have enough to eat, and routine health care was unheard of. "If I was still in my home village, I would probably have cholera by now," Joseph says.

Joseph's mother was able to enroll him in a mission school, and he eventually pursued his law degree. His matriculation was a process of fits and starts, as he had to withdraw from school several times because of lack of money. But he finally completed his coursework, arguing along the way with professors who he felt did not devote enough class time to human rights law. "I was definitely one of the poorest students in the school, and for that reason I was oriented toward human rights the whole time," he says. "Seeing my mother and neighbors struggle built my conviction to work for the rights of poor people."

Concannon says that it is a minor miracle that Joseph cleared all the barriers in his path to becoming an attorney. "Most people in Haiti don't get even elementary education, and Mario wouldn't have either if the mission school hadn't opened the year he was ready for school. And most people who finish law school can't meet the thesis and apprenticeship requirements to actually become a lawyer," Concannon says. "Part of the reason Mario is so special is that the system is set up to keep people like him out, but he slipped through by a combination of perseverance, intelligence, and luck."

Joseph started his career with a Catholic Church justice commission, representing victims of repression by Haiti's military coup government, before joining BAI. Haitian law training includes strong socialization toward elitism, and one would-be BAI lawyer refused the job when he was informed it would include meeting with his clients in the community. But Joseph embraces the role. Balding now, and thicker than most Haitians, he leans forward into his conversations, speaks quickly and loudly, and gestures intently when making his point. Joseph visits his poor clients in their homes, insists that court proceedings be translated into Creole so that all parties can understand what has been said, and puts his clients front and center in public demonstrations and media campaigns. History proves that challenging the status quo in Haiti is risky business. Some of Joseph's Haitian friends and colleagues have been murdered for their human rights advocacy, and Joseph still operates under constant death threats. Because of the danger, his wife and children have been granted political asylum in the United States.

When Concannon, a US lawyer who had been working with the UN in Haiti, joined BAI, Joseph was suspicious, thinking that his new American colleague might be a CIA agent. "I had never known an example of an American in Haiti who was here to do good," Joseph says. But he eventually overcame his initial misgivings about Concannon, and the two have worked as a team ever since. Concannon worked for BAI in Haiti for several years after the successful Raboteau trial, and then returned to the United States to create the BAI sister organization Institute for Justice and Democracy in Haiti, known as IJDH. Concannon came home at a particularly low moment for Haitian human rights. "We US lawyers had been forced out of Haiti after the 2004 coup that removed President Aristide, and most of us sat around depressed, thinking all our work had been for nothing," says Nicole Lee, a former BAI lawyer and now the executive director of the foreign policy organization TransAfrica Forum. "Compare that with Brian, who created this whole new US-based organization that has proven to be so important to everything we had been working for at BAI." Lee describes the low-key Concannon as a tireless worker who makes the transition from human rights lawyer to political strategist to movement organizer as the needs of the Haitian cause dictate. "I've been in meetings with Brian on Capitol Hill and with the [Obama] administration, and people clearly look to him as the definitive voice on Haiti justice issues," she says. "Over the past ten years, so many people have been wrong about what was going on in Haiti. But Brian has always—*always*—been right."

By representing Jean-Baptiste and other Duvalier victims, Joseph and Concannon and their colleagues have been able to insert themselves into the prosecution process. In fact, they appear to be leading it. Joseph and Concannon shared with the Haitian government prosecutor extensive evidence that the government can use to prove political and financial crimes committed by Duvalier, his family, and his aides. US law firms working pro bono with IJDH drafted questions and submitted them to the *juge d'instruction*, the investigating judge tasked with determining whether Duvalier is to stand trial. The questions were designed to allow the judge to lay the groundwork for proving the essential elements of Duvalier's liability as an accomplice and commander, and thus his responsibility for the crimes committed by his subordinates.

But the investigating judge, Carvés Jean, ruled in January 2012 that Duvalier could not be prosecuted for human rights abuses, and that he should stand trial only for corruption charges. A cartoon soon circulated around Port-au-Prince spoofing the dissonance of that ruling. The cartoon showed Duvalier behind the wheel of a Mercedes stained with blood and filled with human skulls, with a policeman saying, "I am arresting you for stealing a car, Mr. Duvalier!" Joseph and Concannon are helping Duvalier victims appeal that decision, and were heartened by the February 2014 interim appellate ruling.

In a country with virtually no tradition of judicial independence from the executive branch of government, Judge Jean's ruling was no surprise, given President Martelly's clear indication that he has no interest in a Duvalier prosecution. But the Martelly government is also largely dependent on international largesse. "The Duvalier prosecution will only happen if the international community demands it," one Martelly aide admitted to me. So IJDH has spent considerable effort seeking support outside Haiti for bringing Duvalier to justice. The UN and the IACHR have issued strong calls for a Duvalier prosecution, with UN secretary-general Ban Ki-moon telling the Security Council two months after Duvalier's return to Haiti, "It is of vital importance that the Haitian authorities pursue all legal and judicial avenues in this [Duvalier] matter. The prosecution of those responsible for crimes against their own people will deliver a clear message to the people of Haiti that there can be no impunity."[38]

IJDH says there are many ways the international community can make the prosecution happen. The United States and France, in particular, can provide access to key evidence and use their status as Haiti's suppliers of aid as a bully pulpit to call for justice. The international community can provide Haiti's justice system with funding, training, and technical assistance to allow Haiti to handle the complex prosecution of acts that occurred decades ago. Such support is much needed: the Haitian justice system was underfunded and understaffed even before the January 2010 earthquake, which destroyed the Ministry of Justice and the Palais de Justice, where the Supreme Court, the Appeals Court, and the Court of First Instance of Port-au-Prince all were located. Helped by US law firms, IJDH has already mobilized some assistance for the Duvalier prosecutor and investigating judge, and UN high commissioner of human rights Navi Pillay has sent an expert on human rights prosecution to work with Haitian authorities.

The weakness of the Haitian judicial system is just one of the barriers a Duvalier prosecution will have to overcome. Duvalier's lawyers have argued that the Haitian penal code's statute of limitations for his alleged crimes has long since run out, banning his prosecution, an argument seemingly adopted by the investigating judge.[39]

Another challenge is that many victims of Duvalier-era persecution have made it clear to human rights advocates and fellow victims that they are afraid to come forward and testify about their experiences, especially with a Duvalier-friendly Martelly government in charge of Haiti. A month after Duvalier's return to Haiti, a group of these victims sent a letter to then-president René Préval, citing a fear of intimidation and asking for Duvalier to be detained during the investigation of his crimes.[40] Yet Duvalier remains free, and many of his victims remain silent.

In response to the safety concerns, BAI has helped Duvalier victims create their own organization of solidarity, the Citizens' Collective for Prosecuting Duvalier, known by its Creole acronym, KOSIJID. In their appeal of the investigating judge's statute of limitations ruling, Joseph and Concannon argue that the time limits have not yet begun to run on the many cases of "disappearances" during the Duvalier era. That argument is on solid legal ground: various courts in the Americas and France have held that such crimes are unsolved and thus considered permanent and continuous until the victim is found. The French precedent is particularly persuasive, since the applicable statute in France mirrors Haiti's. On other human rights charges, the statute of limitations defense is well refuted by multiple international rulings. For example, decisions by the IACHR, whose interpretations of the American Convention on Human Rights are binding on Haiti, hold that prosecutions for significant human rights violations are not subject to such time limits. Those same international law obligations take Haiti's prosecution of Duvalier out of the realm of the discretionary: article 276(2) of Haiti's Constitution pulls all of Haiti's international treaty commitments into domestic law, including multiple explicit treaty pledges to investigate and prosecute human rights violations and not to allow domestic statutes of limitations to thwart those prosecutions.[41] The UN's Pillay joined Duvalier victim lawyers and human rights organizations in condemning the investigating judge's 2012 statute of limitations ruling.[42]

None of the barriers to prosecution—limited capacity, fearful victims, or procedural arguments—can provide an adequate excuse for the failure to pursue justice, says Mario Joseph. "A Duvalier process and trial would mean so much for Haiti," he says. "It will help people believe in the system of justice if they see a defendant held accountable who stole our country's money and killed and imprisoned people. Not only will it let the people know we are a democracy that will seek justice, it will send a signal to current and future leaders that, if they commit crimes, they too will be prosecuted."

Joseph and other advocates also believe strongly that prosecution needs to occur in Haiti rather than in an international venue, even if jurisdiction could be established elsewhere. They point out that the majority of the Haitian population is too young to remember the Duvalier reign of terror and could benefit from exposure of the injustices of the past. The long-term development of the Haitian justice system would be enhanced by the infusion of international expertise and support, and a model of accountability and transparency would be created in a country sorely in need of visible displays of justice. As Michèle Montas, a Duvalier victim, told Human Rights Watch, "Justice means that the truth shall be known, and that all that happened did not happen in vain."[43]

The most significant barrier between Montas and the other Duvalier victims and the trial they seek is the president of the United States. Through ties of history, culture, and governmental and non-governmental aid, Haiti—whose capital, Port-au-Prince, is a mere ninety-minute flight from Miami—is deeply connected to the United States. The United States can not only push the Haitian government to put Duvalier on trial, it can help protect the safety of the complaining witnesses and provide access to the diplomatic cables and other evidence from the Duvalier era that could help make the trial successful. Yet, since Duvalier has returned to Haiti, the US response has been coolly detached. Shortly after Duvalier's 2011 return to Haiti, State Department spokesperson P. J. Crowley said, "As to his [Duvalier's] status in the country and what happens, this is a matter for the Government of Haiti and the people of Haiti."[44] The US ambassador to Haiti, Kenneth Merten, later echoed that position, as did Secretary of State Hillary Clinton.[45]

This laissez-faire approach to the Duvalier matter is a bitter irony to Haitians, who can cite a pattern nearly two centuries old of the United States regularly immersing itself in Haiti governmental affairs. It is also a position that is deeply disappointing to many human rights activists who had hoped for better from the Obama administration. At a meeting of the National Lawyers Guild in the fall of 2011, Concannon said that it is "disgusting" that a president who is a former constitutional law professor, with a team of advisors with vast human rights credentials, is not pushing for prosecution of Duvalier. Concannon pointed to Harold Koh, then the legal advisor to the State Department and a former Yale Law School dean who worked extensively on Haitian refugee cases in the 1990s; Michael Posner, then-assistant secretary of state for human rights, democracy, and labor, and founder of the Lawyers Committee for Human Rights (now Human Rights First); and Stephen Rapp, ambassador-at-large for war crimes issues, who spent a career prosecuting human rights violators like Duvalier in places like Liberia and Rwanda. "My guess is that if you sat down with these guys over a beer, they would say, 'Yes, of course he needs to be prosecuted,'" Concannon said. "There is no serious legal controversy about it."

That leaves only political controversy. A Duvalier prosecution would inevitably expose embarrassing details of the long US pattern of supporting the Duvaliers financially and militarily despite awareness of the regime's brutality and thievery. US marines helped François Duvalier consolidate power and repel challenges to his regime, the United States was the chief supplier of weapons for the *tontons makouts*, and US aid was so generously distributed to Duvalier that it made up half of Haiti's budget in 1961. "Papa Doc" even used USAID trucks to carry supporters to his political rallies.

If anything, these ties became stronger during Jean-Claude Duvalier's tenure. The United States deployed warships to repel any challenge to Baby Doc's ascension to the Haitian presidency after his father's death, and the younger Duvalier's first speech as president featured the promise, "The United States will always find Haiti on its side against communism."[46] Between 1972 and 1981, the United States gave over $400 million in aid to Haiti, and USAID pledged to leverage the low-paid Haitian workforce to turn the country into the "Taiwan of the Caribbean." Under the avaricious Jean-Claude Duvalier, that aspiration gave way to an economy that featured the exportation of plasma, illegal drugs, and human cadavers. Even after public disclosure of Duvalier's human rights abuses and massive corruption, US assistance continued to flow freely.[47]

The same outsized financial influence of the United States that helped prop up the Duvaliers for three decades still exists in Haiti today. It could be put to the service of seeing that justice is done, activists like Joseph and Concannon say, but there is no indication that the current administration intends to push Haiti to prosecute Duvalier. One Capitol Hill official who agrees with the Obama administration's hands-off approach defended the US position to me. "People in Haiti need food, they need clean water, they need houses to live in," the official said. "The new president needs a chance to succeed and our support in doing so. Wouldn't you rather put US pressure and resources into those essentials than a very difficult and complicated prosecution of someone who has not been in power for a quarter century?"

This view is shortsighted, Concannon says. "If you look at the long term, Haiti is never going to become a successful and prosperous country until we have the kind of accountability that the Duvalier trial would allow us to have," he says. "It is accountability for political violence crimes, and perhaps even more important, it is accountability for stealing the Haitian people's money. And if the lesson is that Duvalier, who did not even try to hide how he stole government funds, is allowed to be going around to the fancy restaurants and clubs in Pétionville [the wealthy suburb of Port-au-Prince where Duvalier now lives], that is a lesson to current officials that there are no consequences to stealing money."

Human Rights Watch's Reed Brody agrees. "Can you imagine any other country where a former dictator accused of political murders and leaving people to rot and die in prison is allowed to just walk back into his country and remain free?" he asks. "But I think people are just shrugging their shoulders, and saying, 'Well, that is Haiti.' In so many ways, Haiti is the floor, the bottom, of what we expect internationally, both economically and in the performance of its government and justice system."

Haiti has largely lived down to those low expectations. A long and troubled history of dictatorships and coups d'état has produced a revolving door of Haitian judges and prosecutors with reputations for corruption and bending to the will of the country's political and economic elite. Impunity for powerful politicians and the wealthy becomes a self-perpetuating cycle: Brian Concannon says several Haitian judges have confided to him about receiving a carrot-and-stick message from litigants, such as "take this bribe or we'll burn down your house." Concannon sympathizes with the judges. "They want to be honest, but have limited protection. So they take an offer they cannot refuse."

Brody says that the Haitian government does not bear sole responsibility for seeing that justice is done in the Duvalier case. "Part of this is the fault of the international community. Where is the outrage we would have if the brutal leaders of Iraq or Serbia were walking around free? We would not allow this anywhere else." Brody begins to recite the names of former dictators thrown in jail for human rights violations—Charles Taylor of Liberia, Slobodan Milosevic of Serbia, the leaders of the Khmer Rouge in Cambodia—many of them for crimes several decades old. "I've got a map on my office wall filled with all the guys that were prosecuted years after they lost power," Brody says. "But not in Haiti."

Instead, the US government and the vast majority of US private organizations and their donors push the Duvalier prosecution to the side and focus their attention on humanitarian relief in Haiti. In so doing, they are following a traditional development narrative. The solutions to Haiti's suffering are usually characterized by images of engineers digging wells, construction workers building houses, and especially doctors treating the sick. But the physician most associated with Haiti relief, Dr. Paul Farmer—the legendary cofounder of Partners in Health, a Harvard Medical School professor, and the subject of the best-selling book *Mountains beyond Mountains* (chronicling his work in Haiti)—places much of his hope for the country in the hands of lawyers.[48] "The current justice system's shortcomings—especially its unavailability to the poor—underlie almost all of Haiti's problems, including political instability, poverty, violence and corruption," says Farmer, who helped found IJDH and serves on its board of directors. "BAI and IJDH raise people's expectations of their leaders and create a viable peaceful avenue for combating the great injustices in Haitian society."

For centuries, the term "rule of law" has been used as shorthand to describe the ideal template for a system of governance that controls both state and individual power. Despairing of the limited supply of philosopher-kings, Plato endorsed instead the rule of law: "If law is the master of the government and the government is its slave, then the situation is full of promise and men enjoy all the blessings that the gods shower on a state."[49] The Magna Carta famously promised that no free man would be imprisoned or his property seized "except for lawful judgment of his equals or by the law of the land."[50] In modern Western democracy, there is no more enduring maxim than the John Adams–drafted statement in the Constitution of Massachusetts directing that the Commonwealth would be a "government of laws and not of men."[51]

Within international legal circles, there is a debate about what the rule of law actually guarantees. Is the law involved "thin," meaning just a narrow guarantee of specific and predictable legal procedure, or "thick," encompassing broad social and economic goals like the rights to health care and food? Scholars who see the rule of law as a "thin" procedural phenomenon argue that clear and enforceable laws meet the criteria as long as there is some minimal restraint on the power of the state.[52] A Duvalier prosecution, for example, would seem to be called for even under this narrow definition. But most contemporary definitions of rule of law are thicker, incorporating the enforcement of guarantees like the rights to housing and education included in international instruments such as the Universal Declaration of Human Rights. The Haitian Constitution, for example, guarantees a broad array of social and economic rights alongside protection for freedom of speech and due process of law.[53] In the words of Michel Forst, writing as the UN's independent expert on the situation of human rights in Haiti:

> Establishing the rule of law cannot be done simply by defending civil and political rights through a reform of the courts and the criminal justice system, the police and the prison system. Establishing the rule of law also means ensuring that public institutions and services are functioning. Over and above the safety of persons and goods, such services must also provide for the enjoyment by all citizens of the economic, social and cultural rights listed in the International Covenant on Economic, Social and Cultural Rights, ratified by the Haitian parliament. The ratification reflects the will of the Haitian authorities to work for the realization of the economic, social and cultural rights of all Haitians, and to work in the long term against poverty and social exclusion.[54]

Human rights advocates like BAI and IJDH push for the enforcement of both thin and thick rights, and most economists who study global development agree that poverty and law are inextricably linked. Nobel laureate Amartya Sen says that enforcing even the "thin" procedural version of the rule of law would have significant impact on rebuilding struggling nations like Haiti. A personal witness to the devastating Bengal Famine of 1942, Sen's signature argument for the link between individual freedom and social well-being is his assertion that no nation with a functioning democracy and free press has ever suffered a famine. Since information flows freely in those settings and democratic governments must respond to the will—and, presumably, outrage—of the people, widespread suffering is averted.[55] Peruvian economist Hernando de Soto champions the rule of law from a neoliberal perspective, emphasizing that private-sector economic development is enabled by strong government institutions providing consistent enforcement of laws, especially in areas of contract and legal title to property. The vacuum of verifiable title to property leads to the inability to obtain credit for assets like houses and small businesses, enforce contracts, or conduct trade outside a very small network. De Soto says that the dysfunctional legal systems of most developing countries stifle entrepreneurship and growth, a point he dramatized in his research by demonstrating that it took 289 days of sustained efforts to legally open a small garment workshop outside Lima, Peru.[56]

It is particularly challenging to build the rule of law in a country where the gun has always trumped the statute, as Raymond Davius knows. A broad-shouldered fifty-five-year-old with a round face and receding gray hair, Davius leans out of his chair to mimic his hands being tied behind his ankles. He then demonstrates how Haitian soldiers would push a stick between his legs and arms so that he was drawn into a helpless ball. This was position Duvalier's army preferred when they beat him with a *baton gayak*, a two-foot-long rod. "After the first three strikes on you, you really can't feel the ones after that," he says.

A former Haitian army officer, Davius left the military in 1978 to join the Christian Democrat party, the same anti-Duvalier group that Myrtha Jean-Baptiste's family belonged to. Davius was seized by government officials soon after. It was the first of many arrests Davius endured, seventeen in all, including imprisonment in the Casernes Dessalines barracks and the National Penitentiary, two-thirds of the notorious Haitian "triangle of death." In 1983, Davius was able to escape to asylum in Venezuela. Now, back in Haiti, he has some scars on his head from the beatings, but the deepest wounds are harder to see. "The effects of this are inside me all the time," he says. The large man's eyes fill with tears as he talks about family and job troubles. "My comportment is not normal compared to other people, and I have problems in my life. People think I am crazy."

He pauses to collect himself, then goes on. "The problem is not as much about Duvalier himself as it is what he represents. If Haiti does not judge Duvalier, we have lost the opportunity to send a message to Haitian leaders who think they can kill whoever they want and steal whatever they want, and not be judged.

"We have a proverb in Creole: *Si pa gen sitire pa ka gen vole.*"

Translation: If there is no tolerance, there would be no thieves.

3 | The Rule of Law, Political Will, and Haiti

W hen the MINUSTAH soldiers showed up in his Fort National neighborhood of Port-au-Prince on January 5, 2005, Jimmy Charles, a twenty-seven-year-old husband and father of two children, was unloading sand from a truck for his father's masonry business. The soldiers arrested Charles.[1] Charles was not told of any charges against him, but it was no surprise that he was being taken into custody. An employee of Téléco, the Haitian telephone company, Charles was an active supporter of the Fanmi Lavalas political party, which had supported President Jean-Bertrand Aristide. Since Aristide's ouster in February of the previous year, the coup d'état government that replaced him had been making sweeping arrests. The names of Lavalas members were announced on the radio, and those who did not go into hiding immediately were rounded up and thrown into prison. The prime minister of the Aristide government, Yvon Neptune, was arrested in June 2004 and held for two years before being released.[2]

The MINUSTAH troops turned Charles over to the Haitian National Police the same day he was arrested, and he was imprisoned at the Anti-Gang Service holding cell at the commissariat in downtown Port-au-Prince. The nine-foot by twelve-foot cell had no running water or toilet, and the temperature routinely exceeded one hundred degrees Fahrenheit. By the time Charles arrived at the cell, it was so crowded that prisoners had to take turns sitting on the floor. Prisoners relied on their families to provide drinking water and meals, so Charles's wife, Mikelsie Jusma, and his father, Jean-Charles Deus Charles, visited him daily to bring him food. Five days after his arrest, Charles was brought before a judge, who declined to hear the case because the police had not submitted any report. Charles was scheduled to go before another judge on January 12.

On the morning of the twelfth, Charles's wife visited him at the cell. When his father came to see him that afternoon, Charles was gone. The elder Charles was told his son had been released, but when he went to his son's home in Fort National, his son was not there. The elder Charles then went to the court where Charles had been scheduled to appear, the Tribunal of Peace of the East Section. Charles had never come to court. Charles's family was getting anxious, and they returned to the Anti-Gang commissariat, where they were told to look at the National Penitentiary to see if Charles had been transferred there. He had not. The next day, the elder Charles found his son's body in the morgue of State University Hospital. Jimmy Charles had been shot eleven times. His body had been delivered to the morgue by an ambulance at 2 p.m. the afternoon he was scheduled to go to court.

Later, a Haitian National Police spokesperson claimed that Jimmy Charles was killed during a shootout between police and "bandits" in the Port-au-Prince neighborhood of La Saline, on the other side of town from Charles's neighborhood of Fort National. A spokesperson for MINUSTAH later repeated the same account of Charles's death. But Charles's family and friends recognized that his death had all the markings of being the latest in a series of extrajudicial executions by Haitian police. "My son was released from detention without being heard by a judge for the sole purpose of being executed," Jean-Charles Deus Charles said.[3]

The Charles family was not alone in their grief. In March of the previous year, within days after Aristide left the country, five young men were arrested by police in the La Saline neighborhood, and their bodies were found the next day in different parts of the city. On the afternoon of October 26, 2004, masked men traveling in vehicles bearing police license plates and dressed in black police uniforms shot and killed thirteen people from the Rue Estimé quarter of Fort National. Two days after Jimmy Charles died, journalist Abdias Jean, who had been investigating the police shooting of two young boys, was himself killed by the police. Three days after that, Ederson Joseph, a schoolchild, was killed by a hooded police officer in the yard of the child's home. Among the hundreds of political prisoners detained by the coup government was a Roman Catholic priest, Father Gérard Jean-Juste, a critic of the government who was arrested twice for a murder that occurred while Jean-Juste was out of the country. Jean-Juste was held for over seven months even though no evidence was ever presented against him.[4] Mario Joseph, who served as the lawyer for Jean-Juste, the Charles family, and other political prisoners, said, "The only reason given for these massive assaults on unarmed people is that 'criminals' or 'bandits' or 'gang members' are present in the community. The process of legal accusation has been reduced to name-calling—the word *chimère* [monster] is used like a death sentence."[5]

Under Haitian law, none of this should have happened. Since Jimmy Charles was not in the process of committing any crime when he was arrested, article 24-2 of the

Haitian Constitution and articles 77 through 80 of the Haitian Code of Criminal Procedure make it clear he could only be legally arrested and detained on a warrant issued by an investigating judge. No such warrant was ever issued. Similarly, the Universal Declaration of Human Rights, which Haiti is bound to respect as a member state of the UN, protects against arbitrary arrest or detention, as does the American Convention on Human Rights, the regional human rights instrument that Haiti ratified decades ago.[6]

The conditions of Charles's detention clearly violated the letter of the law, from his detention without review by a judge (prohibited by article 26 of the Haitian Constitution, articles 7 and 8 of the American Convention on Human Rights, and article 10 of the Universal Declaration of Human Rights) to the brutal conditions he and his cellmates endured (prohibited by article 44-1 of the Haitian Constitution and by article 5(2) of the American Convention). Obviously, extrajudicial execution is an illegal act: article 45 of the Haitian Constitution proscribes any penalties except those issued through legal procedures, and article 25 forbids cruelty toward prisoners. Article 4(1) of the American Convention says, "No one shall be arbitrarily deprived of life," and article 5 of the convention prohibits torture or "cruel, inhuman, or degrading punishment or treatment." The Haitian National Police Code of Conduct firmly condemns abuse of detainees.

Citing these laws, Jimmy Charles's family filed official complaints with the Haitian government and the IACHR. Haitian law mandates that an investigation should have been launched immediately and the family's request for an autopsy should have been granted (per the Haitian Police Code of Conduct, article 25 of the American Convention, the landmark 1989 Inter-American Court of Human Rights *Velásquez Rodríguez* case, various UN resolutions, and other guidelines).[7] The Haitian judiciary should have been independent from the executive branch officials who oversaw the police (per article 60 of the Haitian Constitution and the UN Basic Principles on the Independence of the Judiciary).[8] By law, the investigation into Jimmy Charles's death should have been expeditious and unbiased.

But for Jimmy Charles and for other Haitians, the law on paper reads like a fantasy novel. Six months after Charles's death, Amnesty International issued a report saying that the coup government's prime minister, Gérard Latortue, had failed to live up to his promises to establish an independent commission to investigate police abuses. Amnesty International's investigation showed that, in Haiti, lawlessness had settled in as the norm: "Prosecutions for extrajudicial killings, ill-treatment and other human rights abuses remain notional. Investigations more often than not fail to establish who the suspected perpetrator was and do not conform to international standards. . . . Some parents of victims refrain from going to the morgue for fear of reprisals or because they cannot afford to pay the sum needed to take the corpse away for a proper burial."[9]

A report issued by the Organization of American States (OAS) that same year of 2005 said that the Haitian National Police sometimes wore face masks and dressed in black so as to conceal their identities when firing on the public. The OAS found that prisoners in Haitian jails showed wounds consistent with beatings and torture and that the police investigated only a fraction of the hundreds of human rights complaints it received that year. The report, issued under the name of the General Secretariat of the OAS and citing its own investigation and numerous other international reports, concluded that Haitian police "have been implicated in disappearances, summary arrests and executions, torture, rape and drug trafficking, among other crimes and human rights abuses."[10]

The complaint the Charles family filed with the Haitian government was never acted upon, nor was any independent investigation conducted. The IACHR ordered the Haitian government to respond to the Charles family's petition filed with the commission, but the government never replied. Multiple formal requests for an autopsy were ignored. Charles's body lay decaying in the state hospital for three months, but no autopsy was ever conducted. Instead, the family was presented by the government with a morgue bill for $800, twice the Haitian per capita annual income. It could have been worse for the Charles family: shortly after the journalist Abdias Jean's family spoke to the media in protest of his shooting by the police, the home of his mother and sister was looted.[11]

In such cases, the guarantees of judicial independence enshrined in the Haitian Constitution and international agreements are completely ignored. Through the Ministry of Justice and its control of court budgets and personnel transfers, the executive branch of the Haitian government exercises power over both the police and the judges who would sanction them. When Haitian judge Jean Sénat Fleury threw out the bogus charges against Father Jean-Juste, Fleury was forced off the case and replaced by another judge who reinstated the charges. In December 2005, the interim president of Haiti fired five justices of the Supreme Court and chose five others to take their place.[12] Bernard Gousse was the justice minister at the time of Charles's death, at the time of the arrest of Prime Minister Neptune, and during the internationally condemned spree of executions and imprisonment of political prisoners. Gousse, also a member of the Supreme Council of the Haitian National Police, had publicly alleged that Father Jean-Juste "engaged in terrorist acts." Gousse then engineered Judge Fleury's removal and replacement, followed by Jean-Juste's re-arrest. US ambassador to Haiti James Foley, otherwise a supporter of the coup government, told the State Department that Gousse was "a complete failure on both the security and justice fronts."[13]

Six years later, on July 6, 2011, President Michel Martelly nominated Bernard Gousse to be his prime minister.

After a surge of protest within Haiti and in the international community, including a petition by BAI asking that Gousse be indicted and prosecuted for human rights crimes committed during his tenure as justice minister, Martelly withdrew Gousse's nomination. But the original choice was revealing, as was the rationale offered by

Martelly chief of staff Thierry Mayard-Paul, who said that Gousse had been named because of his experience as a public administrator.[14] From that perspective, the selection of Gousse was almost understandable: respect for the rule of law has almost never been a prerequisite for holding office in Haiti, and it may have been difficult for Martelly to find a seasoned veteran of Haitian government who has an unblemished human rights record.

Haiti has seen thirty-two coups d'état in its two centuries as a nation, extensive foreign intervention in its domestic political affairs, and the gutting and rewriting of its constitution twenty-three times. (Foreign intervention and constitutional revisions have not been mutually exclusive affairs. Franklin Delano Roosevelt claimed credit for writing the version of Haiti's constitution created during the US occupation of Haiti from 1915 to 1934, when Roosevelt served as assistant secretary of the Navy. This document bulldozed generations of Haitian precedent to give US businesses the right to own land in Haiti. Nevertheless, Roosevelt bragged about his role: "I wrote Haiti's Constitution myself, and if I do say it, it was a pretty good little Constitution.")[15]

Now, in the early twenty-first century, Haiti is coming off a debilitating thirty years of Duvalier repression, followed by spates of democracy interrupted by more coups d'état. The January 12, 2010, earthquake dealt devastating blows to the Haitian justice system, with the Ministry of Justice, the Palais de Justice, and many courthouses, police stations, and jails all destroyed or seriously damaged. Judges, lawyers, and police officers were killed.[16] The government of Haiti estimates that as many as 17 percent of Haiti's civil servants perished in the quake.[17] Thousands of prisoners escaped after the earthquake, with fewer than one in ten escapees recaptured since.[18]

As the Jimmy Charles case demonstrates, Haiti's justice system was remarkably weak even before the earthquake. A review by the National Center for State Courts in 2004 revealed that many Haitian courts had been closed for months, with case files lost or looted. Those courts that were open were usually dilapidated and understaffed. The authors of this review concluded that the system "is best described as barely functional."[19] A 2001 World Bank report and a 2009 report by the US Institute for Peace found similarly dismal situations. These reports cited widespread corruption, executive interference in the judiciary, and a lack of security for judges tasked with making potentially unpopular decisions.[20] Judges in Haiti are poorly trained and chronically underpaid. (Haitian lawyers traditionally have been wealthier and better educated than judges, leaving the judges vulnerable to both corruption and derision.) The coup government of 2004 fired over three hundred judges and police chiefs. Even the democratically elected Aristide government ignored the constitutionally mandated separation of powers, putting judges in place through executive order.

Prison conditions were also abysmal before the quake. Cells were horribly overcrowded, and children were held in the same cells with adults. The vast majority of prisoners were pretrial detainees, many of them waiting for trial for longer than the maximum sentence for their minor offenses. During an April 2005 visit to the National Penitentiary, the IACHR counted 1,052 inmates, only 9 of whom had been convicted of any crime. Of 117 women held at Pétionville Prison at the time, only 4 had been convicted.[21]

As Jimmy Charles and his family learned, Haitian law in reality bore little resemblance to Haitian law on paper. But even the formal Haitian law, based on the nineteenth-century French Napoleonic Code, leaves much to be desired. The laws do not adequately respect the rights of women and children, nor do they provide needed protection for victims and witnesses. The formal law is a hodgepodge of codes and various presidential decrees that are sometimes contradictory and not widely published or understood, even within the legal community. Referring both to the rule of law and to the social and economic indicators that place Haiti in the basement of world rankings for health, income, and social services, the OAS in 2005 lambasted the conditions endured by the Haitian people as "a disgrace for our Hemisphere."[22]

In the aftermath of the earthquake, the situation worsened. The Haitian National Police, already labeled by the OAS as "under-resourced, over-worked, and under-compensated," suffered significant losses of lives, equipment, and buildings.[23] The surviving police inflicted their own post-earthquake damage through extrajudicial executions. On January 21, foreign journalists witnessed officers of the Haitian National Police shooting two men for taking a bag of rice that had fallen off the back of a truck. Two days before, in response to an attempted prison escape in Les Cayes, police shot at least thirty-five unarmed inmates, buried the bodies of the victims in unmarked graves, and then reported that a single detainee had done the shooting. On March 5, 2011, a Haitian National Police officer allegedly killed two men who were hanging posters for a presidential candidate.[24]

The justice system was in tatters. The UN reported in 2011 that cocaine traveling from South America to the United States and Europe passes "relatively freely" through Haiti without police interference.[25] The earthquake destroyed evidence housed in the Palais de Justice, and other vital court records were looted in the days after the quake. In late 2011, the American Bar Association Rule of Law Initiative estimated the Haitian courts' criminal conviction rate to be just 3 percent.[26] A September 2012 visit by UN assistant secretary-general for human rights Ivan Šimonović to the Haitian National Penitentiary revealed that only 278 of 3,400 prisoners there (8 percent) had been convicted of a crime.[27] The US State Department reported in 2011 that Haitian prisons were filled to more than 500 percent of capacity, as measured by international standards, and were havens for diseases like HIV/AIDS, malaria, and drug-resistant tuberculosis.[28]

Such figures are disturbing in the abstract. When observed in person, the conditions are haunting. For example, at the Prison Civile de St. Marc, the cells are surrounded by two twenty-foot walls of concrete, three layers of razor wire, and a half-dozen guards holding rifles and revolvers. The cells themselves are about three meters wide and five meters deep. A full-sized SUV probably could not fit into one, but each cell holds a minimum of thirty-six men apiece, day and night. On the day I visited the prison in the summer of 2012, it was over one hundred degrees Fahrenheit in the open air, but an even more intense heat radiated out from the cells. All the prisoners were shirtless and barefoot, very thin, and wearing as little as possible. The startling sight of near-naked dark-skinned men crammed together and crouching on a bare floor evoked images of Africans chained in the hold of a slave ship.

The guards explained that the prisoners are allowed out of the cells once a day, for a few minutes in the morning when they line up to use the single toilet shared by four hundred male and female prisoners. If the prisoners need to relieve themselves at any other time of the day or night, they defecate into a plastic bag or urinate on the floor of the cell. Ideally, they will urinate when dousing themselves with the grimy plastic buckets of water provided for the purposes of both drinking and bathing.

During my visit, a half-dozen men pressed themselves against the bars of cell #5, squeezing together and turning sideways for a view of the visitors. The chalk marking by the entrance to the cell said that thirty-nine inmates were held there. Shelove Davillus wanted the touring lawyers to know his name and that he has four children. Rene Jean-Robert called out too, saying he is thirty-three years old. Both were convicted of being associated with gangs. When asked how long their sentences are, they answer the same: "*Perpetuité.*" Forever. Other men shouted out their names. Oddly, most do not ask for specific help with their case or make a request of any kind. It was almost as if they were putting a message in a bottle, hoping it would drift toward a sympathetic audience. Next to Jean-Robert's head on the cell wall was an exactingly sketched picture of a dreadlocked Jesus on the cross.

According to Government of Haiti figures, 70 percent of its prisoners have not faced trial, although many had been held for lengthy periods of time. When the UN's independent expert on the situation of human rights in Haiti visited a women's prison in Pétionville in 2011, nearly 90 percent of the prisoners had never faced trial. Courts are limited in their coverage of rural areas and unable to provide counsel to most litigants. Judges, police, and court officers were reported to be soliciting bribes to expedite or dismiss cases.[29] BAI works with Partners in Health on a program called "Health and Human Rights Prison Project" to provide medical care and legal intervention for Haitian prisoners. "Almost everyone we see in the prisons can tell us a dollar figure they were offered to dismiss their case," says Dr. Evan Lyon of Partners in Health. "For the very poorest people in the countryside it can be $300; for people in the cities who are believed to have contacts in the US, it can be $10,000. Everybody's got their price, and the ones in prison are the ones too poor to pay it. There is this expression people say around the prison: *Moun rich, pa fè krim*—rich people don't do crime. In all layers of the system, it is transparently corruptible." (Once, in Port-au-Prince, I witnessed police stop several vehicles at a road-block, a notorious venue for soliciting bribes, while allowing a truck to pass through unmolested, despite the fact that garbage in the rear of the truck was fully aflame, spewing chunks of fiery garbage onto the street.) This lack of an efficient and reliable judicial system leaves a vacuum that was filled by vigilante justice in response to accusations of theft and other crimes. The Haitian National Police reported 113 cases of what they called "lynching" in 2011, none of which resulted in arrest.[30]

After the earthquake, an additional 3,500 MINUSTAH troops and police arrived in Haiti.[31] But, as discussed in Chapter 1, their arrival was at best a mixed blessing, as the UN personnel's credibility in enforcing the rule of law was undercut by their own lack of accountability to Haitian justice. That immunity, coupled with high-profile shootings and other accusations of violence and mistreatment of Haitians, cause the troops to be widely resented and mistrusted. For example, many Haitians are aware of the incident that occurred on August 17, 2010, when employees of the Christophe Hotel in Cap-Haïtien heard a voice call from the grounds of a MINUSTAH base, "They are suffocating me!" Later in the day, the UN reported that sixteen-year-old Gérard Jean-Gilles had entered the base and hanged himself from a tree. That explanation was immediately called into question, in part because Jean-Gilles had recently been accused of stealing $200 from a UN interpreter believed to be dating the MINUSTAH base chief. An autopsy of Jean-Gilles's body ruled out the explanation of suicide. But subpoenas to UN staff from the Haitian investigating judge were ignored, and no arrests were ever made.[32]

There were a few post-earthquake bright spots for the rule of law, including the January 2012 conviction of seven police officers in the Les Cayes prison massacre.[33] And the reduction of state-sponsored political violence that occurred under the presidency of René Préval from 2006 to 2011 was a trend that so far has held true post-earthquake.[34] But Préval's successor, Martelly, was elected only after the Lavalas majority party was banned from the contest, a decision international donors privately condemned as being reached in bad faith and aimed at "emasculating" Lavalas.[35] Analysis of the voting by the Center for Economic and Policy Research concluded that, after the banning of Lavalas and the suspiciously large number of ballots rejected by Haitian officials, fewer than 20 percent of eligible Haitians had their votes counted in the November 2010 election.[36] While lengthy pretrial detentions remain the norm for the poor, Duvalier's return to Haiti bolstered the perception of impunity for political violence committed by those in power. *Moun rich, pa fé krim.*

Two years after the earthquake, I visited a courtroom in Port-au-Prince within the grim set of buildings that had replaced the Palais de Justice after its destruction by the earthquake. The day's docket included the trial of a man accused of cheating the driver of a *tap-tap* (one of the privately owned vans or trucks that serve as Haiti's chief mode of transportation) out of eight hundred gourdes (about US$25). The cramped, airless courtroom was filled with some forty male lawyers, witnesses, and police, with only a single woman present. The prosecutor rose from his chair on an elevated platform and gave an impassioned speech; then the defense lawyer provided a more measured reply. The judge took notes during the arguments, occasionally calling for order by ringing the small gold bell by his side. All three men wore black robes. The judge then delivered a long recitation of his verdict, speaking slowly and haltingly so that his words could be transcribed by his clerk, who was using a blue Bic pen to fill the pages of an enormous blank book. The defendant sat by himself on a wooden bench facing the judge. A lean young man who appeared to be no more than eighteen years old, he alternated between staring vacantly and occasionally looking around the courtroom as if trying to catch someone's eye. Ultimately, he was sentenced to a year in prison, but very likely had served far longer than that before the trial was ever held.

I was accompanied in court that day by a Haitian friend who was unusually well-connected with the local power structure—I had previously witnessed him negotiating the release of a *tap-tap* driver who had been arrested after failing to pay a police bribe. When we walked away from the trial, I mentioned that the defendant did not seem to be following the exchanges over his own fate. "That is because he wasn't," my friend said, shaking his head in disgust. "The judge talks in French, the lawyers talk in French, the man whose case is being decided understands only Creole. What kind of justice is that?"

Haitians ask questions like these a lot. International evaluations of the Haitian justice system reliably document the Haitian people's lack of faith in its responsiveness or impartiality, and their widespread belief that the police and courts protect only the elite. Mario Joseph says the image reflects reality. "The justice system is unaffordable for the people of Haiti, but if you are rich or important and your rights are not respected, you can find justice. Conversely, if you are powerful and you abuse human rights, you can find ways to avoid the consequences of your actions."[37]

Among legal scholars, human rights activists, and historians, there is some debate about the meaning of the term "rule of law." But the definition provided in a 2001 World Bank report on Haiti reflects a rough consensus:

> Rule of law is about ensuring that the government is representative of all segments of society, complies with the law and upholds the constitution. It implies that the legal framework will be consistent with international norms and standards, with an accountable executive, and clear separation of powers, an independent judiciary, fair and effective administration of justice, a civilian and democratically controlled security force, public procedures in the adoption of legislation, effective oversight mechanisms and means of redress available to all citizens, and a culture of rights and constitutionalism.[38]

According to a centuries-spanning consensus among philosophers and statesmen, the rule of law is nothing less than the cornerstone of enlightened human existence. From Plato to Thomas Aquinas and beyond, there has been deep support for the primacy of the law as a civilizing force. John Locke, in his second *Treatise on Government* (1690), pronounced, "Where there is no Law, there is no Freedom."[39] More recently, the rule of law has been held up for admiration from the political Right ("the central principle of Civilization is the subordination of the ruling class to the settled customs of the people and to their will as expressed in the Constitution," said Winston Churchill) and the Left ("the rule of law itself, the imposing of effective inhibitions on power and the defense of citizens from power's all intrusive claims, seems to me to be an unqualified human good," said socialist historian E. P. Thompson).[40]

That consensus holds that the benefits of the rule of law reach far beyond abstract concepts of liberty and accountability. In fact, the rule of law is considered to be an essential component of the economic and social success of nations and individuals. British historian Niall Ferguson, in his 2011 book *Civilization: The West and the Rest*, attributes the rise of Western civilization since the fifteenth century to six concepts ("killer apps," he calls them) that the rest of the world lacked.[41] One of them is the rule of law.[42] Ferguson's argument is far from new, as early twentieth-century sociologist Max Weber wrote extensively on the role that stable, predictable law plays in enabling economic transactions that lead to growth and prosperity. More recently, Nobel laureate economist Amartya Sen has concluded that the rule of law and economic and social well-being are inextricably connected building blocks for a country's development:

> It is hard to think that development can really be seen independently of its economic, social, political or legal components. We cannot very well say that the development process has gone beautifully even though people are being arbitrarily hanged, criminals go free while law-abiding citizens end up in jail, and so on. This would be as counterintuitive a claim as the corresponding economic one that a country is now highly developed even though it is desperately poor and people are constantly hungry. . . . [So] in answering the query, "What is the role of legal and judicial reform in the development process?," we must at least begin by noting the basic fact that legal development is constitutively involved in the development process, and conceptual integrity requires that we see legal development as crucial for the development process itself.[43]

Peruvian economist Hernando de Soto has made his own widely cited argument for the rule of law, an argument that is highlighted by a distinctly capitalist celebration of the economic empowerment that flows from clear and enforceable property rights. De Soto reviewed the challenges faced by the poor in several countries, including Haiti, and concluded that the people he observed were severely disadvantaged by the absence of an efficient system of regulating property rights. "Imagine a country where nobody can define who owns what, addresses cannot be verified, and the rules that govern property vary from neighborhood to neighborhood, from street to street," de Soto writes. Clear and legally enforceable titles, along with transparent and straightforward licensing and contract mechanisms, are the keys to development for the poor and their countries, de Soto says.[44] In Haiti, for example, de Soto estimates that there is as much as $5 billion in value in urban and rural real estate, ready to be leveraged for the purchase of equipment, building supplies, labor, and fertilizer, if only the owners could legally verify their holdings.[45] (It should be noted that de Soto's property-centric approach is associated with the neoliberal economic policies that have caused much damage in Haiti, as is discussed further in Chapter 7.)

De Soto's goal of a widespread use of legal titles to raise funds seems a remote one in Haiti, where projects to build roads, water treatment facilities, and hospitals have all experienced setbacks because of unclear titles to needed land.[46] The problem of Haitian land registries being out of date and unreliable was featured in *Where Did the Money Go?*, a post-earthquake documentary on Haiti produced by Michele Mitchell and Ivan Weiss. The film included a scene where a frustrated NGO director tells of trying to buy a piece of land from a purported owner, only to have eight other people show up, all claiming they were the true landowners. "And they all had documents to support them," she said. "The land laws here in Haiti are so fucked up!"[47]

Turkish economist Daron Acemoglu makes a similar case for the necessity of enforceable property rights for the poor. In his 2012 book, *Why Nations Fail: The Origins of Power, Prosperity and Poverty*, coauthored with Harvard political scientist and economist James A. Robinson, Acemoglu argues that inclusive economic institutions are the key to a nation's prosperity. An essential component of that inclusivity is an unbiased system of law. Haiti provides a favorite Acemoglu example of a state that has failed because of an extractive legal system operated by a state that responds only to the interests of the elite. The deficiencies of Haitian economic institutions, which give parents no incentive to educate their children, and Haitian political institutions, which do not build and finance schools, mean that Haiti has "many potential Bill Gateses and perhaps one or two Albert Einsteins who are now working as poor, uneducated farmers . . . because they never had the opportunity to realize their vocation in life."[48] In a 2012 *New York Times Magazine* profile of the economist, Adam Davidson illustrated Acemoglu's rule of law thesis by pointing out that the lack of clear property titles in Haiti creates a disincentive for farmers to grow crops too successfully. A visibly thriving farm, he points out, would attract poaching of the land by the more elite and powerful members of the community.[49]

The views of Sen, De Soto, Acemoglu, and similar theorists have found support from several empirical studies showing a strong link between rule of law and measures of economic development.[50] The rule of law provides the necessary strong foundation and sturdy frame on which a country's economic and social well-being is constructed. There is plenty of historical evidence demonstrating how shaky that structure can be when the rule of law is absent. Simon Bolívar's rejection of the rule of law in favor of "an able despotism," Ferguson argues, doomed most of Latin

America's population to centuries of economic suffering, especially compared to their US counterparts:

> The newly independent states [in Latin America in the early-to-mid-nineteenth century] began their lives without a tradition of representative government, with a profoundly unequal distribution of land and with racial cleavages that closely approximated to that economic inequality. The result was a cycle of revolution and counter-revolution, coup and counter-coup, as the propertyless struggled for just a few acres more, while the creole elites clung to their haciendas. Time and again, democratic experiments failed because, at the first sign that they might be expropriated, the wealthy elites turned to a uniformed *caudillo* to restore the status quo by violence. This was not a recipe for rapid economic growth.[51]

Sadly, no country's history is a better fit for that description than Haiti's, where a long tradition of lawlessness is linked arm-in-arm with a legacy of grinding poverty.

However, rule of law enthusiasts and development experts still find hope for countries like Haiti, in large part by referring to global historical trends that show movement toward transparent, accountable justice systems. De Soto in particular draws parallels between the struggle for property rights in the current developing world and the fits and starts of the United States' progress toward defining similar rights in the nineteenth century.[52] Social scientists as far back as Gunnar Myrdal and T. H. Marshall in the mid-twentieth century have identified trends of rights evolution in democratic societies.[53] Their optimism for growing the rule of law has been followed by money. The arguments of Sen, De Soto, and others provide the intellectual underpinnings of extensive investments in multilateral and bilateral efforts to promote the rule of law in developing countries. It is difficult to pin down a definitive dollar figure for these global rule of law promotions, but the number would be impressively large. In 2004, the senior vice president and general counsel of the World Bank reported that the bank had engaged in over six hundred rule of law projects.[54] One calculation that same year concluded that the World Bank alone had devoted $2.9 billion to rule of law projects since 1990, a figure consistent with the bank's report of spending nearly a half-billion dollars per year on rule of law loans from 2003 to 2008, and almost $5.5 billion per year in a sector it labels "Law and Justice and Public Administration."[55] The US General Accounting Office (which changed its name to the US Government Accountability Office in 2004) reported in 1999 that the United States alone had spent $970 million on rule-of-law programming, much of it in Latin America, in just one five-year period in the 1990s.[56] USAID reported having spent $14.3 million on "rule of law and human rights" initiatives in 2007.[57] Echoing Sen's and de Soto's conclusions, these agencies have claimed that their rule of law programming addresses not only economic development and human rights, but also poverty, democratization, and peacemaking.

Yet, sadly, there is scant evidence that these multi-billion-dollar rule of law programs have succeeded in improving either the economic or political climates in the host countries. The likely explanation for the disconnect between consensus theory and on-the-ground reality is that the funded rule of law programming has been largely designed as a "top-down" approach to achieving legal reform. The focus of these programs—and the money that supports them—has been devoted to state institutions and the elites of the justice system. The World Bank legal vice presidency unit has formally announced that since "judges are the key to an effective and efficient legal system, the Bank's activities concentrate on judicial training; judicial codes of conduct; evaluation and discipline; qualification, appointment and promotion of judges."[58] In development discussions, the term "law reform" is sometimes literally equated with "judicial reform."[59]

The manifestation of this judiciary-centered approach is found in the significant expenditures on courthouse structures, equipment, judge training, and international judicial exchanges. Much smaller amounts are set aside for grassroots interventions. World Bank staff admit that part of the allure of investing in court buildings and equipment is that they are expensive, and therefore help achieve the bizarre-but-true priority for Bank personnel: to ensure that money is spent. "Disbursements are a primary indicator of a project's progress," Linn Hammergren, senior public sector management specialist in the World Bank Latin America Regional Department, has admitted. "The task manager's main concern, then, is to keep the money flowing."[60]

For example, a nearly $70 million law reform project in Guatemala, funded by the World Bank, the USAID, and the European Union, among others, was dominated by court construction and judicial training. The Bank evaluated the results of its investment as "moderately unsatisfactory," using its official project completion report to candidly acknowledge the limited efficacy of money spent on buildings and seminars.[61] "Although so obvious as to hardly bear mention, without counterpart buy-in, a judicial or institutional reform effort will not get far," the report said. "It is the corollary to this statement that is more important[:] buy-in means not just accepting the donor contributions, but rather internalizing and actively pursuing the change goals behind them."[62]

Rule of law assistance programs often include some support for civil society advocates of legal rights, in the form of direct legal services and funding. These allocations are usually bundled under the heading of "access to justice." But the size of these investments is dwarfed by the funds dedicated to construction projects and training programs for the legal system's elites. Erik Jensen, a former World Bank consultant and now codirector of Stanford University's Rule of Law program, calls the access to justice projects "lip service interventions." "Lip-service interventions always find their way into donor reports, but they receive very little if any MDB [multilateral development bank] funding," Jensen wrote in 2003. "Activities related to access to justice for disadvantaged sectors—women, the poor, lower castes—are always a part of the standard package, but, more often than not, the very last part."[63] For example, in Haiti, a $1 million 1999 grant from the US Department of Labor and the International Labor Organization, designed to encourage employers to respect labor rights and standards, was devoted entirely to an organization of employers, with none directed to worker organizations.[64]

Overall, this top-down approach has failed miserably. Despite great hopes, rule of law efforts in recent decades have been largely ineffective in achieving either meaningful legal reform or significant economic development. A 2006 World Bank–sponsored evaluation singled out the prevailing judiciary-centered approach for particular criticism:

> A limiting and unsuccessful emphasis on "form" rather than "function" seems to have dominated much of the rule of law reform over the years. Programs have typically focused on institutional objectives and formal legal structures without a measured understanding of the political and economic dynamics that prevented such structures from existing in the first place. . . . The focus on formal institutions has largely resulted in shell-like institutions, unenforced and poorly understood legislation, and judges and police with little commitment to the rights and values sought to be entrenched through the reform.[65]

New York University law professor Frank Upham has compared the international community's top-down rule of law investment strategy to the Soviet Union's failed economic model, and bluntly pronounced the record of law reform as "dismal."[66] That opinion is in line with empirical evaluations of judiciary-centered reforms, which demonstrate a lack of significant positive effects on the availability or efficiency of justice. For example, analyses of rule of law efforts in Latin America, the former Soviet Union, and Kosovo have all shown that most programs there have had neither indirect effects on economic development nor significant direct impact on the law as it applies to the people.[67]

Unfortunately, the experience in Haiti provides further evidence of the limitations of a top-down approach to building the rule of law. In the last twenty years, the USAID, the UN, the French and Canadian governments, and even the American Bar Association have all invested heavily in promoting the rule of law in Haiti. Programs have focused on the training and mentoring of judges, prosecutors, and police; support for a magistrates' school; construction of a police academy; donations of equipment; and renovations of courthouses. Precise breakdowns are hard to come by, but it appears clear that the money committed to this work was a meaningful portion of the estimated $6.7 billion in international aid that flowed to Haiti from 1995 to 2010. For example, USAID-supported justice programming for Haiti in the late 1990s cost about $97 million, and in 2006 the UN Development Programme and the Government of Canada launched an $11.6 million program to train judges and prison officials and rewrite the penal codes, among other goals. More recently, many international governments pledged that their post-earthquake support for Haiti would target the justice system.[68]

Yet the consensus is that the vast majority of this rule of law programming in Haiti has been completely ineffective. A 2004 assessment commissioned by the largest Haiti rule of law investor, USAID, found the Haitian public to be largely unaware of their legal rights, and that the justice system that serves them was inaccessible and unreliable: "Taken together, the result is that, despite the sizable financial and human efforts expended to improve the Haitian justice system, there are currently few areas where the efforts of past programs can be observed, and overall, past programs have had limited impact on the current state of the Haitian justice sector."[69] The 2005 OAS report reached a similar conclusion, echoing the somber verdict from a 2001 World Bank report: "There is nearly unanimous agreement among the international community that development assistance in the rule of law sector since 1994 has failed to produce tangible results."[70]

These same reports carried both explicit and implicit hints as to the reasons for the programs' lack of success. The reports' authors point to the lack of coordination among rule of law donors, and failures to account for Haitian customs and culture. The USAID-commissioned 2004 report also revealed, presumably unintentionally, a colonial-era attitude that could explain why some international rule of law interventions caused resentment from Haitians. A portion of the report states, "Clearly, efforts to engender a work ethic, self-starting initiative, and self-sufficiency [among Haitians] should be important ingredients for all future programs."[71] The report's authors also note "the need for Haitian citizens to learn how to be responsible members of a democratic society."[72] Absent from the report is any acknowledgment of a significant irony: the same document that lectures Haitians on the principles of democracy also discusses USAID funding for the International Foundation for Election Systems (IFES), which has been widely condemned for undermining Haiti's democratically elected government. IFES employees in Haiti were required to attend antigovernment demonstrations, and IFES used USAID funds to employ persons like Bernard Gousse and Gérard Latortue. Gousse and Latortue became justice minister and prime minister, respectively, in the government that took power when the democratically elected Aristide government was overthrown in the 2004 coup d'état, which occurred just a few months before the USAID-commissioned report was published.[73]

A common thread runs through all the post mortems on rule of law efforts in Haiti: the programs failed because of a lack of "political will" for justice reform. The need for, and absence of, political will is a theme in reports by the World Bank, the OAS, USAID, Haitian judges, various international human rights organizations and advocates, and the US Institute for Peace. The 2004 USAID-commissioned report actually used the term "political will" three times in its executive summary alone. This consensus diagnosis for the failures of Haitian programming mirrors the conclusions reached in examinations of similarly ill-fated rule of law efforts across the globe. Political will is explicitly identified as the chief barrier to achieving rule of law in developing countries in reports by UN leadership, Western law professors, African grassroots legal activists, and economists.[74]

Remarkably, for most of these commentators, the discussion stops there. The political will problem presents something of a black box for development and legal experts who have invested so much so unsuccessfully in places like Haiti. Thomas Carothers of the Carnegie Endowment for Peace says, with substantial justification, that "rule of law promoters are . . . short of knowledge on how the rule of law develops in societies and how such development can be stimulated beyond simplistic efforts to copy institutional forms."[75] Carothers went on to articulate more clearly the unknowns within the rule of law movement:

> Clearly law is not just the sum of courts, legislatures, police, prosecutors, and other formal institutions with some direct connection to law. Law is also a normative system that resides in the minds of the citizens of a society.[76]
>
> Major questions abound, still unanswered. For example, how does the will to reform develop? Can it be generated and if so how? Should we assume that institutions change through gradualist reform processes willed by persons inside the system? Does public pressure play a major role? What about abrupt, drastic change provoked by persons outside the institutions who are dissatisfied with their function or who have their own goals about what institutions to have?[77]

Indeed, these are the critical questions to be asked about efforts to support the rule of law and build respect for human rights. Since questions of social change and political will are unfamiliar to development and legal experts, they should invoke the practice of legal inquiry and call on expert witnesses to explain the phenomena.[78] Fortunately for those who seek answers to the "political will" questions that have vexed rule of law efforts, these questions have been the subject of generations of study in the social sciences.

In order to analyze the dynamics of social change, social scientists have carefully dissected the movements that successfully advocate for broad reform. Multiple studies have examined the roots and growth of efforts like the US civil rights movement of the mid-twentieth century, the Indian independence movement of a slightly earlier era, the South African antiapartheid movement, democracy movements in Russia and Eastern Europe, and the women's empowerment movement in Chile.[79] The results of these studies have led to evolving views about what creates political will for change. Until the 1970s, the dominant perspective in the study of social movements was "classical collective behavior" theory, which held that social movements come about because of the spontaneous behavior of aggrieved parties responding to increased discontent.[80] Following that, the "resource mobilization" and "political process" theories proved to better fit the available data. Those theories hold that social movements derive from more rational and strategic action constrained by external societal forces like governments or elites.[81]

Currently, the most credible observers of social movements find a middle ground. They see a combination of these psychological and structural factors to be present when a successful movement gets its start. For example, a study of the Tallahassee, Florida, civil rights movement found that key roles were played by both impromptu, passionate marches and the activities of existing student, church, and NAACP (National Association for the Advancement of Colored People) organizations.[82] Similar combinations of emotion and structure were present in the resistance to apartheid, opposition to Communist rule in Eastern Europe, and the anticolonialism movement.

Viewed through the lens of this social movement research, it becomes clear why rule of law investments in Haiti and elsewhere have had such limited success in overcoming the "political will" barrier to reform. The strategies of multilateral and bilateral investors in law reform concentrate on winning the hearts and minds of the judicial and political elite, but these efforts are undermined by the fact that the current systems' dysfunctional nature provides substantial benefits to those very elites. As Gary Haugen, president of the law reform organization International Justice Mission, has written, "Elites have little or no incentive to build legal institutions that serve the poor. A properly functioning legal system would only limit their power—and require a substantial commitment of financial and human resources."[83] Or, as the Haitians put it, *Moun rich, pà fé krim*. The history of social movements, including Haiti's own grassroots efforts to overcome slavery and remove Jean-Claude Duvalier and post-Duvalier dictators, shows that successful reforms are not likely to be initiated by the judges, prosecutors, or police. Instead, they will be initiated by the vast majority of Haitians who are economically poor, disenfranchised, and highly skeptical of the current justice system's commitment to democracy and human rights. Thus, the problem with rule of law investments is clear: social change comes from the bottom up, but rule of law dollars have been flowing from the top down.

Social movement history shows that reform-minded organizations like BAI and IJDH provide the platforms on which the aggrieved majority acts. And social movement outcome research shows that the relative strength of these organizations pushing for reform, as measured in terms of size, network ties, internal organization, and fundraising ability, will ultimately determine the success of any reform efforts. An oft-cited example is Aldon Morris's analysis of the organizations supporting the 1960 African American sit-in movement, a pivotal development in the US civil rights struggle.[84] In the Haitian rule of law context, the obvious analogs to these civil rights reform organizations are BAI, IJDH, and other groups pushing for reform. Properly supported, these existing and evolving law reform groups and their leaders are poised to play the pivotal roles that social movement historians, along with iconic movement organizers like Saul Alinsky, have long predicted for them.[85] As Kirsti Samuels notes in her 2006 World Bank report discussing the future of the efforts to instill the rule of law, "Domestic political reform pressure and local political reform champions are essential for real [rule of law] change. There must be a systematic focus on identifying and supporting 'agents of change' who have a driving will to reform."[86]

In Haiti, these hoped-for agents of change are already in place, in the form of BAI and IJDH, their leaders, their clients, and their colleagues. The lesson of social movement studies is that these activists are likely to lead the way toward Haiti's adopting and respecting the rule of law. BAI provides the indigenous leadership that is the foundation of any successful reform effort. And social movement studies show that IJDH, with its US-based fundraising capabilities and access to international media and decision-makers, also provides a needed component of the campaign to instill the rule of law in Haiti. The US women's suffrage movement, the Indian independence movement, the US civil rights movement, the South African antiapartheid movement, and the US farm worker movement, among many others, were all supported financially by individuals and organizations who could readily obtain funding and attention to sustain the movements.[87]

A dramatic example of the value provided by outside supporters of social movements is provided by Craig Jenkins and Charles Perrow's study of US farm worker movements. In comparing a failed 1946–1952 attempt by the national Farm Labor Union to organize farm workers with a successful effort by the United Farm Workers in 1965–1972, Jenkins and Perrow found no difference in the levels of farm worker discontent, the talents and dedication of the organizers, or the methods of contention. The difference between success and failure, they concluded, was the support of outside "liberal" groups like church organizations and organized labor, which was far more substantial for the latter movement. Jenkins and Perrow conclude that this scenario was not just fortuitous to the second movement, it was a prerequisite for its success: "Are deprived groups like the farm workers able to sustain challenges, especially effective ones, on their own? We think not. . . . For a successful outcome, movements by the 'powerless' require strong and sustained outside support."[88]

The global movement against apartheid in South Africa provides a notable recent example of an effective local-transnational advocacy partnership with characteristics very similar to the BAI-IJDH relationship. A lesser-known precedent can be found in Chilean legal advocates' documentation of human rights abuses during the 1970s and 1980s. Indigenous advocates compiled damning evidence of injustice, which was then used by transnational human rights groups to pressure the Chilean government and obtain consistent UN condemnation of the government's human rights record.[89]

In this tradition, BAI and IJDH engage in an ambitious agenda of human rights advocacy. Their docket includes community-based programs on rape accountability and prevention, housing rights, and prisoners' rights, along with international advocacy for fair elections in Haiti, earthquake response, and immigration rights for the Haitian diaspora. BAI helps organize street-blocking protests by camp dwellers facing eviction, and loud, aggressive demonstrations in protest of the UN's cholera response. BAI even houses multiple grassroots organizations and an independent newspaper in its Port-au-Prince offices. High-profile litigation, such as the claims on behalf of Duvalier victims and cholera victims, serves a vital movement-building role by "framing" the grievances of the Haitian people. Erving Goffman, in his influential 1974 book, *Frame Analysis: An Essay on the Organization of Experience*, outlined the process of individuals constructing their own reality by organizing events in a way that gives coherent meaning and guides their future action.[90] Framing includes the use of provocative words and language to mobilize action, with notable contemporary US examples being anti-abortion advocates' labeling of late-term procedures as "partial-birth abortion," or the Occupy movement's "We are the 99%" slogan. As Robert Benford and David Snow put it, the social movement organizer's task is to create frames that will "move people from the balcony to the barricades."[91]

It may seem obvious that a dysfunctional system and its political leaders would be blamed for a widespread lack of justice. But research on the psychological phenomenon of "system justification" shows a common human predisposition to defend and justify the status quo, even among those who are most harmed by the existing system.[92] Therefore, social movements must organize around issues that are framed in sympathetic terms, and the terms must be understandable to the population at large, the media, and the leaders who are being pressed to make changes. When advocates like BAI and IJDH directly confront tangible, ground-level instances of injustice, such as sexual assaults by the Haitian police or government evictions of post-earthquake camp dwellers, they become ideal frame articulators. The lawyers and other advocates provide the empirical credibility of the collective action frame, which is a key factor in determining whether the frame will have resonance. Specifically, social movement history indicates that collective protest stands a better chance of success when movements identify victims of injustice and amplify their victimization into "injustice frames" in advance of calls for change.[93] A recent example was provided by the brutal death of a young antigovernment activist at the hands of Egyptian police, which led to the rallying cry "We are all Khaled Said" that animated the 2011 Arab Spring antigovernment protests in Cairo.

The framing process is particularly crucial when the aspiring movement is presented with a galvanizing moment or crisis. High-profile grievances, whether the subject of formal litigation or not, are often ideal vehicles for providing both the galvanizing moment and the opportunity to frame the issue as an injustice applicable to a broad population. The most iconic US example of both framing and galvanizing is the litigation challenging racial segregation in public schools, which culminated in the 1954 US Supreme Court decision in *Brown v. Board of Education* rejecting the concept of "separate but equal." Ironically, the Brown decision had little immediate effect on school segregation, but it has been described by Richard Kluger as "the catalytic event that began the Second Reconstruction paralleling the one after the Civil War," and as the "parent" of the mass civil rights movement.[94]

A similar triggering effect was caused by a 1971 International Court of Justice ruling against continued South African control and apartheid-themed occupation over an area then called "South-West Africa." The ruling led to statements of support from church leaders, educators, and tribal chiefs, followed by widespread strikes that led to more favorable labor agreements and continued the momentum toward the eventual liberation of South-West Africa into the independent nation of Namibia. Subsequent public interest litigation in southern Africa helped chip away at tangible components of apartheid, such as pass laws and prisoner abuse, as well as apartheid's veneer of invincibility.[95]

As BAI and IJDH show by their work with community organizing and international lobbying, legal rights advocates can also operate in venues far beyond the courtroom. In 2007, lawyers in Pakistan conducted high-profile street demonstrations against President Pervez Musharraf's attempts to dismiss the country's chief justice and impose emergency rule.[96] In another example, lawyers teamed with traditional social movement organizers to educate and empower black villagers to block a forced removal in apartheid South Africa. Also in South Africa, legal advocates supplemented rights-oriented litigation with nonviolent resistance to attempts to remove blacks to "homelands," and helped inform and empower the country's labor movement, which played a key role in opposing apartheid.[97] An historical example of the key non-litigation role that lawyers can play in framing a grievance and triggering broader action is found in the removal of Guatemalan dictator General Jorge Ubico y Castaneda in 1944, when forty-five lawyers wrote a series of articles in a Guatemala City newspaper and became the first citizens to publicly call out the general about corruption in the judiciary. The articles triggered teacher and student protests, demonstrations, and a public strike. Within a month, Ubico resigned.[98]

Jean Sénat Fleury is not a social movement historian, but he certainly knows about the challenge of building the rule of law in Haiti. Fleury worked in the Haitian judicial system for eighteen years, moving up from a role as local justice of the peace to become an instructor at both the National Police Academy and the School of Magistrates. He eventually became a respected *juge d'instruction*, or investigating magistrate. In November 2004, Fleury was assigned the case of Father Jean-Juste. Jean-Juste had been dramatically arrested and jailed by the coup government he had been criticizing, and Minister of Justice Bernard Gousse had publicly accused the priest of terrorist intentions and murder. But in Fleury's courtroom, the government could not produce a single witness, document, or other evidence to link Jean-Juste to any illegal activity. Fleury ordered that Jean-Juste be released. Justice Minister Gousse in turn decreed that all of Fleury's cases be taken from him. Another judge was assigned to the Jean-Juste case, and the priest was rearrested. Fleury resigned in protest.

Fleury has since written several books and continues to advocate for the rule of law in Haiti. His 2009 book, *The Challenges of Judicial Reform in Haiti*, is dedicated to his friend Laraque Exantus, a prosecutor who had been investigating the 1993 murder of Justice Minister Guy Malary, a killing that was rumored to be an operation of the Haitian military and police. Exantus himself was kidnapped from his home in February 1994, and was never seen again. In his book, Fleury strongly agrees with the consensus that most of the international efforts to reform Haiti's justice system have failed, and that the current system achieves the double distinction of being both distrusted and inaccessible. Like every other indictment of the Haitian justice system, Fleury's book singles out political will as the foundation essential for any meaningful reform: "Without the political will to make the changes that guarantee each citizen's constitutional rights, the State will inevitably sink beneath the combined flood of financial crime, removing the last defenses against brutality and harm from smuggling, armed gangs, and the anarchy of an atrophied banking system that drowns legitimate businesses."[99]

Speaking from his home in Boston, where he immigrated to after his clashes with the Haitian government, Fleury talked about the requirements for creating that political will in Haiti. "There are many poor people in Haiti, and these people's voices need to be heard. The work of organizations like BAI can give a voice to these people, and the international partnership gives them credibility, and helps keep them safe from reprisals within Haiti."

Fleury has worked with Mario Joseph and Brian Concannon on many cases, including the Raboteau and Jean-Juste litigation, and he praises them personally as skilled and effective attorneys. But Fleury puts special emphasis on the grassroots organizing and communication efforts by BAI and IJDH: "Giving a voice to the people who do not have access to justice is more important than their work inside the courtroom. When justice is difficult to find in a courtroom, and it certainly is in Haiti, you have to push to find it outside."

4 | The Raboteau Trial

The Haitian military leaders who had overthrown the elected government led by Jean-Bertrand Aristide in 1991 knew they were governing in contradiction to the popular will. They had removed Aristide in September of that year, less than ten months after he won 67 percent of the votes cast in the first true democratic election in Haitian history. So the Haitian army, led by Lieutenant General Raul Cédras, systematically and ruthlessly cracked down on any resistance to their rule. "We the people elected Aristide," pro-democracy activist Marie Denise Fleury would say later. "When the people have said yes, it is like a tattoo. When the people have said yes, you have to cut the people to erase this ink."[1]

The army's efforts to erase this resistance were bolstered by the paramilitary group FRAPH, the Revolutionary Front for the Advancement and Progress of Haiti. "The armed barricades that were common at this time were manned not by the military, but by FRAPH," said Colin Granderson, who led the UN/OAS Civilian Mission in Haiti during the years of the coup government. "Clearly, FRAPH had significant money with which to organize and have a presence. And the FRAPH leaders flaunted this; they were everywhere."[2] Much of that money appeared to come from the United States, and it was later confirmed that FRAPH leader Emmanuel "Toto" Constant was on the payroll of the Central Intelligence Agency.[3] Working together, the Haitian military and FRAPH killed an estimated three thousand Haitians in the three years following the 1991 coup. They tortured, raped, and displaced thousands more.[4]

The attacks were not random. "During the coup years, there was a period distinguished by the systemization of repression that took the form of attacks against a specific part of the population," said Camille LeBlanc, Haiti's minister of justice in 2000–2001.[5] In other words, the army and FRAPH were intent on killing off their opposition. A part of the population that attracted special interest was located in a small, crowded, and very poor shantytown section of the coastal city of Gonaïves. The area was called Raboteau.

"Gonaïves is very important in our history," says Fritz Dèsir, then and now a resident of Raboteau. "Every country has a center of resistance. For Haiti, it is Gonaïves, and Raboteau in particular." Opponents of the coup government began to congregate in the Raboteau area, some of them coming from the nearby communities and some traveling from other parts of Haiti to join like-minded colleagues. As Dèsir tells it, the movement's philosophy was straightforward: "We elect a president, and this president should be returned to Haiti. So we try to express our resistance *pacifik*—peacefully." They conducted demonstrations in the narrow streets of Raboteau, carrying signs that said *Fok prezidan konstitisyonel la tournen* (The elected president must return) and *Aba Cédras* (Down with Cédras), and singing songs with verses like *Nou pap aksepte viv nan kondisyon sa yo* (We do not accept living in this condition). When OAS observers were present in the area, the soldiers would allow the protesters to demonstrate. When the observers left, the soldiers' forbearance went with them. In response, the demonstrators planned sudden, quick protests that lasted only until the military and FRAPH forces stormed in to break them up. The demonstrators would then run and hide in homes or flee to small fishing boats in the nearby Gulf of Gonâve, which leads to the Caribbean Sea. "We called the sea 'The Embassy,'" says Charles Eddy Joseph, one of the movement leaders. "It was our safe place, where they could not get to us."

After the soldiers left, the movement leaders would return to shore. But during these same months, tens of thousands of Haitians took to the sea with more long-term escape in mind, many heading to the United States in small boats. The resulting refugee crisis and an international activist campaign focused attention on Haiti's military leaders, and in 1992, newly elected US president Bill Clinton publicly committed to supporting Aristide's return. Feeling the pressure, the military and FRAPH increased their presence in Raboteau. Observers like Father Daniel Roussière of the Gonaïves branch of Commission Justice et Paix, a Catholic human rights group, saw storm clouds gathering. "This was not about killing a few people, but killing the resistance movement. To kill this resistance, they had to strike the Haitian people in one of the hearts of the resistance, which was Raboteau," he said.[6] The military and paramilitary felt the need to send a message, said Michèle Pierre-Louis, the longtime director of the Foundation for Knowledge and Freedom and later the prime minister of Haiti from 2008 to 2009. "Clinton had taken power and Aristide's return is on the horizon," Pierre-Louis said. "[So the military says] 'You want to participate [in the government]—well, see what will happen to you. And we have the power to do it. The power to exterminate you. Because you don't count in this society, and we want it to stay that way so that you will never count.'"[7]

The first concerted blow against the Raboteau resistance occurred on April 18, 1994. Military and FRAPH members attacked the area, apparently looking for leaders of the pro-democracy movement, especially a man named Amiot Métayer. Typically, movement leaders like Métayer stayed out of sight as much as possible, so a favorite strategy for the coup government was to attack the family and community of the leaders so as to lure the preferred targets out. Troops stormed into Raboteau on the eighteenth, but leaders like Métayer and Charles Eddy Joseph were able to escape to the sea. Apparently acting on the mistaken belief that Raboteau resident Valcius Valcin was Métayer's father, soldiers began beating the man with clubs and rifle butts. "He was an old man, blind for twenty-seven years," says Marie-Denise Fleury, who witnessed the attack.[8] The next morning, Valcin died from his injuries.

In the early morning hours of April 22, the military and paramilitary returned to Raboteau, this time with a much larger force and a more sophisticated plan of attack. Mary Nicolas remembers waking up before dawn on the twenty-second to the sounds of soldiers breaking down her front door. As she and her family fled out the back, gunfire sounded behind them. Charles Eddy Joseph ran too, and saw several others gunned down as they fled. Soldiers had circled the neighborhood before charging into homes, and were spraying automatic weapon fire. The soldiers grabbed people and forced some into the sewage canal. Fleury was kicked by soldiers and had a gun held to her head. Jean Claude François saw several people being beaten by soldiers. Many Raboteau residents ran to the reliable escape route of the sea, but "The Embassy" was no longer a sanctuary for them. While Haitian army and FRAPH members chased people out of the neighborhood, other military soldiers and members of the paramilitary lay in wait on the shore and in boats, machine guns in hand. When the Raboteau residents ran to the harbor and tried to climb into boats to make their escape, the armed men opened fire.

No one is sure how many people were killed in Raboteau that morning, but the consensus is that between ten to twenty people were murdered, dozens injured, and several others arrested and tortured. The attack plan included a regimen for disposing of the bodies in a way that would eliminate evidence of the massacre. Victims' legs were tied together and pieces of iron or brick affixed to them so that the bodies would sink when thrown into the sea. Some corpses that did not completely sink floated to shore a few days later. Other bodies were buried in shallow graves that were soon dug up by pigs and dogs. For several weeks, residents would see animals walking the streets of Raboteau, carrying human body parts in their mouths.

As the Raboteau community grieved, the Haitian diaspora kept up the pressure on the US government to return Aristide to leadership. Their calls for action were buttressed by brave eyewitnesses who snuck out of Haiti to deliver reports of coup leaders' abuses, Haitians who conducted hunger strikes in immigrant detention centers in the United States and on Guantanamo Bay, and an international network of sympathetic journalists and activists.[9] Finally, in October 1994, the Clinton administration helped restore Aristide to his elected post in Haiti, but only after first compelling Aristide to provide amnesty for those who had carried out the coup.[10] The US military allowed the Haitian military and FRAPH high command to flee Haiti, and the United States seized tens of thousands of pages of documents from army and FRAPH headquarters, including gruesome evidence of torture sessions whose victims had been depicted in photographs that were pinned to office walls like trophies. (For several years, the United States refused repeated requests to return the documents to the Haitian government.)[11] After a popular poll showed 62 percent of Haitians supported eliminating the military, Aristide disbanded the army.[12]

The amnesty Aristide was forced to grant covered only the actions of the actual September 1991 coup, and none of the many atrocities that occurred in the following three years. So Aristide founded Bureau des Avocats Internationaux, and charged it with the mission of providing non-Haitian attorneys to assist the Haitian government in the prosecution of human rights violators. Under this original model, BAI received government funding and was supervised by Miami attorney and longtime Aristide advocate Ira Kurzban. Aristide and Kurzban's aim was to bring the talents and resources of international lawyers to the process of reforming the Haitian justice system.[13]

Florence Elie, the coordinator of the Raboteau trial for the Haitian government, said that these prosecutions were the first step toward Haiti moving past the tragic coup years. "After a long period of repression, it is very important that the victims be recognized—that the truth be brought up so that everyone can have the cathartic experience and make sure that it is behind us," she said. Elie is herself the widow of a political murder victim, the assassinated Haitian justice minister Guy Malary. "We need to make sure we have the strength to build instead of always going back to the past," she said.[14]

It was a sound philosophy. But, for Haiti, it was a novel one. The formal legal system had never before played a role in dispensing justice after a regime change. After Jean-Claude Duvalier was forced out of Haiti in 1986, several villages created ad hoc tribunals to prosecute the *tontons makouts* presidential militia, but dozens more *makouts* were hunted down and killed by vengeful mobs.[15] A chant from a Vodou justice-seeking ceremony reflected the prevailing view of the official legal system: "There is a state, but there is no justice. Lend me a chair so I can sit and watch them. It's their country. They'll do what they want."[16] Haitian lawyers and judges could not afford to be any less cynical, Brian Concannon says, even in the heady days after Aristide was returned and the army dissolved. The lawyers and judges were "worried about making enemies because they didn't know who would be on top next time," Concannon says. "Based on Haitian history, it has been a fair bet that there'll be a coup on a fairly regular basis."[17]

But the Raboteau community resisted any urges to take matters into their own hands, and instead looked to the official legal system for justice. After Aristide's return, they redirected their activism toward pushing for prosecution of those responsible for the April 1994 attacks. They created a Raboteau victims organization and conducted regular demonstrations in the town square, singing "If you are not corrupt, arrest the criminals / We demand they be judged, those murderers, judge them! / Don't you hear us?"[18] Reed Brody, now an attorney with Human Rights Watch, worked at BAI for a time in its early days. "The impetus for justice came from below," he says. "In Raboteau, it was the strongest. Precisely because the victims themselves were demanding justice is why, in Raboteau, you could break through this inertia, remove the obstacles, to overcome the fact that the US was holding the documents, that the really top [army and paramilitary] guys were out of the country."[19]

The first test for the BAI and Aristide government plan to prosecute human rights violations came in the trial of the alleged killers of Guy Malary. After speaking out in opposition to the coup government, Malary had been gunned down in broad daylight in Port-au-Prince on October 14, 1993. Two men, former Army corporal Jean-Romique Antoine and civilian Robert Lecorps, were charged with the murder and brought to trial in July 1996.[20]

Concannon was newly hired by the BAI and did not participate in the trial. But he watched the proceedings, and saw several problems. The prosecution relied too heavily on accounts of eyewitnesses and did not bolster the testimony with enough documentary evidence, Concannon thought. The chief prosecutor did not interview the Malary murder eyewitnesses before trial, and the same prosecutor signaled his lack of interest in the case to the jury. That jury was made up of wealthy and well-connected Haitians. One juror was the anchorman for the government-controlled TV station during the coup period, and two others seemed to be personal friends of the defense counsel. BAI lawyers participated in trial preparations but did not actually represent the victim in the case, nor did they have a Haitian lawyer on their team. Overall, Concannon thought, the prosecution's case was weak. When the fifteen-person jury returned a not-guilty verdict for the Malary defendants, he was not surprised. Concannon had recently been assigned to the Raboteau case, and he vowed to learn from the mistakes he saw.

Even before the unsuccessful Malary trial, BAI was reconsidering the original Aristide-Kurzban plan to staff the organization with only non-Haitian lawyers. With other BAI lawyers working on the Malary case, it was left to Concannon to interview and hire two Haitian attorneys. He chose Mario Joseph and one other attorney, and proceeded to finalize the hires. "Then I mentioned something I thought would not be a controversial point," Concannon recalls. "I said, 'By the way, we have to have no boundaries here. Even though you are lawyers, if you have to go to a poor person's home to interview them, you'll need to be willing to do that. You'll need to make photocopies yourself a lot of the time. We'll be representing the poorest of the poor in Raboteau and meeting them where they are, so you'll need to get in the mud figuratively and literally sometimes."

Both of the lawyers looked at Concannon and said, "Absolutely not." The Haitian culture and strong message of law school training both hold that lawyers exist above the level of the poor masses and are expected to maintain that distance. Then and now, Haitian lawyers spend their days in their offices or in court, where they make speeches that are eloquent but often somewhat disconnected from the realities of their clients' lives. Concannon's offhand request to break down barriers was offensive to Joseph and the other attorney. They had no intention of debasing themselves and their profession the way the young American lawyer was suggesting. The hiring negotiations broke down, and the three agreed to think about their positions and get back together later. Ultimately, the Haitian lawyer slated to be hired with Joseph at BAI turned down the job. By that time, Concannon understood better. "I am sure he is still proud of standing up and defending the dignity of Haitian lawyers from the imperialist jerk who would demean his noble profession," Concannon says. "I get it now, but we were going about the advocacy process in a different way."

Joseph decided to accept the job. It was not the first time Mario Joseph found himself traveling a different path than that of the typical Haitian lawyer. Joseph describes his childhood in warm terms: his memories include swimming and fishing in the Artibonite River with his brother, his cousins, and his friends. "Even if you have money or can be close to a beach, to me the best place to relax is the river," he says.[21] But Joseph's family also knew hunger. They had no access to electricity, and many of his relatives never went to school.

Joseph's background of rural poverty meant that he struggled to afford his own schooling at every turn. At one point, he started his own small school, teaching math to young students, saving the meager tuition money he received from those students to pay the bills for his own legal education. Even as a first-year law student at the State University in Gonaïves, Joseph began sitting in the Peace Courts (the lowest court level in Haiti), helping peasants translate French court documents into Creole. "Mario was always different from other Haitian lawyers," Kurzban says. "He comes from a background where he really understands what it means to be voiceless, poor, dispossessed, and he chose the path of speaking for people who are the most vulnerable."

So Joseph was happy to sign on to work with BAI, and eager to take on the challenge of representing the poor who were victimized by human rights abuses. He was not quite so eager to be working with Concannon. The two young lawyers—Joseph was then thirty-three, Concannon thirty-two—eyed each other warily across a wide gap of culture, privilege, and language. Concannon appreciated Joseph's clear affinity with Haiti's poor and never questioned Joseph's integrity, an unusual quality among Haitian lawyers participating in a deeply corrupted system. But Concannon felt that Joseph was, like many other Haitian attorneys he had observed, more attentive to oral presentations than the written work of practicing law.

If anything, Joseph was even less impressed with his new partner. Interviewed for a 2003 report by the Harvard University Project on Justice in Times of Transition, Joseph said that he knew that Concannon was proud of his French and his efforts to master Creole. But Joseph did not think Concannon's French was up to par and thought Concannon was deluding himself about his Creole skills. For several months, while he weighed whether Concannon was in fact a CIA agent sent to undermine the Aristide administration, Joseph measured every word he said in front of his American colleague. He did not think he would have to hold his tongue long, because Joseph thought the Raboteau trial would be prepared for and wrapped up within a few months. After that, he was sure, Concannon would leave Haiti.[22]

Years later, Joseph spoke about the experience of starting work at BAI. "All of my colleagues ridiculed my work, or dismissed it because I was using my talents on behalf of people without much social status. They thought I was bringing down the exalted position of the attorney. But as we developed our program, people saw that we had talented lawyers from the US coming down to volunteer to work with us. And most importantly, they saw us winning: winning in Haitian courts against more prestigious lawyers, and winning in international courts."

By now, Mario Joseph's name appears to be attached to the suffix "Haiti's most prominent human rights lawyer." To international advocates, human rights agencies, and even the *New York Times*, it is his unofficial title.[23] In 2013, he was one of three finalists for the Martin Ennals Award for Human Rights Defenders, an award bestowed by a coalition of ten international human rights organizations, including Amnesty International, Human Rights Watch, and the International Commission of Jurists, and sometimes referred to as the Nobel Prize for human rights.[24] The recognition is derived in part from the enormous breadth of Joseph's hybrid work as a lawyer/organizer/activist/spokesperson. In the current cholera case, for example, Joseph interviews and retains the clients, drafts or reviews all legal pleadings, helps organize the street demonstrations, coordinates the intra-Haiti media outreach, and is the chief liaison between the Haitian lawyers and other individuals involved with the case, including advocates with the international human rights agencies, lawmakers, and global media personnel. "The level of work he does simply cannot be done by one person, so I am still not sure how he pulls it all off," says Kurzban. "He has to be the voice of the people who have no voice all over the country, and that seems to be an impossible burden."

Paul Farmer says that Joseph is one of his heroes, in part because he empowers others who work for justice in Haiti. "Pro-democracy and human-rights activists know that if they are arrested or 'disappeared,' Mario will be there to fight for their freedom. That gives some people the courage they need to act, and others the patience they need to act non-violently," Farmer says. "By helping Haitians enforce their civil rights, including their rights to organize, to send their children to school, and to free and fair elections, Mario is making profound social changes in Haiti."[25]

Part of the challenge of being a human rights leader in Haiti is managing the actions of angry comrades in a society where violence has been a common reaction to injustice. During a Port-au-Prince march near the National Palace to commemorate the one-year anniversary of the earthquake, demonstrators looked up to see large pieces of concrete flying through the air. Some of the Haitians participating in the demonstration were throwing rocks at MINUSTAH soldiers patrolling the area surrounding the group. Joseph's response was to immediately expel the rock-throwers from the demonstration. Some hard feelings ensued, but a message was delivered:

no matter how justifiable your frustration may be, nonviolence is a nonnegotiable component of being a part of the cause he and BAI are working for.

People who know Joseph bring up his bravery so often that the praise becomes eerie, as if one is hearing the prelude to martyrdom. Joseph's era of living dangerously began immediately after the 2004 coup. He and BAI were closely associated with the departed Aristide, whose supporters were targets of the coup government. Joseph left Haiti after the coup only long enough to settle his wife and children in Miami, where they eventually received political asylum because of the danger to them in Haiti. Then, just ten days after Aristide was forced out, and against all advice, Joseph returned to Port-au-Prince and BAI. Since then, shots have been fired into his office and he has received multiple death threats, including a bullet sent to him in an envelope. Amnesty International issued an Urgent Action alert in 2004 regarding Joseph's safety, and he often stays in different places for security reasons.[26] As recently as October of 2012, another Amnesty International alert was issued for Joseph's safety after the former chief prosecutor of Port-au-Prince claimed he had been ordered to arrest Joseph.[27] At the same time, Joseph received a new series of death threats.

No one in Haiti takes such threats lightly. One of Joseph's fellow Haitian prodemocracy activists, Lovinsky Pierre-Antoine, was abducted in August 2007 and has never been heard from again.[28] "Mario is the most courageous person I know," says Kurzban. "You have to appreciate Haiti to understand how his life is in danger every day. In Haiti, ministers of justice have been executed, and human rights advocates have been executed. If Mario is perceived as a threat to the old-line Duvalierists or the elite, they will execute him. They have no compunction about that."

Joseph's personal commitment and his own life history of overcoming poverty have earned him the loyalty of Haiti's poor and the praise of international supporters of human rights. "You have the sense of this person who was born and put on this earth to do what he is doing," says international philanthropist and IJDH supporter Karen Ansara. One of Joseph's gifts is his ability to project a powerful presence when making public speeches, a quality Ansara refers to when she calls Joseph the Martin Luther King Jr. of Haiti. "When he speaks, it is riveting because he speaks with so much passion and real experience to back it up. He is a prophet. He is the person who speaks truth to power."

Like all talented speakers, Joseph varies his approach according to his audience. On December 9, 2011, wearing a T-shirt and baseball cap, he addressed a protest outside a MINUSTAH base in St. Marc. Joseph sharply condemned the UN for its role in the cholera outbreak and led the crowd in turning directly to the UN soldiers lined up in front of the base. "Who brought us the *kolera*?" he yelled in Creole, pointing to the base. "MINUSTAH!" the crowd responded. He repeated the call-and-response several times, and the crowd pointed to the soldiers each time. "This is just the beginning," he said. "Next time, we will protest in Mirebalais, where they defecated in our water!" The crowd cheered. "We need *jistis*!" Joseph yelled. "Can we wait?" "No, we can't wait!" the crowd responded, jumping up and down and waving their hands. Then all joined in a hand-clapping, jumping chant of "*Jistis ak reparasyon* [justice and reparations], *jistis ak reparasyon, jistis ak reparasyon!*"[29]

A few months later, wearing a suit and tie, Joseph was the guest of honor at a gathering of human rights lawyers in New York City. In decidedly more measured tones, and in English, he said:

> I cannot address a group of people so committed to using the law to advance social justice without discussing the roots of injustice in my country, Haiti. Some of the roots of our injustice lie underneath Haitian soil, from decisions and actions by political, social and economic leaders. . . . But many of the roots of Haitian injustice extend north, starting in places like New York and Washington. . . . If the roots of our injustice extend to powerful countries, it is essential that the fight for our justice extend there, too. Right now the fight for justice in Haiti is a heavy load, because we feel we are fighting the UN, the US, and many other powerful actors. I invite everyone here to join the Haitian people in this struggle. Together we can make the load light enough to carry, and establish the just society that my people deserve.

The New York lawyers gave him a standing ovation.

Within Haiti and beyond, Joseph is reversing the popular imagination of what a Haitian lawyer can be, says Mildred Trouillot-Aristide, the wife of Jean-Bertrand Aristide and a lawyer and human rights activist herself. "Mario has established himself as the human rights–centered and victim-driven voice on legal, political, social, economic, and health injustices that plague Haiti," Trouillot-Aristide says. "That says a lot—because it is far from the typical role or perception of the Haitian lawyer. Beyond Mario's considerable legal work, I think that his legacy will be his contribution in changing the lawyer's image in Haiti and setting new national standards on defending human rights—while showing young lawyers what is possible."

An object lesson of Joseph's role was provided one day in 2009, when a team of physicians from Partners in Health and lawyers from BAI arrived at a rural prison near Hinche and set up in the prison yard. The prisoners were allowed to go out of their cells to see the doctors and lawyers, and dozens of men came streaming out. In their wake, however, was another man, crawling in the dust, using his elbows to propel himself forward while his legs dragged uselessly behind. Dr. Evan Lyon of Partners in Health and Joseph spoke to the man and learned he was imprisoned because his son had been accused of stealing a cow. The son had fled to the Dominican Republic, so the man was put in jail in his place. Shortly after his arrest, the father suffered what appeared to be a paralyzing stroke. "I have never seen any problem of any kind fixed so quickly in Haiti," Lyon recalls:

Mario just sprang into action, heading immediately to the local courthouse to gather documents and find this guy's file. Within an hour, we were in front of the local judge and Mario has me explain the medical situation and he argues the legal perspective. Sure enough, this guy was given his release.

One of the nice things about Mario is that he didn't say, "Look at me, look at the nice thing I did." Instead, he just said it was silly that this kind of intervention needed to happen in the first place. He provided a very meaningful and staggering critique of the state of the law that this man would be put in this situation.

IJDH staff attorney Nicole Phillips has observed Joseph working on the international stage, translating for him in meetings with UN delegations and at human rights conferences. She has watched delegations of global activists line up to hug him, saying "You are my brother!" She remembers accompanying Joseph to multiple meetings at the US Social Forum in Detroit five months after the 2010 earthquake. Joseph was shocked to learn about the massive evictions connected with the US foreclosure crisis, and found solidarity with others who were fighting for housing rights just as he was doing in Haiti. It being so soon after the earthquake's devastation, emotions were still running high, and activists from around the world wanted to speak with Joseph and share their sorrow. "He was so patient and so willing to talk to people, over and over again, about the suffering going on in Haiti," Phillips says. "On a personal level, he was coming from a place that was truly selfless, and you can't help but connect with that."

As Joseph and Concannon would later admit, they began their work on the Raboteau case with very little idea of the scope of the challenge ahead. "A human rights case in Haiti presented a completely blank page," Concannon says—except for the black mark of the Malary trial.[30] So the first mandate of the Raboteau prosecution was to avoid the mistakes of the Malary prosecution.

By Concannon's estimation, the biggest problem in the Malary trial was that the Haitian system was simply not yet prepared to handle some critical prosecution tasks, including detailed fact investigations. He and Joseph decided that BAI's role would be a flexible one, with the overall goal of providing whatever support the official Haitian system needed for the Raboteau case. "Our main contribution was to accept no excuses for failure: we took it upon ourselves to make sure that the system worked at every level necessary to have a fair trial. We didn't do it all ourselves—there were lots of others doing great work. But we would never accept that the case wasn't going to work because someone else didn't do their job," Concannon says now. "I think this is an important point, and one that has defined our work from the beginning. I have seen over and over again, in legal and development programs, both that the programs are not calibrated to the actual challenges, and that the foreign actors define success by their completion of certain defined tasks, rather than ensuring an overall result. The programs inevitably fail when engaging with reality, so then the *blan* [Creole for "foreigners"] throw up their hands and say, 'We did what we could . . .' and blame Haiti or Haitians for their predictable failure."

Joseph and Concannon began spending most of their days in Gonaïves, away from the BAI offices and their homes in Port-au-Prince, searching for witnesses and victims during the day and staying in the homes of friends at night. With Haiti's low rate of literacy, the most effective form of mass communication was by radio, so Joseph and Concannon began speaking on radio shows, encouraging those with information about the massacre to come forward. By now, over two years had passed since the attacks, and it was impossible to create a reliable, factual picture of the events from scratch. So Joseph's and Concannon's efforts were aided by the work of a courageous Raboteau justice of the peace, Jean-Baptiste Dorismond. Dorismond had defied the obvious wishes of the brutal coup government by going door-to-door the day after the 1994 killings, interviewing witnesses and documenting damage caused to homes. The French priest Father Daniel Roussière also assisted in the immediate aftermath of the attacks, gathering medical records and collecting witness statements.

Based on their fact-gathering and research of the Haitian penal code, Joseph and Concannon drafted a complaint for their victim clients. In October 1996, they filed the claim in court, marking the beginning of the formal legal process. An investigating judge, the *juge d'instruction*, had already been working on the Raboteau case, but it would be several more years—and multiple intervening changes in investigating judges—before a final *ordonnance*, or criminal charging instrument, was issued by Judge Jean Sénat Fleury of the Gonaïves Trial Court. (As described in Chapter 3, Fleury was the same judge who would in 2004 order the release of Father Gérard Jean-Juste, only to have the coup government's justice minister order Fleury removed from the case and Jean-Juste rearrested.) An investigating judge in the Haitian judicial system has many duties that are similar to those of the charging prosecutor in the US system, and the judge does not preside over the same trial that he investigated. Joseph and Concannon worked with Fleury to produce a 173-page-long *ordonnance* outlining the charges, a document still considered to be the most thorough ever prepared by the Haitian justice system.

BAI's original vision was to provide a "jumpstart for the justice system," in Concannon's recollection. "We were supposed to provide some investigating, legal advice, and other consultant-type help to get investigations rolling, then have the system take over. This made sense to me at the time, but as the Malary case made clear, it was like jumpstarting a car that had no brakes, steering wheel, or pistons." So Joseph and Concannon turned to Haiti's *partie civile* process, which allowed them to work side-by-side with prosecutors and judges like Fleury. It was important, they believed, for the prosecutors and judges not only to be familiar with the case and to produce solid legal instruments. They also needed to embrace the radical notion that the Haitian legal system could pronounce justice on the powerful on behalf of the poor. "Judges and prosecutors and ministers [of justice] were afraid that this was a real good way to fail publicly," Concannon said. "That made people very reluctant to take a chance."[31] So Joseph and Concannon wrote legal memoranda about the case in French, and shared the results with judges and prosecutors up to and including the Minister of Justice. They both charmed and cajoled, regularly taking prosecutors and the investigating judges to dinner, but also complaining loud and long when necessary, with Concannon usually playing the role of the heavy. "The amount of straight legal work . . . what a lawyer would do for the victims in an ideal world, was not a tenth of the time that we spent on that case," Concannon says. "Most of the time was spent on . . . pushing other people or helping other people to do their job."[32]

The most effective pretrial advocacy was performed by the Raboteau Victims Association itself. Despite receiving multiple anonymous threats, they continued to hold weekly demonstrations, demanding arrests and trials. Haiti's top military and paramilitary leaders had escaped when US forces returned Aristide to power, but, beginning in 1998, multiple other Raboteau defendants were arrested. Some of the arrests were made by police, but the Raboteau community took its own initiative, too. When former paramilitary members were recognized on the street in Gonaïves, community members circled them and made citizens' arrests, blocking their escape until the police arrived to take them to jail. Graffiti started appearing on walls throughout Haiti: *Fok kriminel—yo jije*. Translation: The criminals must be judged.[33]

Raboteau victims also overcame a problem that threatened to derail the case altogether. In 1998, the minister of justice assigned a new, politically well-connected chief prosecutor to the Raboteau trial. The new prosecutor was not familiar with the case. Worse, he seemed not very interested in its success. This lackadaisical approach came as no surprise to Haitians, as this prosecutor had a history of indifference to human rights abuses. As a local justice of the peace in 1993, he allegedly had ignored the mass arson of homes in the Cité Soleil area of Port-au-Prince by the paramilitary group FRAPH. Joseph and Concannon went through the official channels to protest the prosecutor's appointment, to no avail. Visions of the failed Malary trial, with its unprepared and unmotivated chief prosecutor, returned. "If the chief prosecutor absolutely doesn't want the case to go forward, it won't," Concannon says. "He has plenty of ways of blocking it."[34] But the Raboteau victims persisted, writing open letters, talking to radio shows, and demonstrating in the streets to demand that the prosecutor be removed. Finally, the minister of justice relented, and replaced the prosecutor. "We made this trial; it is because of us that this trial happened," Raboteau victim Deborah Charles would say later.[35] No observer of the Raboteau process would dispute that claim.

The trial would include some features previously unknown to Haitian criminal prosecutions. The UN/OAS mission in Haiti recruited retired Argentine military officials to analyze and testify regarding the Haitian military's chain of command and the likely responsibility of leadership for the well-planned Raboteau massacre. The prosecution team also retained forensic anthropologists who matched DNA from

Raboteau victims with their survivors, who were acting as plaintiffs in the case. The forensic experts were also able to document the likely causes of death in several corpses discovered after the attacks. Raboteau would become the first criminal trial in Haiti to use DNA evidence.

It would also become one of the most document-intensive trials in Haitian history. Concannon believed that one of the fatal flaws of the Malary prosecution had been the failure to bolster eyewitness testimony—which in the Haitian court system is subject to cross-examination by both defense lawyers and jurors—with paper evidence less susceptible to credibility challenges. Although valuable documentary evidence was lost when the United States seized the files at the FRAPH and military headquarters, other documents did show the military units' movements and other preparations prior to the attacks, and established individual defendants' presence in Gonaïves.

While the US-trained Concannon focused on the paper trail, he began to realize that the trial plans would still have to reflect the Haitian culture's long tradition of favoring oral presentations over documents. Although Haitian lawyers and judges are obviously quite literate, and jury members are required by law to be as well, an estimated 51.3 percent of the Haitian population does not read or write.[36] The resulting preference for oral presentation and memory is reflected in even the most educated of Haitians. Concannon had noticed that Joseph's writing abilities were less honed than those of a comparable US lawyer, but he also soon discovered that Joseph could, with a mere minute of preparation, speak for fifteen minutes in a well-organized presentation. The Georgetown Law–educated and Boston law firm–trained Concannon could not come close to matching that. With all the major players in the Raboteau trial coming from the oral tradition, Joseph and Concannon's challenge was to honor that tradition while buttressing the dialogue with on-paper evidence.

The final piece of trial preparation may have been the most critical of all: who would be the people determining the verdict? Juries are a relatively rare phenomenon in Haiti, as the law calls for their use only in *crimes de sang* (crimes of blood)—essentially, murder. All other cases are decided by a judge. Haiti's jury pools, most notably in the Malary case, had been notoriously skewed toward the elite, in part because of the literacy requirement and in part because justice officials wanted to retain their fellow elites in the decision-making roles. Such a jury would have little in common with the exceedingly poor Raboteau victims. So Joseph and Concannon successfully argued for the justice system to develop a more representative jury pool, including people outside of the provincial capital of Gonaïves.[37]

Joseph and Concannon found hope for an impartial Raboteau jury from a major human rights case that went to trial in Port-au-Prince in August 2000, just a month before the Raboteau case was scheduled to be heard. Police officers, including high-ranking commanders, were tried for the execution of eleven civilians in the Port-au-Prince neighborhood of Carrefour-Feuilles. The jury found seven officers guilty, including the police chief of Port-au-Prince. The sentences were alarmingly slight—just three years for each defendant despite the multiple murders. But to Joseph and Concannon, it was heartening that the jury had actually been willing to rule against high-powered defendants. After four years of preparing a case they had once thought would be ready in just a few months, and after side-by-side efforts that had gradually built a sense of trust in each other, the two lawyers were finally ready for trial.

The Raboteau massacre trial began on September 29, 2000. The proceedings were conducted under a large tent erected in the Gonaïves courthouse parking lot, since there were too many defendants, witnesses, lawyers, and observers to fit into the indoor courtroom. Twenty-two defendants had been arrested and held for trial, with another thirty-seven to be tried *in absentia*. But, from the Raboteau victims' perspective, the trial seemed to be lost as soon as it began.

In the courtroom, the ten defense lawyers, all wearing black robes, far outnumbered the prosecutors. Joseph, as the victims' civil lawyer, was placed at a separate table, away from the all the other attorneys. The non-Haitian Concannon was not allowed to sit at the counsel table, so he pushed his way to a spot at the front of the audience, where he would be close enough to hand notes to Joseph. The defense lawyers were far more experienced and had far greater national reputations than young Joseph and the prosecutors, and these defense lawyers kicked off the trial with loud and dramatic speeches, damning the proceedings as a sham and painting the victims as greedy or deluded liars. After the opening statements, some of the Raboteau victims were in tears. "They said to me, 'Brian, we appreciate all you did, but we can't beat these guys,'" Concannon recalls. "I told them not to worry—that these guys were good at giving speeches, but that all the work we had done preparing would pay off soon. I only half-believed it myself."

Those impassioned speeches by defense counsel were in French, still the dominant language in Haitian courts. Speaking French fluently is a signal of accomplishment and elite status in Haiti, and Haitian attorneys jealously defend the propriety of conducting their arguments in the language mastered by the country's most highly educated citizens. But with the Raboteau trial being broadcast live on national radio, and much of it shown on television as well, the vast majority of those hearing the trial understood only Creole. A broader-than-typical jury pool meant that most of the jurors were not extremely fluent French speakers, either. So Joseph, alone among the lawyers involved in the trial, chose to argue his case in Creole. "French is the colonial language—the language of exploitation," he explained. "The people are still being exploited in that language. We chose to argue in Creole, because we are the lawyers of the poor and illiterate."[38] Beyond its demonstration of solidarity with the victims and its political symbolism, the strategy had a more tangible benefit: jurors who seemed to nod off when the other attorneys spoke in French noticeably perked up whenever Joseph took his turn in Creole, their preferred language.

Once the witnesses began their testimony, the jury usually had to wait a while to hear from Joseph. The Haitian court process calls for the judge to question the witnesses first. Typically, the judge's inquiry begins with a broadly worded invitation, such as "Tell me about the events of April 22, 1994," which elicits a long narrative from the witness. Then the prosecutor gets to ask questions of the witness, followed by the defense lawyers and the jury members themselves. Only after that parade was completed did Joseph get his opportunity, on behalf of the victims he represented, to pose his questions.

The defenses put forth by the accused consisted of two overlapping arguments: First was what Concannon called the "Holocaust-denier" argument, claiming that the story of a massacre was a complete fiction. The second defense argument was based on alibi, claiming that the particular solider or paramilitary member was nowhere near Raboteau on April 18 or 22. As the trial moved forward, a pattern became set: The judge allowed a soldier defendant to claim he had been elsewhere when the killings took place, and the prosecutors offered some rhetoric in opposition. Then, Joseph would respond by presenting official military records to show that the accused had in fact been stationed at or near Gonaïves on the days in question. Some defendants then claimed they had been transferred to another location, prompting Joseph to show the jury further documents showing that the transfer had occurred after the massacre, not before.

"It seems crazy, because it was probably 1992 technology we were using, but it was like the musket versus the arrow," Concannon says. "We simply had a banker's box of indexed documents that showed the soldiers' whereabouts—we started calling it the 'magic box'—and Mario used it to follow up all the flowery talk by the other lawyers with a real fact-based question that totally undercut the defendants' stories." By now, the Raboteau victims were feeling much better about the course of the trial.

Yet it was still not clear whether the documents were having a positive effect on the jury. The defense lawyers seemed to ignore the clear pattern of documentary evidence undercutting their clients' alibi defenses, and the government prosecutors were not mentioning it either. While waiting for his turn to examine the witnesses, Joseph would write down the questions he wanted to ask when he finally got his turn. In the audience, Concannon scribbled a similar list. Both grew increasingly anxious as the victims' key points were omitted from the questions of the other lawyers, including the prosecutors. Was anyone paying attention to the evidence presented, or was it just another Haitian trial focusing on rhetoric and bombast? Finally, the jurors had their chance to ask questions. As the jurors grilled the witnesses, Joseph and Concannon began crossing planned questions off their lists. The jurors were watching the same trial as Mario Joseph was, and asking his questions before he ever had to. The prosecutors eventually took notice. The prosecutors who at first had scorned the use of so many documents started easing up to Joseph and Concannon during trial breaks, asking, "Do you have a folder for me, too?"

As they had done in the lead-up to indictment and then again to trial, the Raboteau victims seized control of the stage, as shown in footage from the documentary *Pote Mak Sonje: The Raboteau Trial*. (The title derives from the Creole proverb *Bay kou bliye, pote mak sonje*—whoever strikes the blow forgets, whoever bears its scars remembers.) The film shows Deborah Charles testifying that, on the morning of April 22, she awoke to an explosion of gunfire, and said aloud, "We will die today." She nearly did. Charles was among the Raboteau residents who fled to the sea—the embassy—to escape the invading soldiers, only to be ambushed by other soldiers as she clambered aboard a small fishing boat. "I was hit by three bullets while climbing into that boat," she testified. "Judge, I would like to show you." Charles then walked around the witness stand so that all could get a better view while she brandished her left leg, with its three ugly bullet-hole scars. Rosiane Profil testified about trying to climb into that same boat, and showed her own bullet wounds, high enough on her upper thigh that Judge Napela Saintil embarrassedly gestured to her, indicating that she should lower her dress. Profil ignored him until she was sure the jury had seen the damage. Marie Claudette Senatus pointed directly at the defendants who had crashed into her home, knocked her down, and held her at gunpoint. "Even if you had hit me with clubs, I would recognize them," she said. "I am telling the truth."[39]

After sitting through defense lawyer speeches, some of the Raboteau victims took advantage of the judge's open-ended questioning to make their own points. "These people had no pity on any one," said Pierre Michel. "They shot and crushed anything in their way. They made many suffer. They chewed us up and spit us out like sugar cane. Today, with them in court, we should talk to them. We should not be ashamed. In front of this audience, we should say what they did."[40]

The victims' eyewitness testimony was challenged by the defense lawyers and sometimes the defendants themselves. Many defendants argued that the massacre never happened. The grim physical refutation of that claim was provided by a forensic expert who analyzed the bodies recovered in the days after the attack. People in the courtroom cried during the exhibition of skeletons with holes caused by high-powered bullets and when witnesses described the discovery of corpses with ropes tied around their necks. Documents from the Haitian military archives showed arms shipments to the Gonaïves barracks and also demonstrated that commanders knew of the planned attacks. Command responsibility was further established by the testimony of Argentine military experts, who said that Haitian army leadership at the very least knew about the planned assault and did not try to halt it. Colin Granderson, the former director of the UN/OAS mission in Haiti, took it a step further. Granderson testified that the Raboteau attacks were part of a sophisticated system of repression that included planning attacks on pro-democracy activists and covering up the evidence afterward.

On November 10, 2000, six weeks of testimony and arguments came to a close. After four hours of deliberation, the jury returned with a verdict of guilty for sixteen of the twenty-two defendants in custody. Twelve of the defendants were convicted of premeditated murder, and were sentenced to life in prison. Six days later, a summary, judge-only version of the trial was held for the thirty-seven *in absentia* defendants, and the judge issued guilty verdicts and sentenced them all to life imprisonment as well. The judge also ordered the defendants to pay the victims and their families damages in the amount of US$140 million.

The largest, most complicated, and most ambitious trial in Haiti's history had concluded with a result that was a near-total affirmation of human rights and the rule of law. One of the jurors, Marc-Antoine Thebault, expressed pride in being a part of the historic event. "Haitian justice has been seen as something you could buy at market. If I go to market, I can buy justice. That is how we thought about justice in Haiti. But, after this trial, and with this trial, it gives a new face to Haitian justice. It is through this trial that the Haitian justice system had to rise again to say, 'No! Impunity has to be punished in Haiti.'"[41] Rosiane Profil felt the victims' determined activism had finally borne fruit. "I feel strong and proud. I explained everything [to the court] with anger," she said. "We were always in the square marching and doing sit-ins for justice. Now that we have found it, I have to be happy."[42] UN officials had observed the trial and praised its fairness and transparency. The UN independent expert for Haiti, Adama Dieng, said that the trial was a "landmark for justice in Haiti."[43]

Interviewed shortly after the verdict, Mario Joseph tried to put the victory in context. "It is like a war. We have won a battle, but there are other battles to fight before we have succeeded. And the big battle is impunity—impunity in Haiti."[44]

On the day Mary Nicolas welcomes me into her small home in Raboteau, almost eighteen years have passed since the events of April 1994. Nicolas shows me where the soldiers broke down the door on the early morning of April twenty-second, then reaches into a box and produces fifteen bullet shells she found in her yard the morning after the attacks. "*Se souvenir,*" she says, laughing a little. She ushers me inside to a front room where we sit beneath a poster of *Les Dix Commandments*, family photos, and a clock with a Baby Jesus being held by a Virgin Mary. Four other members of the Raboteau Victims Association arrive, and we sit knee-to-knee on folding chairs. Nicolas apologizes for the cramped quarters. "My house is small, but I am the only one of us who is stable economically," she says.

In fact, none of the Raboteau Victims Association members here has a steady income. Some of them do not appear to have a home at all. Haiti's grinding poverty has not spared human rights heroes. "Every year, we commemorate the events of April 1994, but now we do not have the economic power to commemorate like we used to," says Fritz Dèsir. I recall a scene from the *Pote Mak Sonje* documentary where the transcendent witness Rosiane Profil is interviewed sometime after the trial. She explains how her family survives on the bits of food scraped from the bottom of street vendors' cooking pots. A young boy sits beside her. "He is a fifty-cent child," she tells the camera. "When you try to make fifty cents to eat, you become pregnant in the process."

The men and women of Raboteau want to talk about President Michel Martelly's hopes to revive the Haitian army, and about the government's plan to provide pensions and back pay to former soldiers. The government of Haiti has never paid any reparations to the victims of army atrocities, they say, not to mention taking any steps to make sure a similar attack does not happen again. "It is the same people who made our blood flow who will get the pay, and who will again be in the army," says Marie Denise Fleury. Those gathered in Mary Nicolas's home make it clear that they are still activists, and they still feel responsible for responding to the death and devastation visited on their community in 1994. They mention several times that the Raboteau attacks were aimed at pro-democracy activists like themselves, but the violence gathered up many others who just happened to live in the area. "There are still people in this town who bear the scars, and they were victims because of us," says Enold Prophet. "If they [the military and FRAPH] had found us, they would have tied us to the back of a *machin* [car] and drug us through the town."

Sitting next to me is Charles Eddy Joseph. I recognize his name and face from the *Pote Mak Sonje* documentary. He was one of the most visible pro-democracy leaders in Raboteau—one who barely dodged bullets on both April 18 and April 22. For the first half hour of conversation, Joseph says nothing, just clenching and unclenching his fists. Occasionally, he puts on and took off a pair of sunglasses, although the room is near-dark. Suddenly, he stands up, points around at the gathered group and shouts, "The people in this room are the reason people died, so it is our responsibility to speak out and deliver a declaration!" Angrily, he lists all the ways the trial verdict has been unfulfilled, saying the abusers live well but the victims continue to suffer.

"To me, the country has no law!" He is still yelling.

Marie Denise Fleury seems to want to calm him down. "We have law, we just do not respect it," she says.

"That is the same thing!" Joseph says.

There is no evidence in Mary Nicolas's living room that these people are some of the recipients of a $140 million court verdict. In fact, virtually none of that judgment has ever been collected. The one exception occurred when a San Francisco-based NGO, the Center for Justice and Accountability, worked with IJDH and BAI to obtain a $400,000 judgment in Florida against one of the Raboteau defendants living in exile in the United States, Haitian army colonel Carl Dorelien. Dorelien had won the Florida Lottery in 1997, and in 2008, $400,000 of the lottery winnings were seized and delivered to the Raboteau victims. Although the money technically belonged only to one victim, Mari-Jeanne Jean, the widow of a man killed in the massacre, she divided it up and shared it among ninety-nine people. To date, it is the only portion of the judgment ever collected.[45]

The United States deported three members of the army high command convicted in the Raboteau massacre, including Dorelien and Major General Jean-Claude Duperval, the highest-ranking soldier ever deported from the United States to face human rights charges. But most of the high-ranking army and FRAPH officials never served a day of their Raboteau sentences. Lt. General Raul Cédras and General Philippe Biamby live in Panama. FRAPH leader and CIA informant Emmanuel Constant lived with government protection in New York until he was convicted of mortgage fraud in 2008. Those who did go to prison did not stay long. Former FRAPH member Jean Tatoune escaped from the Gonaïves jail in August 2002. The surviving defendants who faced trial (two died in prison) escaped from the National Penitentiary in February 2004 during the second overthrow of Aristide. The three members of the army high command who had been deported from the United States escaped the same day. None of the escapees has ever been rearrested for the Raboteau case.[46] During that same period surrounding the 2004 coup, the judge in the Raboteau case was physically attacked, a prosecutor in the case had his law office burned, and several of the Raboteau victims had their homes burned. One Raboteau victim was executed in front of the Gonaïves police station. No arrests were ever made for these crimes.

On April 21, 2005, the Cour de Cassation, Haiti's Supreme Court, issued an order on appeal of the jury trial verdict in the Raboteau massacre. By that time, none of the original defendants was still in prison. But the court vacated their convictions anyway, ruling that the case should not have been submitted to a jury. The Supreme Court reversal was remarkable, because the trial judge's 1999 decision to impanel a jury followed the letter of the Haitian Constitution and was never challenged by the defense lawyers at trial or on any of three appeals. Amnesty International condemned the appeal decision as "politically motivated" and a "major setback in the fight against impunity in Haiti."[47]

Back in Raboteau, we leave Mary Nicolas's home to walk to the nearby harbor. We pass by pigs rooting around in some sparse garbage and barefoot kids playing soccer with a bundled-up rag in the cobblestone street. Charles Eddy Joseph and Fritz Dèsir share their hopes of somehow talking to members of the US Congress about forcing the Haitian government to pay reparations to the Raboteau victims. They have drafted a petition on the military back-pay issue they intend to read on Gonaïves radio the next week. I ask a final question: did they ever believe the perpetrators of the massacre would be brought to justice? They shake their heads no. There is a pause, and then Marie Denise Fleury says, "But I did hear one soldier that day tell another that they needed to kill any witnesses so they could not testify. So they were scared of *jistis*."

We arrive at the water's edge and they point to the places where bodies floated ashore in the days after the attack. "When we started the movement, the water was like the embassy for us," Joseph says. "After April 22, it became a cemetery." Since some of the bodies were never retrieved from the sea, the Raboteau Victims Association erected a stone monument in the shallow water by shore. They pose for a photo in front of the tomb, which has several names listed and one carved inscription in Creole: *Konbyen Moun Pou Yo Touye Anvan La Jistis Fleri*.

Translation: How many people do they have to kill before justice blooms?

5

How Not to Save a Country

*Lost Opportunities in the
Post-Earthquake Response*

Late in the afternoon of January 12, 2010, Mario Joseph walked into the annex office of Haiti's provisional electoral commission. His mission was to obtain copies of some documents the BAI and IJDH needed as they prepared a petition in connection with the Haitian elections scheduled for the following month. But Joseph was told the documents he sought were not available, and he was instructed to come back the following day. Less than an hour later, the 7.0 magnitude earthquake struck Port-au-Prince, collapsing the electoral commission building and killing everyone inside.

By then, Joseph had returned to the BAI offices. The BAI building shook violently and some damage was done, but the structure did not collapse. Everyone in the office was safe, so they rushed home to check on their loved ones. The wife of one BAI security guard was killed, but the other BAI workers' immediate families had survived. Then everyone began hearing about the deaths of close friends and relatives. Joseph's family was safe in Miami, so he walked from the office to his home. It appeared to have suffered little damage, but like many Haitians he would not sleep indoors, afraid the aftershocks would bring the building tumbling down around him. For more than a month, Joseph worked every day on earthquake response in his office, and slept for only a few hours each night, and then only in his car or in a small shed. When he first traveled to the United States after the earthquake, Joseph was scheduled to speak at a conference at University of California Hastings Law School. The conference organizers inquired whether

Joseph would prefer to stay in a hotel room or with people in the community. Either way was OK, Joseph replied, as long as he could sleep in a one-story building.

On the afternoon of the quake, Brian Concannon was at his then-home in Oregon, on a telephone conference call with a group of Latin American solidarity activists coordinating their advocacy around the upcoming Haitian elections. IJDH and BAI were enjoying the most stable period of their organizations' history. After a seemingly perpetual state of crisis response since IJDH was founded after the 2004 coup d'état, the democratically elected Haitian government led by President René Préval was making strides in human rights and in providing basic services. The funding of BAI and IJDH was stable, and the mechanics of the Haiti-US advocacy partnership were finally coming together.

During the call, Concannon was also monitoring his e-mail, and he saw a message pop up about a 7.0 magnitude earthquake in Haiti. He did not know the significance of the number. But when Concannon told the group, one of the call participants, Dale Sorenson, said, "Oh my God, 7.0!"

"She is from San Francisco, so I knew that was bad," Concannon recalls. He immediately hung up from the conference call and started dialing the BAI office phone lines, and then the numbers of everyone he knew in Haiti. He could not get through. Eventually, he reached Joseph's wife, Rosemie, in Miami. She had just received a brief message that Joseph was OK.

"From the time I heard Dale's reaction, all I could think about was the precarious buildings in Haiti, and how many people must have been in them," Concannon says. As he made dozens of calls and monitored the news from Port-au-Prince, Concannon rode a roller coaster of emotions. "The numbers [of people killed] kept getting worse, but for the people I knew, it was mostly good news at first. Every time we heard that someone was OK, it was a cause for celebration. But then you would hear another number, and know that the bad news about individuals would come eventually." Indeed, the numbers would be horrific, with estimates of over two hundred thousand killed, another three hundred thousand injured, and two million Haitians left homeless.[1] The thousands of buildings destroyed included most of the important government buildings and many historic landmarks. For days, people disembarking from planes at Port-au-Prince would cringe at the smell of decaying bodies that hung over the entire city.

CNN and other stations began showing the carnage nearly nonstop, but Concannon decided not to look at much of the TV coverage. "I was concerned it would disable me—and the psychological impact of seeing the earthquake aftermath did do that to many people—and I felt a strong need to be as effective as possible in helping respond and getting the word out." Concannon's message, delivered in a multiday blitz of media interviews and conferences, focused on the international response to the crisis:

I immediately thought back to the series of tropical storms that hit Haiti within
a couple of weeks in August and September of 2008, and really devastated
the country. [The four storms caused mudslides and flooding that killed eight
hundred people and destroyed most of the country's crops.][2] The Haitian
government simply did not have the capacity to respond to the storms. It did
not have the ability to create a civil defense system or complete forestation
projects that would have reduced landslides and flooding and make the country
less vulnerable to the storms. As the same storms went through the Caribbean,
they really whacked the other countries much harder than they did Haiti.
But these countries had much less devastation than Haiti because they had
governments that could provide basic services.

The limited capacity of Haiti's government at the time of these storms was neither a surprise nor an accident. It was the desired result of the international community's longtime push for a neoliberal economic policy for Haiti. Neoliberal
philosophy elevates the roles of markets and private enterprise, and discourages reliance on the government to provide services, including health care, education, and
security. (Chapter 7 includes a fuller description of the twentieth-century history of
international pressure on Haiti's leaders to privatize industries, lower taxes, eliminate tariffs, and limit wages.) Instead of bolstering the Haitian government, US and
international assistance to Haiti has prioritized support for non-governmental organizations that provide services in the country. Those organizations, totaling untold
thousands in a country with a population of ten million people, are so ubiquitous
that Haiti is often referred to as the "Republic of NGOs" or "The NGO Republic of
Haiti."[3] At least one observer has estimated that 80 percent of the country's basic
services in Haiti are provided not by the government but by NGOs.[4] External aid to
Haiti, routed almost exclusively through organizations other than the government,
exceeded the government budget even before the January 2010 earthquake. Since
the earthquake, the relief dollars have poured into Haiti at a rate that is four times
the government's internal revenue.[5] Haiti is now one of the most thoroughly privatized countries in the world.

Yet it is far beyond the capacity of these non-governmental organizations to
tackle large-scale problems like countrywide emergency response, environmental
protection, and health-care systems, much less to address infrastructure needs like
water and sewage treatment. "It has been the orthodoxy of international development policy for the past thirty years that government is the source of all ills, and
all we need to do is make government smaller," Concannon says. "I have always
felt that Haiti is a good example of the limitations of that approach." Concannon
references the infamous goal of US neoliberal activist Grover Norquist to reduce
government to the size where it can be drowned in a bathtub. "When you do shrink
government to the size where you can drown it in a bathtub, you get something like
Haiti," Concannon says. "I saw it myself in Haiti in 2002 to 2004, when there was

a development assistance embargo on the country. We saw the police and the courts and every part of the state become much less able to perform very important public service work because the government was being decreased due to lack of funds."

Pooja Bhatia, a US writer who lived in Haiti for several years before moving to New York in 2011, underscored Concannon's point in a *Daily Beast* article published a few months after her return to the United States:

> Haiti is the apotheosis of the small-government state; for most citizens, the state is functionally absent. Even in Port-au-Prince, the capital of the overcentralized country, public services are unreliable at best. Those who can afford to do so order water by truck, get electricity by generator, and fly to Santo Domingo or Miami for health care. Those who can't afford it—and 80 percent cannot—bathe in a shallow stream or carry buckets from afar, light a stubby candle, and see a leaf doctor. . . . And the much-ballyhooed "resilience" that Haitians exhibited after the earthquake was little more than a practice of self-help cultivated over centuries. Haitians must fend for themselves and their kin because no one else, least of all the state, will help them.[6]

Earl Kessler, an urban disaster consultant for USAID, told *Rolling Stone* magazine after the earthquake, "I wish I could organize a trip of Tea Party activists and take them to Haiti, so they could see what happens if they have a country with no government."[7]

The Haitian government's helplessness in the wake of the tropical storms of 2008 was so obvious that it seemed destined to inspire a change in the international community's approach to Haiti. In April 2009, Concannon attended a conference hosted by the IDB and attended by leaders of the World Bank, the US State Department, and other international donors and creditors who had led the effort to shrink Haiti's government.[8] As one USAID official had admitted in 2004, "We used to work with the [Haitian] government. Now we don't. Now we work with NGOs . . . Donor groups just have to come in to implement their own agenda."[9]

But that approach seemed to be on the verge of change, as evidenced by the theme for the 2009 conference, "Towards a New Cooperation Paradigm for Growth and Development." The need for a new approach to Haiti was echoed in speech after speech delivered by the world's leading development actors, including the secretary-general of the UN, the World Bank president, and the US secretary of state. "Everyone got up and said the same thing: these tropical storms showed Haiti is vulnerable, and it is vulnerable because the government can't provide basic services. And the government can't provide basic services because the international community has been going around it for the last thirty years," Concannon recalls. "Everyone was saying the right things about how you go about it: you need to empower the government, you need to develop capacity."

But when the earthquake hit Haiti less than nine months later, that new paradigm had not yet taken root. So Concannon, recognizing that the tragedy would trigger international support for Haiti at a level never seen before, focused his post-earthquake efforts on trying to prevent the international community from repeating the mistakes of the past. He was asked to contribute to an online *New York Times* forum called "The Help That Haiti Needs," published just four days after the earthquake.[10] Concannon's contribution was titled "Work with the Haitian Government":

> Haiti's lack of infrastructure and history of corruption should be considered in shaping the international response to Tuesday's earthquake. But these factors should be a reason for investing in infrastructure and good governance, not for bypassing Haiti's government.
>
> . . . Haiti's devastation exposed the disadvantages of an extremely limited government. The earthquake itself was a natural phenomenon, but its horrible toll was largely the product of manmade factors like the failure to prevent shoddy construction on precarious slopes (or provide safer housing) and a healthcare system already stretched to the breaking point.
>
> . . . An effective international response to the earthquake will minimize the damage of the next stress in Haiti, by including both short- and long-term measures to develop the government's capacity to provide basic, honest services to its citizens.[11]

Concannon assumed he would be on the "radical fringe" of the *Times* discussion, but his views were largely echoed by several other invited contributors. A University of Virginia professor called for the international community to revise its neoliberal policies toward Haiti and put the state in the center of the recovery efforts.[12] Amy Wilentz, author of *The Rainy Season*, pointed out the limited capacity of NGOs to transform Haiti.[13] A senior fellow from the US Institute for Peace agreed that strengthening the government's capacity was key, and invoked the promises of the April 2009 Haiti donors conference.[14] Their views were well supported by research showing that direct assistance to the governments of Mali, Tunisia, and Zambia in Africa had led to significant improvements in public health and education access, and that fears of direct budget assistance being lost to corruption were unfounded.[15]

Concannon wrote the *Times* post in the midst of a frantic week of phone calls, e-mails, and interviews. In part because his wife was due to deliver their second child within a few weeks, he did all this without leaving his home. Concannon had a working phone and computer with a fast Internet connection—real assets for his friends and colleagues in Haiti, where most connections and power were down. So Concannon spent hours each day linking Americans with relief supplies to Haitians who could distribute them, talking in English to the people in the United States and quickly switching to Creole to confirm details with Haitians. He helped arrange for a medical team from New York to take over the BAI offices, running a clinic there and sleeping on-site. Concannon also gave interview after interview to media hungry for perspective on the Haitian situation, and he steered every exchange toward the need for relief efforts to work through the Haitian government. Concannon would rise at 3 a.m. to do early interviews for East Coast media by telephone or Skype, work feverishly all day, and get to bed about 1 a.m.

A few weeks later, Concannon's wife, Marcy, went online to watch some of the archived video interviews, and noticed that for a Saturday interview, Concannon was wearing the same blue shirt he had worn the preceding Wednesday. In fact, Concannon had not taken the time to change his clothes during most of the week, sitting at his desk wearing pajama pants and pulling on a sport coat and tie when a Skype interview was scheduled. "It seemed he was always popping out of bed in the middle of the night to give an interview in Creole," Marcy Strazer recalls. "Sometimes in the evening I would ask him who he gave interviews to that day, and he would not even remember. When the earthquake first happened, I wondered what use he could be stuck up there in Oregon, but it turned out to be the place he could accomplish so much."

At the same time, Mario Joseph shook off his own trauma and helped set up the emergency medical clinic at BAI. He made sure to reserve space for the many Haitian community activists who soon gravitated to the BAI offices to mourn the dead and organize Haitians in response to the crisis. Just two days after the quake, IJDH and BAI sent in a request to the IACHR, asking for a hearing on the need for the international community to respect the human rights of Haitians in the earthquake response.[16] The activists congregating at BAI soon grew alarmed at the numbers of Haitian people going without food, water, and shelter, despite the large amounts of donations pouring in from all over the world. Joseph helped them create and distribute five thousand survey forms to grassroots groups, gathering some of the first data to demonstrate what would prove to be a chronic gap between global donations and those suffering in the ruins of Port-au-Prince.

The generosity of that worldwide response was breathtaking. International governments and multinational agencies ultimately allocated over $12 billion in humanitarian and recovery funding to Haiti. Another $3 billion was donated by private individuals or organizations. Half of the entire US population ultimately donated to Haiti recovery efforts. A celebrity-packed "Hope for Haiti" telethon raised $275 million, and Haitian American singer Wyclef Jean gathered stars to rerecord Michael Jackson's "We Are the World" as a Haiti relief fundraiser. Physicians, nurses, and emergency response workers from around the world volunteered to fly to Haiti to help.[17]

Tragically, the opportunity presented by this historic display of global compassion has been wasted. The international community has ignored the admonitions by Brian Concannon and others to work through the Haitian government and Haitian institutions. Instead, the post-earthquake relief and recovery effort is destined to be seen as an object lesson in shortsighted and self-interested approaches to international aid. It is the kind of foreign aid failure that has been excoriated in treatments like William Easterly's *White Man's Burden: Why the West's Efforts to Aid the*

Rest Have Done So Much Ill and So Little Good, and Dambisa Moyo's *Dead Aid: Why Aid Is Not Working and How There Is a Better Way for Africa*.[18] Worse, the botched response to Haiti's earthquake carries the potential to discourage the donors who greeted the news of January 12, 2010 with sympathy and selflessness.

The mistakes could have been avoided, and there is a way to do better in the future. Rule of law advocates like Joseph and Concannon argue that a rights-based approach to aid and development can be a vehicle for getting much-needed assistance to the world's poor in a manner that respects their dignity and autonomy, while at the same time building the capacity of the government they turn to for services and protection of their rights.

As the saying goes, when your only tool is a hammer, every problem looks like a nail. So it was predictable that the government of the United States first responded to the humanitarian crisis of Haiti's earthquake by mobilizing for military action. The United States, whose military budget nearly equals that of the rest of the world combined, immediately sent five thousand troops to Haiti. Ultimately, twenty-two thousand US troops would be placed in Haiti after the earthquake. (Thirty-three cents of every assistance dollar the US government has pledged to Haiti was actually directed to the US military as reimbursement for its expenses.) US troops seized control of the airport and seaport of Port-au-Prince, self-designated the US Southern Command as the "principal agency" in Haiti, and prioritized military flights over humanitarian flights.[19] An Air Force plane flew over Haiti five hours a day, broadcasting a message warning Haitians not to try to leave on boats for the United States "They will intercept you and send you back where you came from" was the message recorded by Raymond Joseph, Haiti's ambassador to the United States, and delivered by loudspeaker throughout the countryside.[20]

The United States' occupation-style approach led to criticism from Haitian officials and leaders of neighboring countries like Ecuador, Nicaragua, Venezuela, and Cuba, many of whom had historically been generous to Haiti.[21] Criticism from these sources may not have bothered US officials much. The day before the US military mobilized in Haiti, the neoliberal US Heritage Foundation think tank published a statement that the earthquake had security implications for the United States, and that an effective response by Venezuela or Cuba could "diminish US influence in the region."[22]

International accusations of US insensitivity followed the circulation of a video showing US soldiers hurling sacks of food overboard from an army helicopter, keeping their distance from Haitian earthquake victims who scrambled below to grab what they could. Such media images fueled a perception of post-earthquake Haiti as a cauldron of danger and chaos, a perception that seemed to justify the militaristic response. BBC reporter Matt Frei broadcast from Port-au-Prince on January 18, showing video of a few Haitians searching through the remains of collapsed stores. "Looting is now the only industry here," Frei said. "Anything will do as a weapon.

Everything is now run by rival groups of thugs." Frei speculated that, for Haiti, "what may be needed is a full-scale military occupation."[23]

But fears of widespread looting and violence proved unfounded. The international media who followed only US soldiers and emergency responders missed the story of Haitians responding bravely and selflessly in the aftermath of the quake. Those on the ground after the earthquake witnessed neighborhoods organizing to rescue victims from the rubble, and farmers from the rural parts of the country giving shelter and food to hundreds of thousands who fled decimated Port-au-Prince. Other farmers brought food directly to victims in the crippled city. This grassroots humanitarian response was no surprise to Haitians and close observers who had witnessed neighborhood groups repair streets and clean up trash even during the violent chaos of the years following the 2004 coup d'état.[24]

When the military and the media mischaracterized post-earthquake Port-au-Prince as a security crisis rather than a humanitarian crisis, the Haitian people paid dearly. Incoming flights from relief agencies, including the UN World Food Program and Doctors Without Borders, were turned away from the Port-au-Prince airport so that more troops could be brought in. Search and rescue teams from around the world mobilized to go to Haiti, but were similarly unable to get flights into the airport. While willing would-be rescuers were forced to wait at home, Haitians died under piles of concrete.

The United States was accused by witnesses to the post-earthquake response of making a priority of lifting its citizens out of Haiti and directing rescue efforts toward buildings frequented by foreigners.[25] For example, a US general would boast about devoting six separate teams of rescuers to the ruins of the Hotel Montana, which housed mostly foreigners, while Haitians struggled without help to dig survivors out of the rubble of buildings that housed primarily Haitians.[26] Associated Press reporter Jonathan Katz would later say, "What you saw were people coming and going wherever they pleased, and what ended up happening was that they all ended up in the same couple of spots. You could say two things about this: they were focusing on citadels of the rich and powerful and then, not coincidentally, those are the places that the news media tended to congregate as well. . . . It was very hard to watch these things and not feel that I was watching a television show, as opposed to a serious rescue effort."[27]

Marines arrived in devastated areas of Port-au-Prince, ready to respond to disturbances that did not exist but without the food and water Haitians desperately needed. For four days after the earthquake, the UN World Food Program had planes full of food, medicine, and water turned away from the airport by the US military.[28] "Their priorities are to secure the country," World Food Program air logistics director Jarry Emmanuel told the *New York Times*. "Ours are to feed."[29]

Ten days after the earthquake, Dr. Evan Lyon of Partners in Health / Zanmi Lasante made an explicit connection between the overblown security concerns and widespread suffering. In an interview for *Democracy Now!* from the General Hospital in Port-au-Prince, Lyon said:

> It is a peaceful place. There is no war. There is no crisis except the suffering that is ongoing. . . . This question of security and the rumors of security and the racism behind the idea of security has been our major block to getting aid in. . . . In terms of aid relief the process has been incredibly slow. There are teams of surgeons that have been sent to places that were, quote, "more secure," that have 10 to 20 doctors and 10 patients. We have a thousand people on this campus who are triaged and ready for surgery, but we only have four operating rooms, without anesthesia and without pain medications.[30]

The mistaken perception of violent chaos would prove to be enduring. For weeks after the quake, many of the large relief agencies refused to distribute supplies without military escorts, significantly limiting Haitians' access to urgently needed assistance.[31]

Nicole Phillips was one of many friends of Haiti who was devastated by the news of the earthquake's destruction. Since 2006, she had been volunteering with IJDH. In order to spend more time on international human rights law, she cut back her hours at the San Francisco labor law firm where she worked. But the news of January 12, 2010, made her question that arrangement. "I think we all had the same reaction of 'Wow. What can I do?' It seemed a time for emergency responders and doctors, but what could we lawyers do to help?" Then news of a post-earthquake housing crisis and an explosion of gender-based violence made its way out of Haiti. It became clear that lawyers would indeed be needed to advocate for those left homeless, hungry, and victimized, so Phillips made a decision. "I knew two things: First, IJDH would need all the help it could get, and two, that they did not have any money to pay me," Phillips says. "I always wanted to do a job that, if I did not do it, no one else would. I knew that if I left my law firm, forty people could step in and do the work. But it was clear that I could really be of help with Haiti."

So Phillips quit her law firm and became a full-time volunteer for IJDH. Within three months after the earthquake, she was living in a tent pitched on the concrete driveway of BAI's offices. Each morning at 6 a.m., she woke to a line of two dozen people waiting to talk with her about their destroyed homes, their evictions from the camps, their unmet health-care needs, their desperate search for food and water. Phillips, fluent in French and, in her estimation, "still learning" in Creole, participated in multihour meetings where women took turns, one after another, telling how they had been raped. The scope of suffering was unlike anything Phillips had ever imagined. "I was devastated, and everyone I worked with was devastated," she remembers. "But I couldn't be concerned about my own well-being when I was so much better off than the vast majority of people I was interviewing in Haiti." Phillips pressed down her own emotions in order to continue on. When she returned to the United States, she went to a physician, who said that her body was still in shock mode.

Having abandoned her law firm job for one-hundred-hour workweeks and no pay, Phillips lived off of a tax refund, loans from her mother, and a few thousand dollars from teaching a law school class connecting San Francisco law students to Haiti. When she returned to the United States between stays in Haiti, friends bought her lunches and dinners, but the conversations did not always go smoothly. "I was angry all the time," she says:

> I was angry about the responses of our government and the US and international NGOs in Haiti, how they weren't listening to the Haitians. I was angry that we don't think about the rest of the world in the US, and I could not explain to others the pain I was seeing in Haiti. It was hard for me to connect with people around me who weren't constantly talking about social and economic injustices. My heart was in Haiti and not the US, and I did not really know how to connect the two.

Slowly, Phillips began to adjust to her new reality. The first time she was invited to travel to Washington to speak about Haitian human rights issues, she told Concannon about the opportunity, and he responded enthusiastically. But Phillips, who had traveled the country staying in nice hotels as part of her legal career, was not prepared for Concannon's travel suggestion. "He said, 'That is great. Here is a list of people in the DC area who have been friends of the cause. Call them, say hi, and ask if you can stay with them.'"

Phillips laughs about it now, and says she has enjoyed getting to meet Haiti supporters by staying in their guest bedrooms or sleeping on their spare couches. Her family continues to supplement her income, which has been slashed by two-thirds since she began devoting herself full time to human rights. "In order to do this work, we all need support. But that is not a bad thing in many ways, as it takes a community to get change to occur."

Phillips has no regrets about changing her life in response to the earthquake. She had long wanted to pursue a career in human rights, and IJDH and BAI provide the kind of grassroots connections she learned to appreciate while representing labor unions. She is effusive about the inspiration she gains from Concannon and Joseph and the Haitian activists she has come to know. There is even the occasional hint of glamor in the job, which now pays her a small salary: Phillips has had the chance to meet Haiti-supporting Hollywood figures like Matt Damon, Olivia Wilde, and Patricia Arquette. Then she heads back to work, preparing pleas to the UN and international human rights agencies. "Law students and even lawyers dream of getting an opportunity to make a difference like this," Phillips says. "I am incredibly lucky that it is now my daily life."

As the desperation rose in the weeks after the earthquake, the international community and those on the ground in Haiti became increasingly vocal in questioning the post-earthquake response. US ambassador to Haiti Kenneth Merten shrugged off the criticism. Six weeks after the earthquake, Merten asserted that the response was on track to be a historic success. "I think, frankly, it's working really well, and I believe that this will be something that people will be able to look back on in the future as a model for how we've been able to sort ourselves out as donors on the ground and responding to an earthquake," Merten said.[32] By then, the United States and the rest of the international community had already adopted the catchphrase that, for Haiti, they would "Build Back Better." Yet the problems of the first weeks of response persisted, including the critical gap between generous pledges of international support and the lack of services on the ground in Haiti.

The office of the UN special envoy for Haiti tracked public sector donors' performance in fulfilling their pledges made in early 2010, shortly after the earthquake. As late as September 2012, the special envoy reported that only 52.3 percent of the pledged money had been disbursed, and that the rate of disbursement was dropping steadily. Importantly, disbursement does not equal spending, and an alarmingly small percentage of the money delivered from donor countries has reached Haitians in need.[33] For example, as of April 2012, almost $300 million in donations had been delivered to the Haitian Reconstruction Fund, which is tasked with then transferring the money to the UN, the World Bank, or the IDB. But only $56 million of that money had been disbursed, with the rest sitting unused, despite the desperate need for projects like removing debris and building homes and schools. "Funds remain in the bank and are not being allocated in the citizens' interests," Josef Leitmann, the head of the Haiti Reconstruction Fund, admitted in early 2012. "This is nothing to be proud of."[34] A June 2013 report for the US Government Accountability Office found similar problems with U.S funds allocated for infrastructure reconstruction in Haiti, revealing that less than one-third of the $651 million Congress allocated for Haiti reconstruction to the USAID had been spent three years later, and that mismanagement and mistaken cost estimates meant that only 20 percent of the planned fifteen thousand permanent houses would be built.[35]

Even when relief funds were spent, it was often not clear how they had been used. In a December 2012 report, Julie Walz and Vijaya Ramachandran of the Center for Global Development expressed frustration at the opaque nature of the aid process:

> Despite extensive efforts, our ability to trace the money is limited by a lack of transparency and accountability—indeed, three years after the quake, much remains unknown. For instance, who exactly got the $1.3 billion—36% of the total—that was disbursed as grants to International NGOs and contractors? As we have blogged previously, we can look at procurement databases to track primary contract recipients, but we cannot go much further. We can see, for

instance, that $150 million was disbursed to Chemonics, but we have no idea about how that money was spent.[36]

In an April 2013 report analyzing USAID distributions for Haiti, the Center for Economic Policy and Research echoed this complaint about the lack of transparency. Yet the report's coauthors, Jake Johnston and Alexander Main, said that the available information does make it clear that most of the USAID dollars spent for Haiti went to top US contractors, most based in the Washington, DC, area. Less than 1 percent of US government expenditures have gone to Haitian businesses or organizations.[37]

The failures of the post-earthquake recovery efforts can be attributed in large part to the international community's insisting on a Haiti reconstruction plan that ignored the call by Brian Concannon and others to work through and empower the Haitian government. Instead of helping the Haitian government to direct earthquake relief and recovery, the international community first allowed the US military to control the country in the weeks after the earthquake. They then turned over recovery planning to two institutions, the Interim Haiti Recovery Commission and the Haiti Reconstruction Fund. The performance of both proved to be abysmal.

As the name suggests, the Interim Haiti Recovery Commission (IHRC), designed and promoted by the international community and adopted under a state of emergency law by the Haitian Parliament, was intended to serve as a bridge entity. The commission would oversee recovery efforts for eighteen months before transferring authority to the government of Haiti. The commission was cochaired by former US president Bill Clinton, who also serves as UN special envoy for Haiti, and Haitian prime minister Jean-Max Bellerive. Only half of the commission members were Haitian, with the other members representing countries that pledged more than $100 million to Haiti's recovery.[38]

Almost immediately, Haitian members of the commission's board found themselves pushed out of the loop on project selection and staffing decisions. The Haitian board members lodged a formal complaint at a December 2010 commission meeting, alleging that they were mere "rubber stamps" and "tokens." Their statement read in part, "In reality, Haitian members of the board have one role: to endorse the decisions made by the Director and Executive Committee." At another commission meeting, Haitian ministers of parliament were turned away at the door since their names were not on an attendee list.[39] One Haitian senior official later told *Rolling Stone* magazine, as part of an article by Janet Reitman that was sharply critical of the post-earthquake response, "Behind closed doors, the feeling of the Haitian government was that this was just another foreign group they had given permission to come in and take over the country. But what could they do? The Haitian government knew it didn't have the capacity to tackle this reconstruction on its own."[40]

It is undeniably true that the Haitian government did not have a reputation for either transparency or efficiency. But the commission that bypassed them failed in those respects as well. The commission was roundly criticized by the international community for failing to release its criteria for reviewing proposed projects, no full list of projects proposed was provided for public review, and commission meeting minutes were not easily available. In September 2010, the commission drafted a framework to guide reconstruction. But it did not publish the document in Creole, the language of the vast majority of Haitians, and it did not consult with any of the hundreds of thousands of IDP camp residents whose fates would be affected by the plans. The commission was created to coordinate the international response, but the commission was never fully staffed. Several major development efforts, including a multi-million-dollar Port-au-Prince reconstruction project by the Prince Charles Foundation, simply ignored the commission process.[41]

In October 2011, the commission's mandate expired with a whimper. The commission thus left its operational partner, the Haiti Reconstruction Fund, hanging. The fund, itself administered by a board with only a single Haitian member, was tasked with allocating funding for projects approved by the commission. With the commission legally defunct, the fund was left without an operational mandate, leading to the hundreds of millions of dollars in pledged recovery funds sitting untouched in a bank account.[42]

The international community's preferred path to pursuing Haiti's recovery was a wide detour around the Haitian people, and the commission's failure to engage Haitian leaders and the population was just one of several indicators of that intent. The US government was not the only donor to make this mistake. Less than 1 percent of the overall short-term humanitarian relief funding was delivered to the government of Haiti, and less than 20 percent of the long-term recovery funds have been directed through the Haitian government.[43] The cost of this policy was highlighted by a frustrated Dr. Joia Mukherjee, Partners in Health's chief medical officer, two months after the earthquake:

> The entire process [of earthquake response] has bypassed the government in its entirety, and this is very worrisome for the people of Haiti. There are not funds for general operating costs, like paying people's salaries. For us, the most clear example is the general hospital, the only Level 1 trauma center in the country, the only public referral hospital in the city—salaries haven't been paid for four and a half months. You have doctors and nurses and other staff living in their cars, living on the street, living in tents and they haven't been paid.[44]

Using official figures, the Center for Economic Policy and Research showed in 2013 that USAID gave only 0.2 percent of its humanitarian funds to Haitian firms, ignoring the baseline principle of economic development that working with local organizations creates jobs and develops capacity.[45] Haitians were regularly excluded from the critical decision-making in earthquake recovery. A "cluster" system of UN agencies, NGOs, and international organizations working in Haiti was created by the UN Office for the Coordination of Humanitarian Affairs, with the laudable goal of synchronizing the many simultaneous efforts. But the operations were planned and the group meetings conducted at the heavily guarded UN logistical base in Port-au-Prince, where many Haitians were denied admission. Most early meetings were held in English without Creole translation.

These practices were sharply criticized in a 2011 Humanitarian Response Index report prepared by the aid watchdog organization DARA. The DARA report also cited the US government for being nontransparent and most donors for not being flexible enough to partner with Haitian organizations. "The international community cannot claim that it has helped Haiti build back better," the report concludes. "[It] missed an opportunity to redress years of neglect and inattention to the issue of building capacity, resilience and strengthening preparedness for future crises."[46] Mark Schuller, a professor at Northern Illinois University and at the l'Université d'État d'Haïti (UEH), uses a Creole proverb to explain the post-earthquake response in context with Haiti's long-troubled relationship with the United States and the international community: *Rat mode, soufle*—first the rat bites, then it blows on the wound. The United States and the international community had helped cause this post-earthquake hardship, and the efforts to respond to the disaster were not improving the situation.[47]

With the Haitian government and people largely excluded from post-earthquake recovery planning, the international community proceeded to make a series of significant strategic errors, many of them repeating the same mistakes Haiti's donors and creditors had made in preceding decades. The United States spent $140 million sending food to Haiti in the months following the earthquake, ramping up an already much-criticized practice of flooding Haiti's markets with subsidized US-grown food priced so cheaply that Haitian farmers could not compete.[48] As Brian Concannon wrote in his post-earthquake *New York Times* article, the food aid policy served the interests of the United States, but it had proven to be devastating for many Haitians: "Aid often conforms to the needs of US campaign donors over the needs of Haitian victims. Food aid, for example, reduces stockpiles of excess, subsidized US corn better than it fights hunger. It sometimes even increases hunger in Haiti by undermining otherwise sustainable local farmers. When farmers cannot sell their grain because Uncle Sam is giving it away, they close down their farms and move—to a shoddy house on a precarious slope in the city."[49]

Chavannes Jean-Baptiste, director of the Haitian farmers' collective Peasant Movement of Papay, told the Pulitzer Center for Crisis Reporting that the United States should have responded to the crisis by buying food from struggling Haitian farmers. "After the earthquake, the country needed food to help the victims in some places. But it's not really necessary to send to Haiti a lot of food from the United States," Jean-Baptiste said. "We received too much food, when locally it was possible to find food to buy to help people."[50] One US think tank proposed that the United States provide its food aid in the form of buying a full year or two of Haiti's rice crop, a purchase that would have provided an enormous boost to Haitian farmers and cost only a fraction of the committed US aid funds to Haiti.[51] But powerful US agribusinesses have long demanded that food aid be in the form of US food shipped overseas, and the proposal gained no traction.[52]

Instead, within two months after the earthquake, Haitian president René Préval felt compelled to publicly call on the United States to stop sending the country food aid that was blocking Haitian farmers from supporting their families.[53] The self-interested nature of the US food aid policy toward Haiti is not an anomaly: a majority of US foreign aid across the globe is "tied aid," and thus contingent on the purchase of US-originated goods and services.[54] USAID has promoted foreign aid as "really an investment in America," and they have the numbers to prove it.[55] For example, the Organisation for Economic Co-operation and Development reported that a full 93 percent of US foreign assistance in 2005 came back to US providers of goods and services, a number that far exceeds any such return received by other donor countries.[56] It is an intentional exaggeration, but in Haiti I have several times seen versions of a political cartoon depicting an emaciated Haitian spoon-feeding an obese—and whining—tycoon labeled as the United States.

The international community also managed to botch a golden opportunity presented by a massive post-earthquake exodus from Port-au-Prince to the Haitian countryside. In the decades before the quake, the same neoliberal policies of tariff reduction and subsidy blocks that allowed imported food to undercut Haitian farmers spurred a mass migration to Port-au-Prince by millions of farmers looking for work. (A stark remnant of that migration remains in the form of Cité Soleil, a community near the Port-au-Prince airport that was originally designed to house manual laborers for export industries. Cité Soleil is now one of the Western Hemisphere's largest and most notorious slums, characterized by overcrowding, violence, stark poverty, and lack of services.) Port-au-Prince in 1982 had a population of about 750,000, but was swollen to three million people by the time of the earthquake. Before the quake, as many as fifteen thousand Haitians were moving from the rural areas to Port-au-Prince every month. Overcrowded shanty towns, known as *bidonvilles*, sprang up to accommodate them.[57] The buildings in these new areas were usually patchwork affairs of cheaply made and poorly supported concrete that proved no match for the tremors of January 12, 2010. According to one estimate, 86 percent of the homes destroyed in the quake had been built between 1990 and 2010.[58]

But the quake also provided an unexpected opportunity to improve life in Haiti. Over a half-million survivors streamed out of Port-au-Prince for the countryside, a natural decentralization that could have relieved the dangerous congestion in Port-au-Prince. Columbia University economist and development expert Jeffrey Sachs was among many who saw the possibility for supporting a much-needed long-term population shift. Writing in the *Guardian* two weeks after the quake, Sachs said that supplies of fertilizer and seeds, along with irrigation and storage silos, could allow these migrating Haitians to stay in their home villages and double or even triple the country's food production within just a few years.[59] Instead, the international community virtually ignored the rural areas of Haiti, with little aid being directed toward the agricultural sector. Worse, cash-for-work and other programs were created in the city, causing hundreds of thousands to return to urban areas from the countryside. As Haitian political science professor Chenet Jean-Baptiste put it, the post-earthquake response mistakes gave more rope for Haitians to be dragged back into Port-au-Prince.[60] Why was the advice of Sachs and others like Oxfam International ignored? Why was the rural population not well supported by the international community after the earthquake? The DARA report suggested a chilling answer: "Most donors preferred to support the response in the capital, where their aid was most visible."[61]

In providing that aid, contrary to the rhetoric from the April 2009 "New Cooperation Paradigm" conference on Haiti, the international community only increased its reliance on NGOs. Almost 100 percent of USAID funds for Haitian humanitarian relief went to NGOs, to the UN, or other US agencies.[62] Haiti's swollen NGO population is supported by so much government funding—as much as 70 percent of their budgets, estimates Peter Hallward in his book *Damming the Flood: Haiti and the Politics of Containment*—that the term "non-governmental" seems a misnomer. Yet there is one government that most of these organizations are not integrated with: the Haitian government. In fact, NGOs recruited many doctors and nurses away from cash-strapped Haitian hospitals and clinics.[63] "All of the millions that are coming into Haiti right now are going into the hands of the NGOs," Haitian president Préval complained in early March 2010.[64]

Unquestionably, most NGOs are well intentioned, and many did important and valuable work in response to the earthquake. But the overall return on those millions delivered to NGOs has been unimpressive. As an evaluation of the earthquake response by the Global Public Policy Institute and Groupe URD (Urgence, Réhabilitation, Développement) said, "Did the aid systems save lives? Yes, but not that many. . . . Did the aid system eliminate suffering? Yes, but too superficially."[65] An April 2011 audit by the USAID Office of Inspector General showed that, despite receiving grants totaling $138 million, its NGO grantees completed only 7,179 transitional shelters—less than a quarter of their target number—and some of the shelters were substandard.[66] In September 2010, the same inspector general had criticized the performance of for-profit contractor Chemonics, the single largest recipient of USAID funds for Haiti post-earthquake. In carrying out USAID-funded cash-for-work programs, Chemonics was cited for failing to follow safety procedures to protect Haitian workers clearing rubble, and for nontransparency in selecting its workers and rubble-removal sites.[67] USAID delivered contracts for Haiti projects to a partnership that included the Kuwait-based company Agility Logistics, even after Agility Logistics was indicted for defrauding the United States of over $1 billion in contracts for services in Iraq, Kuwait, and Jordan.[68]

Another USAID contractor, a New York firm called Dalberg Global Development Advisors, received $1.5 million to assess land for new housing, but was cited for shoddy work by the *Rolling Stone* report, in which a USAID official admitted, "These people may not even have gotten out of their SUVs."[69] One of the few Interim Haiti Recovery Commission projects to be completed was the Clinton Foundation's project to build hurricane shelters that could also be used as schools. The shelters were built for the Clinton Foundation by a company called Clayton Homes, owned by Warren Buffett's Berkshire Hathaway. But an investigation by the *Nation* magazine revealed that the shelters were not resistant to hurricanes and did not include promised running water or toilets. Many of the shelters had unhealthy levels of formaldehyde and began to sprout mold and rot within months of construction.[70]

The Clinton Foundation's choice of Clayton Homes was a curious one, given that the company had already been sued for high levels of formaldehyde in trailers it sold to FEMA after Hurricane Katrina. Questions have also been raised about the Clinton-Bush Haiti Fund's decision to direct $2 million to the construction of a luxury hotel, the Royal Oasis, in the upscale Port-au-Prince neighborhood of Pétionville.[71] Another high-profile hurricane relief effort, Yéle, has been accused of financial improprieties and self-dealing by the New York attorney general's office. A charity cofounded by Haitian American rapper Wyclef Jean, Yéle had effectively shut down as of October 2012, with promised projects left uncompleted and creditors alleging unpaid obligations.[72]

The American Red Cross has been criticized for a lack of transparency in how it has spent—or not yet spent—nearly $500 million in donations for Haitian relief operations. Haitian Americans have protested outside the Red Cross headquarters in New York City, chanting "Where is the money?" Graffiti spray-painted outside a Red Cross–supported tent in Port-au-Prince camp reads, in Creole, "Get out Red Cross and your committee of thieves." It is not surprising that the Red Cross has struggled to mobilize in Haiti. Before the earthquake, the Red Cross had fifteen people in Haiti. Partners in Health, which had five thousand workers in Haiti, received a fraction of the donations given to the Red Cross.[73] "So often after these major disasters, marketing alone—divorced from the quality or importance of the work an organization is doing—will drive support," Thomas Tighe, chief executive of Direct Relief International, told the *New York Times* shortly after the earthquake.[74]

It bears repeating that most NGOs and their staff members in Haiti are well intentioned, and many provide valuable services. "The earthquake has brought in a great deal of outside energy to Haiti, and there is good that comes with that," says Evan Lyon of Partners in Health. "But there are just so many people involved in the country now that there is often a sense of chaos. If they could organize themselves through Haitian institutions, that would help. But so few do that, and even though there is more energy and money in Haiti, there are also a lot more cooks in the kitchen, and I don't think that is helping Haitian autonomy and democracy."

Lyon's Partners in Health practices what it preaches, using private funds to build a hospital in Mirebalais that is owned, and will eventually be operated by, the Haitian government. In contrast, some international companies' eager responses to the earthquake crisis were transparently profit-motivated, leading to charges of "disaster capitalism" perpetrated by "trauma vultures." Three weeks after the earthquake, US ambassador Merten sent a cable to the State Department in Washington he titled "THE GOLD RUSH IS ON!" In the cable, obtained by WikiLeaks, Merten reported that former US Army general Wesley Clark had made a sales presentation to President Préval on behalf of a foam core housing manufacturer, and that the Florida-based AshBritt corporation was one of many companies to descend on Haiti post-earthquake. "Each is vying for the ear of the President in a veritable free-for-all," Merten wrote.[75]

Soon enough, AshBritt bought itself an advantage in the struggle. Lewis Lucke led the original earthquake relief effort for USAID, meeting with President Préval and the Haitian prime minister multiple times in his official capacity in the weeks after the quake. Then Lucke stepped down from his government role in April 2010, signed a $30,000 per month agreement with AshBritt, and promptly helped AshBritt and its Haitian partner GB Group secure $20 million in post-earthquake construction contracts. Lucke later sued AshBritt and GB Group for an additional $500,000 for his work securing government contracts for the private companies. Lucke was anything but apologetic for his public-to-private efforts. "It's kind of the American way," he told the newspaper *Haïti Liberté*.[76]

A year after the earthquake, public health researcher Deepa Panchang conducted several dozen anonymous interviews of NGO officials in Haiti. As summarized in the anthology *Tectonic Shifts: Haiti since the Earthquake*, the response by NGO officials revealed disturbing misconceptions about the Haitian people. One core belief among some NGO officials was that Haitians who had homes were actually choosing to stay in IDP camps in hopes of receiving benefits from NGOs. They were "waiting for houses, cars, helicopters," said one NGO official. Another said that the camps' conditions were generally acceptable to Haitians living there. "Although I haven't talked to any [camp residents], I think they're pretty pleased," the official said.[77] Similarly rose-colored reporting was often extrapolated to a broader audience, as NGOs eager to impress current donors and recruit new support distorted the systemic nature of Haiti's crisis by highlighting small victories in spite of the dark larger picture of post-earthquake suffering. Predictably, such reports elevated self-promotion over any goal of presenting a balanced portrayal. The Clinton Foundation, for example, produced two videos and issued multiple reports praising its ill-fated hurricane shelter/school project.[78]

But, if one was willing to look, less approving views about NGO performance in Haiti were easy to find. NGOs were accused of bypassing existing Haitian grassroots organizations and using aid dollars inefficiently, if not dishonestly. *Aba* NGO *vole!* (Down with NGO thieves!) was a common graffiti statement on the concrete walls of Port-au-Prince. The 2011 video *Haiti: Where Did the Money Go?*, produced and written by Michele Mitchell and Ivan Weiss, showed an IDP camp where over five thousand people shared just six toilets, despite multiple visits by representatives of international NGOs. "They just take down information and that's it," Jean Cene, the leader of L'Ouverture Camp, told Mitchell. "What I can say they've done with the money is spend it on nice hotels to sleep in, and nice cars to drive. The people, meanwhile, are stuck in the same misery."[79]

Even when NGO money was spent on Haitian projects, the lack of coordination and long-term commitment led to resentment and limited impact. "What we do [in Haiti] is what the donors want and see as being good for us, not what we want and need," Jacky Lumarque, president of Haiti's Université Quisqueya, told the Center for Public Integrity's *iWatch News*. "The NGOs go from project to project without taking the time to develop a strategy for us to respond to our own needs and develop self-sufficient organizations. At the end of their projects, everything vanishes and we're back where we started."[80] In a report issued a year after the earthquake, Oxfam echoed the same concerns about NGOs bypassing Haitian involvement and not coordinating their efforts.[81]

In December 2010, the head of the OAS mission in Haiti, Ricardo Seitenfus, gave an interview to the Swiss newspaper *Le Temps*. In the interview, Seitenfus sharply criticized the international community's approach to Haiti, including the focus on a military response and empowerment of NGOs at the expense of the Haitian government. "There is a maleficent or perverse relationship between the NGO's strength and the weakness of the Haitian state," said Seitenfus. "We want to make Haiti a capitalist country, a platform for export to the US market. It is absurd."[82] Anthropologist Tim Schwartz, who has studied NGOs in Haiti for several years, provided a bleak assessment of their performance. "My own research on the matter suggests that at least 90% are rife with corruption, functionally inert, or give money intended for the poor to people who do not need it," he said.[83] Haitians have their own wry assessment of the situation, joking that a Haitian government minister taking 10 percent from a foreign aid project is corruption, but a Washington consulting firm skimming 40 percent is overhead. Haitian physician and businessman Dr. Reginald Boulos complained to the *New York Times* in 2012 that foreigners do everything in Haiti at a cost five times what Haitians would charge.[84]

Professor and anthropologist Mark Schuller provided a detailed critique of the NGO system in Haiti in his 2012 book, *Killing with Kindness: Haiti, International Aid, and NGOs*. Schuller based his analysis in part on an in-depth comparison of two Haitian NGOs that had contrasting approaches to community inclusion, but were both hampered by the demands of international funders. Top-heavy organizational structures better suited to writing reports than to providing services, lack of collaboration with other NGOs, and programs that reflected donor preferences over the needs of the community are all predictable outcomes of a system structured to compete for the attention of donors outside Haiti. "Foreign funders still wield powerful influence, recalling the old saying that 'the one who pays the piper calls the tune,'" Schuller concluded.[85]

Two years after the earthquake, Nigel Fisher, the UN's chief humanitarian officer in Haiti, said, "The NGOs still have something to respond to about their accountability, because there is a lot of cash out there."[86] But accountability is hard to come by when the international community has chosen to direct its Haiti programs via the privatized system of NGOs. Being an NGO means being largely free of systematic scrutiny, especially compared to a governmental entity that must answer to citizens, taxpayers, and media. Even if an NGO is considered accountable to its donors, that demographic does not include the Haitian people whose lives are affected most directly by the organization's actions. As Schuller wrote, "If a state-sponsored development project failed or merely lined the pockets of insiders, citizens would be in the streets protesting, because there is at least in theory some accountability, some responsibility to the citizenry. [But] NGOs . . . are first and foremost private voluntary initiatives. That is why any NGO can point to individual successes post-earthquake, while close to 40% of camps still lacked water a year following the quake."[87]

As Schuller states, despite the international outpouring of generosity, hundreds of thousands of Haitians suffered in misery for months and then years after the earthquake. By the summer of 2010, the International Organization for Migration registered 1.3 million Haitians living as internally displaced persons, most of them located in greater Port-au-Prince.[88] Two different surveys of camp residents conducted that summer—one directed by Schuller and carried out by a team of UEH Faculté d'Ethnologie students, and one conducted by the LAMP for Haiti Foundation and other groups, including IJDH and BAI—present an anguished picture of deprivation.[89] Forty percent of the camps had no access to water; 30 percent had no toilets.[90] Many respondents said that they were forced to defecate in small plastic bags and then throw out the bags wherever they could.[91] Standing rainwater and mud with a smell "reminiscent of pig farms," as Schuller's report described it, was common, even in the camps with latrines.[92]

Three-quarters of the families interviewed reported that someone in their household had gone at least a day without eating in the week prior to their interview, and more than half said that they had to rely on purchased bottled water for drinking water.[93] Oddly, more families reported a lack of food and abysmal living conditions than claimed to be suffering from hunger or despair about their state of affairs. The researchers concluded that the discrepancy likely indicated that camp residents had resigned themselves to perpetual deprivation. "The conflation of these factors suggests that camp conditions have deteriorated to the point that unacceptably poor health has become indistinguishable from daily life," wrote the authors of the LAMP for Haiti report.[94] IJDH attorney Nicole Phillips, who led the research team, later put it more bluntly. "The tragedy was that the people in the camps had endured so much for so long that they were past complaining about it," she said. "They had just kind of accepted it."

Hundreds of thousands of residents were evicted from IDP camps by alleged landowners with questionable title, while NGOs operating or serving the camps almost always refused to defend the residents' rights to remain. Deepa Panchang's survey of NGO officials connected to IDP camps did not yield a single respondent who had initiated any legal process to stop the evictions.[95] BAI lawyers reported that NGOs working in camps were reluctant to force alleged landowners to prove their rights to the property. The NGO community in Haiti proved to be similarly hesitant to demand a UN response to the cholera epidemic triggered by UN negligence. Mark Schuller has optimistically written that the massive failure of the post-earthquake response has been a pedagogical moment for the current international aid system and perhaps even a "Waterloo" for the broken NGO model.[96] But the international community's cholera response has thus far repeated the familiar dysfunctional pattern: as of mid-2012, the Red Cross, still sitting on unspent millions in post-earthquake donations, had received more funds from the international community to support a cholera response than the Haitian government has.[97] As Haitian rights activist Melinda Miles has written, "An opportunity to set a good example to the rest of the world has instead established a model of how best to act against the interests of a devastated people and render them invisible."[98]

These dismal results are not inevitable. Increasingly, individuals and organizations from the international community and NGOs have recognized that it is counterproductive to ignore the government of the country they wish to help. Paul Farmer has recently written about his own journey toward this realization:

> Since 1983 I have worked in Haiti in many capacities, including as a physician aiming to improve medical care. I operated as many non-governmental organizations [NGOs] still do today: my assumption was that my colleagues and I could do a much better job of caring for the poor and the sick than any Haitian public institution. This was an unconscious assumption: ignorance, not arrogance, was the primary driver of this approach. After ten years of struggle in my initial headstrong, do-it-yourself mode, I began to see that my philosophy, not the Haitians,' needed to change. If Haiti was ever to have healthy, robust means of caring for its citizens, then working with and through public institutions was the only way to achieve meaningful results.[99]

Farmer was not the only one to recognize that his approach needed to change. A survey of Haiti-based humanitarian workers and volunteers in mid-2010 showed that most were committed to measuring their organizations' performance and accountability using widely accepted sets of standards and metrics.[100] The most widely used standards, including those developed by the Sphere Project and the Humanitarian Accountability Partnership, incorporate explicit calls for respecting the human rights of aid recipients. As far back as the 1990s, the UN and other international agencies have urged that assistance be grounded in the recognition of human rights obligations.[101]

In the days after the earthquake, Mario Joseph and Brian Concannon led a team of advocates (which included members of the New York University Center for Human Rights and Global Justice, the Robert F. Kennedy Center for Justice and Human Rights, and Partners in Health / Zanmi Lasante as well as personnel from BAI and IJDH) that submitted briefings and testimony to the IACHR. They urged that the response to Haiti's disaster be delivered with what they call a human rights–based approach to international assistance, a method they consciously contrast with a charity-based philosophy.[102] (Somewhat more poetically, Partners in Health and Farmer usually refer to the same rights-based approach as "accompaniment"—a process of working shoulder-to-shoulder not just with individual Haitians but with the country's government.)[103] Already, with the aftershocks still rumbling in Port-au-Prince, it was clear that most of the international community was looking at Haitians as a charity case and the government of Haiti as a roadblock to be ignored or steered around. So Joseph and Concannon argued that international assistance be grounded in legal entitlements and obligations.

The key to this approach lies in recognizing that the government of Haiti is the entity charged with fulfilling those legal obligations to its citizens. Various human rights instruments and customary international law recognize that the government of Haiti holds the primary duty to guarantee its citizens the rights to food, water, housing, and health care, all of which were so scarce after the earthquake. International law also dictates that the people of Haiti have the right to active participation in their government's decision-making. International actors are themselves bound by multiple international legal instruments, including the UN Charter (which requires states to take "joint and separate action" to protect economic and social rights); the International Covenant on Economic, Social, and Cultural Rights; the OAS Charter; and the American Convention on Human Rights. Those instruments compel states to take action to assist other states and their citizens who are in crisis, but they must do so in a manner that respects the rights of those left vulnerable, which includes working through local governments whenever possible. The law does not apply just to governments. International courts have held that non-state actors like the UN and NGOs have the requisite "legal personality" to be similarly bound by international human rights law.[104]

In addition, many of the states and non-state organizations that generously rushed to Haiti's aid after the earthquake did not arrive with clean hands. Many bear some legal or moral obligations for the disaster to which they responded. In the 1980s, the International Monetary Fund, at the urging of the United States and other nations, compelled Haiti to adopt the neoliberal policies of lowering subsidies for domestic agriculture and slashing tariffs on imported rice.[105] As discussed in Chapter 1, in the late 1990s and early 2000s, the IDB, again at the urging of the US government, refused to distribute hundreds of millions of dollars in approved loans to allow Haiti to make several infrastructure upgrades, including improvements in its water and sanitation systems.[106] And the UN's responsibility for the devastating cholera epidemic is documented in that same chapter.

In their presentations to the IACHR, Joseph and Concannon argued that a rights-based approach to earthquake relief would be characterized by five qualities reflecting Haitians' legal rights: capacity development, participation by Haitians, transparency, accountability, and nondiscrimination. In real terms, they said, international human rights law requires aid providers to work through the Haitian government whenever possible. The law also requires that there be mechanisms where complaints about aid providers could be received and redressed if rights are violated. In short, the law requires that Haitians be treated not merely as spectators of the process determining their fate.

The IACHR agreed. Three weeks after the earthquake, it issued a statement. "The IACHR reminds the Haitian government, the international community, the non-governmental organizations, and the many volunteers on the ground of the importance of respecting international human rights obligations in all circumstances, in particular non-derogable rights and the rights of those most vulnerable."[107]

But, as Paul Farmer pointed out, working with Haitians and their institutions is not just required by law. It is also the most effective and enduring method for providing assistance. As the international donor community agreed in the "New Cooperation Paradigm" conference nine months before the earthquake, Haiti's unique vulnerability to natural disasters was largely caused by too many outsiders, well-meaning or not, who treated Haiti like a blank space to be filled with whatever project or short-term approach the donor saw fit to pursue. It is simply good development practice to respect the sovereignty of the host government and its need to develop long-term capacity, along with treating affected individuals as rights-holders rather than charity cases.

Working with the Haitian people would have reduced long-term dependence and avoided duplication of efforts. Creating accountability measures and leveraging local expertise would have boosted efficiency. One can easily imagine how greater transparency and involvement with the Haitian people could have avoided post-earthquake faux pas like the USAID contracts with shoddy providers or NGO support of questionable projects. Certainly, greater involvement of the Haitians occupying the IDP camps would have prevented NGOs from concluding as a group, as they did in mid-2010, that the Sphere Minimum Standards call for one toilet for every twenty persons was "unrealistic" in Haiti's camps, and that free water distribution to the camps was unsustainable. Instead, the NGOs ignored Haitian perspectives, stopped the free water, and settled for a goal of one toilet per one hundred persons— just in time for the cholera outbreak.[108]

Perhaps surprisingly, given this disappointing reality of aid on ground in Haiti, a rights-based approach to assistance is explicitly embraced by UN agencies, multiple states, state collaborations like the European Union, and most large international-level NGOs. At a special session of the UN Human Rights Council on

January 27, 2010, the council committed to pursuing a human rights approach in its response to the Haitian earthquake.[109] In a mid-2010 survey of 138 organizations working in Haiti, 85 percent reported using a rights-based approach.[110]

Accepting the rhetoric of a rights-based approach to assistance is a useful first step. But good intentions need to be accompanied by true accountability for respecting the human rights of the persons affected and the role of the host government as representing those persons in the short and long term. As the UN Office of the High Commissioner for Human Rights has stated, accountability is the "raison d'être of the rights-based approach."[111] In international aid in Haiti and elsewhere, international actors are far more likely to embrace rights-based language than they are to set up processes to hold themselves responsible for practicing what they preach. The UN's shirking of responsibility for the Haitian cholera crisis provides an unfortunate example of this phenomenon. The crying need for accountability is another reason for international assistance providers to closely coordinate with the Haitian government. Governments are designed to be responsive to affected persons, who retain power as voters and citizens. These affected persons can never have the same ability to oversee the actions of NGOs and foreign donors.

Which, of course, was Brian Concannon's argument to the world two days after the earthquake. Haiti was vulnerable on January 12, 2010, in significant part because insufficient attention had been paid to nurturing a transparent Haitian government responsible for enforcing the law, providing basic services, and protecting the rights of the people it serves. Sadly, Haiti is even more vulnerable today, because most of the billions of dollars donated for its recovery have served only to fund repetition of the mistakes of the past. As Edmond Mulet, the UN's chief in Haiti, admitted in an interview one year after the earthquake, "Unless we address the rule of law in Haiti, all the efforts on reconstruction, on development, on peacekeeping, will be in vain."[112]

At first, Yvonne Jolivan does not have an answer to my question.[113]

Thirty-four years old, but thin and weathered and looking older, she stands barefoot in the entry to one of the many tattered tarp and plywood structures at a place called Grace Village in Carrefour, Haiti. Jolivan holds eleven-month-old Jofte, the youngest of her five children, in her left arm. He reaches inside her dirty green tank top, trying to find her breast. Like almost all of the three thousand people living in this camp for persons still displaced by the January 2010 earthquake, Jolivan is without a job, any source of income, or even clean water and a toilet. My question is: how do you feed your kids?

She shrugs her shoulders and answers in Creole. "When I wake up in the morning, I thank God, and God knows if we are going to eat that day." That seems pretty intangible to me, so I press for some details. When the family does eat, how do they get the food? She shrugs again. "Sometimes people ask me to clean their clothes for them, and if I receive money I can buy food for the children and go to the street to buy water." Finally, she admits to the challenge. "*Li se difisil*"—things are difficult.

It is March 2013, over three years after the earthquake. And the only thing Jolivan knows when she wakes up in the morning is that her family has shelter, meager as it is. But now that is at risk, too. Things are getting even more difficult.

A Christian pastor and his church say that they own the land that Grace Village sits on, and they have ratcheted up their efforts to remove Yvonne Jolivan and the five-hundred-plus families living there. According to multiple residents I spoke with and a thirty-page petition filed in mid-February 2013 by BAI and IJDH with the IACHR, those eviction efforts have included violent, armed assaults; rocks thrown into the camp area; the destruction of tents; and the forced removal of many previous camp residents. The petition also alleges that non-governmental organizations have been blocked from providing water and latrines for camp residents by the pastor, Bishop Joel Jeune, the president of Grace International, a church and not-for-profit corporation registered in the State of Florida.[114]

One former camp resident, Marcel Germain, has provided sworn testimony that Grace International security guards have attacked and even killed some Grace Village residents. Other residents, speaking with anonymity, paint the picture of a reign of terror designed to push the residents off the land. Some American and Haitian human rights lawyers have witnessed Grace International security shooting guns in the camp and forcibly removing a camp resident.

In an interview, Bishop Jeune categorically denies accusations of violence, and points the finger back at the camp residents. Hundreds of former Grace Village residents have been removed from the camp to more permanent homes at a settlement called Lambi Village. Even though there are not enough homes for all the Grace Village residents at the new site, Jeune says, all of the tent dwellers can sign up for a waiting list. But the remaining Grace Village residents want money instead of a place to live, Jeune claims. He notes that some other post-earthquake camps in Haiti were disbanded in part by offers of cash for residents to move. "I don't have a number to give you, but many, many, many of these people have their own house, and they put it for rent and they come to stay here," he says. "They are waiting for that money."

The destruction of Grace Village tents was conducted by Haitian National Police and UN troops, not by him or his staff, Jeune insists. He himself is afraid to go to the camps because the residents throw rocks at him, not the other way around. "I don't see how I can sue anybody for defamation, but I know as Christians we have to suffer. When Jesus was trying to do good, they turned against him, too," Jeune says.

Some of Grace International's US-based church and not-for-profit partners back up this version of the standoff. But, beyond the competing allegations, it was clear that the camp I visited in March did not look anything like a "model for proactive, healthy, and efficient camp management," complete with water wells, showers, toilets, and a trash disposal system. That is the place described in the Grace International web site (*www.graceintl.org*), which invites donations. Several US churches and religious mission organizations have partnered with Grace and supported its call for funds. (The Grace International website says the organization's partners have included the UN World Food Programme and Doctors Without Borders. Through spokespersons, WFP said that it has not been a direct partner with Grace, and Doctors Without Borders declined to comment for this book on their relationship with the organization.) The not-for-profit's US tax return reports $2.8 million in contributions and grants received in 2008 alone. Jeune says most of that figure represents in-kind contributions from volunteers, and that the money goes primarily toward Grace's school and nutrition programs.

If Grace International once harbored nurturing intentions for the tent dwellers, those feelings seem long gone now. Jeune has issued eviction notices to Grace Village residents and told me that the church needs to reclaim the camp land for its school-yard to expand. I asked one of Grace's supporters, Scott Campbell of the Vancouver, Washington–based Christian mission Forward Edge, if he agreed with the residents' and advocates' claim that Grace and Jeune are waging an eviction and intimidation campaign. "Is it an eviction campaign?" he responded. "Well, they are long overdue to leave. As for intimidation, that is a strong word."

The Grace Village residents share their plight with scores of other Haitians. In early 2013, 350,000 people still lived in IDP camps around Port-au-Prince, and the UN estimated that 20 percent of them are facing eviction. There was literally no place for them to go. An estimated two hundred thousand homes were destroyed in the earthquake, with less than nineteen thousand homes repaired. Six thousand new homes have been built. Even Grace International staff and supporters acknowledge that Lambi Village cannot house all the camp residents if they are removed.

Which should come as no surprise. Haiti's housing crisis is far beyond the scope of any remedy created by a pastor or church group, even assuming all of the intentions are noble. And no non-governmental organization has the same duties of fair treatment and the provision of basic services to Haitian citizens that its government has accepted through a myriad of human rights treaties and its own constitution. So when the IACHR ruled on the Grace Village residents' and BAI's and IJDH's petition on March 26, it addressed its order to the government of Haiti, not Grace International.

Responding to the evidence that Haitian National Police helped forcefully evict some Grace Village residents, the IACHR admonished the government to prevent the use of violence. The IACHR also ordered the government to ensure that clean water and police protection is provided to the residents.[115] The IACHR order was a preliminary measure, so Grace Village residents and their advocates hope that future rulings will address the fact that evictions have occurred without court orders. Remarkably, no resident or advocate has yet seen proof that Grace International or Bishop Jeune owns the land on which the camp is based. They also hope that future IACHR rulings will address the fact that official complaints to the government about Grace International have been ignored, and that protesting camp residents have been arrested and imprisoned without warrants or charges. The Haitian Constitution and international treaties guarantee the Grace Village residents better access to housing and services, but those promises are being disregarded.

The Grace Village heartbreak is a microcosm of the post-earthquake disaster in Haiti. The global generosity that was offered at historic levels has yielded only lost opportunities. Aid money promised has not been delivered; money delivered has been wasted. The US government and world community ignored the post-earthquake calls by Brian Concannon, Paul Farmer, and others for rights-based development assistance that could have empowered and improved the Haitian government, creating an enduring solution to Haiti's problems. Instead, shortsighted and self-interested reliance on disjointed private charity has led to a new, post-earthquake reality that is a disaster all its own.

Ultimately, the important question is not whether Grace Village residents are being victimized by an abusive alleged landowner or have simply worn out the patience of a benevolent mission. The important question is whether the rights of some of the world's most vulnerable citizens are going to be respected. Can the world community learn from the massive mistakes made in the earthquake recovery, and do better?

To Yvonne Jolivan and her family, this is not an abstract question. "I just hope someone can help us relocate," she says. "Because our situation here is chaotic."

FIGURE 1. Since 1996, in both Haiti and in the United States, Brian Concannon (left), of the Institute for Justice and Democracy in Haiti (IJDH), and Mario Joseph (right), of the Bureau des Avocats Internationaux (BAI), embody the global North-global South partnership for human rights in Haiti. (Photo: Daniel Ramirez)

FIGURE 2. The UN base outside Mirebalais, Haiti, where sewage dumped into Haiti's chief waterway in October 2010 led to the cholera outbreak that killed thousands. (Photo: Fran Quigley)

FIGURE 3. Concannon, Joseph, and IJDH attorney Bea Lindstrom file lawsuits in Haitian courts, draft international petitions and reports, conduct media outreach, author scholarly articles, and mobilize Haitian activists and their supporters, all in an effort to defend the human rights of the Haitian people. (Photo: Daniel Ramirez)

FIGURE 4. "When the epidemic (of cholera) first hit, we thought we would sit out," Brian Concannon says. "We did not think this was a place for lawyers. . . . Eventually, though, we got tired of looking at our feet when Haitians said, 'Who is going to do something about this?'" (Photo: Daniel Ramirez)

FIGURE 5. The residents of Camp Django held press conferences and conducted demonstrations to protest illegal eviction from their internally displaced persons (IDP) camp. Their advocacy did not prevent their eviction, but other activist efforts have kept vulnerable persons in their homes. (Photo: Fran Quigley)

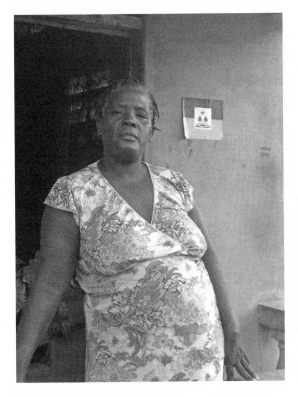

FIGURE 6. Jacqueline Olonville had never engaged in any human rights activism before cholera introduced by UN troops (MINUSTAH) sickened her and killed thousands. Now she has joined the trailblazing lawsuit demanding accountability by the UN. "MINUSTAH came here and killed our families and God's children, so I want them to leave and give us back our country," she told a rally in St. Marc, Haiti. (Photo: Fran Quigley)

FIGURE 7. Mario Joseph's and Brian Concannon's call for the international community to channel its post-earthquake response through the Haitian government was ignored, and the resulting mismanagement and ineffectiveness has been criticized across the globe. (Photo: Daniel Ramirez)

FIGURE 8. Part of Joseph's portfolio includes reaching out to the international community through media interviews and participation in documentary films. His open challenge to powerful Haitians has earned him death threats and forced his family to leave the country for their safety. "Mario is the most courageous person I know," says BAI founder Ira Kurzban. "You have to appreciate Haiti to understand how his life is in danger every day." (Photo: Daniel Ramirez)

FIGURE 9. Mario Joseph conferring with residents of an internally displaced persons (IDP) camp as they resist eviction attempts. "When the rule of law does not exist, you have to build it," he says. (Photo: Fran Quigley)

FIGURE 10. Activists demonstrate in front of the government social affair ministry. One of the group was arrested after he spoke out in opposition to government policies. "[President] Martelly, we are asking for work, we are asking for food, and you give us prison," they chant. (Photo: Fran Quigley)

FIGURE 11. Haiti's National Palace was one of thousands of Port-au-Prince buildings destroyed in the January 2010 earthquake. (Photo: Fran Quigley)

FIGURE 12. Concannon lived in Haiti for nine years before returning to the United States. "My place to best help the people of Haiti was not in Port-au-Prince but back here in the States, making the US safe for democracy in Haiti," he says. (Photo: Daniel Ramirez)

6 | Beyond the Courtroom

When the earthquake hit Port-au-Prince on January 12, 2010, the home of the thirty-eight-year-old woman and her husband collapsed on them. The husband was killed, and the woman was trapped for several hours before she was able to escape. Two days later, as the woman was searching for her husband's body in the rubble, she was grabbed by two men carrying guns. They pulled her into a nearby tent and raped her.

Less than four months later, when the same woman was using the latrine after dark at an IDP camp, two other men forced their way into the stall. One pressed a knife against her waist, and then they raped her.

The woman has since made several attempts to commit suicide by drinking bleach. So far, her daughters have been able to stop her.[1]

A few weeks later, a twenty-four-year-old woman, also a widow, was taking trash to a dumping site at the same camp. Four men forced her into a car and drove to a deserted street, where all four raped her. Then, one grabbed the woman by the throat and ordered her to open her mouth. She did so, and the man bit off the end of her tongue.[2]

There was no systematic effort to collect all reports of gender-based violence after the earthquake, but there is no question that attacks occurred with alarming frequency. New York University's Center for Human Rights and Global Justice conducted a 2011 study of four different IDP camps in and around Port-au-Prince. Fourteen percent of families living in the camps reported that at least one of their household members had been victimized by sexual violence in the first year after the earthquake. Nearly one in five of the reported victims was under the age of eighteen.[3]

A random survey sample by University of Michigan researchers yielded an estimate that over ten thousand people were sexually assaulted in Port-au-Prince in the first six weeks after the earthquake.[4] As recently as the early months of 2012, BAI was still receiving an average of four new rape victims in its offices every week, more than half of them children. Even these disturbing numbers likely underestimate the extent of the crisis; it has been well demonstrated that fear of retaliation and stigma create a reluctance to report attacks. As one Haitian woman told the NYU researchers, "If you speak about it, they will kill you."[5]

In the wake of the rape epidemic, unwanted pregnancies followed. A UN and Government of Haiti study in the fall of 2010 reported pregnancy rates in the IDP camps at three times the urban average before the earthquake, with two-thirds of the pregnancies unwanted.[6] Haiti has one of the highest HIV rates in the Western Hemisphere, with one of every fifty adults HIV-positive, so the rapes are feared to have infected many victims with the virus.[7] Lack of access to prenatal and obstetric care in Haiti led to maternal mortality rates that were among the world's worst even before the earthquake devastated Haiti's meager health-care system. Post-earthquake, a 2011 Human Rights Watch study told harrowing stories of women and girls giving birth on street corners and tent floors.[8] Abortion is a criminal offense in Haiti, but the drug misoprostol, which can induce abortion, is often sold on the street. Haitian health providers reported a post-earthquake spike in patients with complications from self-administering misoprostol or using unsterilized metal objects to induce abortions.[9]

Before the earthquake, women in Haiti already had it bad. Although Haitian women are referred to as *poto mitan* (the pillars of society), they bear the worst of Haiti's poverty and lawlessness. Before the earthquake, less than a quarter of women had access to modern methods of contraception, and one in every ten Haitian girls had a child or was pregnant by age seventeen. Girls usually entered the education system later than boys, and early pregnancies and domestic obligations meant they usually dropped out earlier, too. Most women found their economic opportunities limited to the informal sector, and, when they did get jobs, their salaries were lower than men. In a country where land ownership is so important to peasants' survival, women in common-law marriages—known as *plasaj* and constituting the majority of conjugal relationships in rural Haiti—have no legal right to the land they may cultivate for decades. Sixty percent of female-headed households lived in extreme poverty. Women have long been significantly underrepresented in political leadership and in government, with only a single female in the thirty-member senate as of 2011, and just five women in the ninety-nine-member Chamber of Deputies. A woman has not served on the Cour de Cassation (supreme court) for the past twenty years. Even the rape crisis after the earthquake had plenty of brutal precedent, with one Haitian official estimating in 2000 that as many as 90 percent of Haitian women had experienced gender-based violence in their lives. Rape was regularly used as a weapon of terror and political repression during Haiti's military regime in 1991–1993 and during the 2004–2006 conflicts.[10]

After the earthquake, things got even worse for Haitian women. Of course, the quake directly maimed and killed tens of thousands of women, including leaders in government and journalism and inspirational women's rights activists like Myriam Merlet, Magalie Marcelin, and Anne Marie Coriolon.[11] Historically, women tend to bear a disproportionate share of the harm after disasters. Sexual violence increased in tense, lawless post-disaster settings like those created by Hurricane Katrina and the South Asian tsunami of 2004, as well as in the aftermath of Haitian hurricanes and tropical storms. The night of the Haitian earthquake, 4,500 prisoners escaped from the Haitian National Penitentiary, further destabilizing a chaotic situation filled with despair and violence.[12]

The IDP camps, which had almost no security presence and limited lighting after dark, proved to be the most dangerous settings of all. The camp tents and shacks offered virtually no physical barriers to intrusion, and women were attacked while walking to fetch water or to reach latrines. Many frightened women resorted to defecating in plastic bags or in the open after dark, which itself carried risk. As a 2011 report coauthored by BAI and IJDH put it, "These [post-earthquake] conditions have created an environment in which people feel frustrated, desperate, and dehumanized—emotions that all too often are channeled into sexual violence against women and girls."[13] Neither the US military presence immediately after the earthquake nor the long-term presence of MINUSTAH troops in Haiti provided any meaningful protection for camp residents.

Violence and deprivation walked hand-in-hand. Eighty-four percent of the IDP camps' residents in NYU's survey reported going at least one day without eating in the previous week, and the study found strong correlations between sexual victimization and a family's lack of access to food, water, and adequate sanitation.[14] Women who were forced to go far from home to search for food and water put themselves at risk of attack during their quest, and often had to leave children at home unattended and vulnerable. Hunger and thirst forced many struggling women, particularly girls whose parents died in the earthquake, to resort to so-called survival sex. In one IDP camp focus group interview by the NYU researchers, every woman present reported being asked at least once to trade sex for goods and services. For some women, there is little choice but to agree. "People will try to survive by the way they can," one woman living in an IDP camp told Human Rights Watch. "So, for US $0.60 or $1.25, you have sex just for that. It's not good to make prostitution, but what can you do? You have to eat."[15]

In response to this epidemic of sexual violence after the earthquake, the reactions to the victims by Haitian police and judicial officials ranged from indifference to outright hostility. The widow who was raped twice, once while searching for her husband's body in the earthquake rubble and once in an IDP camp latrine, later saw one of the rapists return to the camp two months after she was attacked. A friend caught the man and held him down, and others called the police emergency number.

There was no response, and eventually the man broke free. The victim fears he will return and retaliate. The same fear kept the rape victim whose tongue was bitten off from initially making a police report at all. No arrests have been made in her case, even though she has since seen one of her attackers on the streets of Port-au-Prince.[16] These women know too well that if the attackers do return, they are unlikely to be deterred by any official police presence, as law enforcement is largely absent from the IDP camps.[17] In fact, one of BAI's clients is a fifteen-year-old girl who was raped by a Haitian National Police officer and another man.

Under Haitian law, a woman who has been raped has several options for seeking legal intervention. She can immediately call the police, or make a later complaint to the police, justice of the peace, or the office of the prosecutor (also known as the *parquet*). All have the authority to order the accused to appear in court in cases of flagrant offenses, or *flagrant délit*, and the police have the duty to investigate, gather evidence, and make arrests for flagrant offenses. Haitian law defines a flagrant offense as one where the person is caught in the act of committing a crime or soon after, usually within forty-eight hours.[18]

In reality, as the capturers of the widow's rapist discovered, it was difficult to get Haitian police to respond to an emergency situation. Calls to the police at nighttime were often not answered, or the caller was told that the police could not respond because they were sleeping. On other occasions, rape victims were told that the police did not have a car or gas to allow them to travel to the scene of the crime.

So advocates urged women to make their complaints in person at the police station if possible. But the reception at the station was often intimidating. Police sometimes wrongly sent complainants to another agency or accused the woman of fabricating the allegations to obtain money—a particularly common reaction when the victim was poor. When a nineteen-year-old woman whose mother had been killed in the earthquake was raped in one of the IDP camps, the police told her, "When you catch the gangsters who raped you, then call us."[19]

That reaction was common in the months after the earthquake, according to advocates and UN officials, who report that Haitian National Police rarely investigated a rape complaint if the attacker's identity was not immediately apparent.[20] Women reporting rapes were questioned about whether they were wearing provocative clothing or somehow triggered the attack, with one Haitian judge recently telling a women's advocacy group that he did not believe in rape. "I've seen male judges blame the victim and imply it's their fault because, for example, they wore a short skirt," says Mario Joseph.[21] A UN report in June 2012 followed a sample of sixty-two rape reports delivered to the Haitian National Police in 2010. Only twenty-five of the sixty-two cases were reviewed by a prosecutor and only eleven of those cases were thoroughly investigated. None of the cases came to trial before the summer of 2012.[22]

The Haitian government was undeniably weakened by the earthquake—twenty-seven of twenty-eight national government buildings were destroyed and almost one in every five Haitian civil servants was killed or injured. But even prior to the disaster, the official precedent for ignoring or demeaning rape victims was well established. Rape was not even criminalized in Haiti until 2005. A 2009 IACHR report on violence against women in Haiti documented biased and negligent pre-earthquake treatment of gender-based violence, including one horrific story of a boyfriend beating his teenage girlfriend, pouring gasoline on her, and setting her on fire. The young man was released after one month of detention. The report concluded, "Most cases of discrimination and violence against women are never fully investigated, prosecuted, and punished by the justice system in Haiti. The Commission observed an alarming pattern of systematic impunity that sends a social message that discrimination and violence against women will be tolerated."[23]

Even when a Haitian rape victim was able to have her official complaint accepted, she faced significant odds against obtaining justice. Most Haitian rape victims do not seek medical treatment because they are worried about the cost, fear retaliation by their attacker, lack transportation to care, or lack awareness of available services.[24] This poses a significant problem for prosecutions, since rape complaints without an official medical certificate are usually ignored in the Haitian legal process. Complaints supported by a medical certificate that does not conform to the preferred format are often rebuffed as well. As one Haitian lawyer reported hearing a prosecutor's clerk say, "This is an easy case; there's no medical certificate."[25] BAI complained to the UN Commission on the Status of Women in late 2011 about the de facto requirement of a medical certificate in order for a rape complaint to be pursued. That practice, BAI said, "reinforces the belief in the justice system that women's testimony is inherently untrustworthy."[26]

The Haitian judicial process is notoriously slow and confusing for victims, most of whom cannot afford legal representation. If a case survives the complaint stage and gets referred to an investigating judge (*juge d'instruction*), the case often bogs down for months and even years. The caseloads are high, and the courts do very little work in the summer months. "Justice does not really work during the summer," says former BAI attorney Esther Felix.[27] The slow pace of the process provides too many opportunities for corruption, Felix says, because attorneys and intermediaries sometimes pay for beneficial scheduling of cases, or to have a case held back until the victim drops the pursuit of her complaint. In one recent case, a clerk solicited a direct payment from a BAI client's mother in return for a promise of a favorable ruling.[28]

Court proceedings are conducted in French, when most Haitians speak only Creole. The court staffs' failure to provide information to the victims sometimes allows the accused to be released because the victim did not appear at a hearing. Like the police station environment, the court hearings can be extremely intimidating for rape victims. In one BAI case, a judge sat the accused adult rapist next to his fourteen-year-old victim, and many judges put the victims on the defensive during aggressive questioning from the bench.[29] Intimidation comes from outside the courtroom as well, as the mother of a teenage rape victim told the IACHR: "Since my daughter was able to identify at least one of her rapists, his father, a former military official, has called several times. First, he offered money if we would just 'leave it alone.' Then he mentioned that he knew I didn't live with a man so it would be easy to kill me if I caused problems for his son."[30]

In Haiti after the earthquake, rape was easy to commit and very unlikely to be punished. Most rape victims, especially those living in the same IDP camp as their attackers, weighed the likelihood of retaliation as higher than successful prosecution and made a rational choice not to lodge an official complaint. Jayne Fleming, a US-based human rights lawyer, submitted an affidavit to the IACHR in late 2010 describing the cases of twenty-three post-earthquake rape victims she represented in efforts to obtain humanitarian parole in the United States. Of those twenty-three victims, only two made a police report. In those two cases, the police did not make any arrests, and the rapists threatened the families of the victims, forcing them to go into hiding.[31] The NYU researchers found that rape victims were more willing to tell survey interviewers about their rape than they were to make an official report to the police. As one of the women told an NYU interviewer, "Justice does not exist in Haiti."[32]

When justice is so elusive, what is left for Haitian women and their advocates to do? "Since the rule of law in Haiti has been almost non-existent, you have to build it," says Mario Joseph. On paper, at least, there is some framework on which to build.

Despite Haiti's failure to criminalize marital rape or adopt a special law prohibiting domestic violence, Haiti has signed a variety of regional and international human rights treaties, including the International Covenant on Civil and Political Rights, the Conventions on the Rights of the Child, the American Convention on Human Rights, and the Inter-American Convention on the Prevention, Punishment and Eradication of Violence Against Women ("Convention of Belém Do Pará"). All these instruments place extensive obligations on the government of Haiti to prevent, investigate, and punish acts of violence against women. The 2005 reform of the 1835 Penal Code of Haiti finally made rape a criminal offense, setting a minimum sentence of ten years for rape against a woman and fifteen years for rape against a girl (under fifteen years of age). The 1987 Haitian Constitution, inspired by the populist organizations that put an end to the Duvalier regime, is a sweeping and progressive mandate of civil, economic, and social rights.[33] Adopted with the support of 90 percent of the Haitian people, the Constitution has been called (in the words of Haitian economist Fritz Deshommes) "an excellent warhorse [that] must be equipped, nourished, and cared for in order to achieve the real re-foundation" of the Haitian state.[34]

Also, despite the grim history of women's suffering in Haiti, the nation has a noble legacy of solidarity and activism to draw from. Most recently, Haitians responded bravely and unselfishly in the aftermath of the earthquake. Long before international rescue efforts could begin, Haitians mobilized to dig out survivors from the rubble, often with their bare hands, and they cared for the injured, and took in family members and even strangers left homeless by the destruction. The activist and author Beverly Bell, writing in the collection *Tectonic Shifts: Haiti since the Earthquake*, quoted Mesita Attis of the market women's support group Martyred Women of Brave Ayibobo: "If you heard your baby in the ruins crying, 'Mommy, Mommy, Mommy,' fourteen people would run to help you. If you did not have a piece of bread, someone would give you theirs."[35]

The post-earthquake solidarity and resilience sprung from a well sunk deep in Haiti's culture. A sense of collective responsibility is steeped in the tradition of the world's only successful slave rebellion and the powerful Creole egalitarian rallying cry, *Tout moun se moun*—everyone is a person. As Bell writes:

> As tenacious as oppression and deprivation have been throughout Haitian
> history, the country's highly organized grassroots movement has never given up
> the battle its enslaved ancestors began. The movement is composed of women,
> peasants, street vendors, human rights advocates, clergy and laity, workers, and
> others. The mobilizations, protests, and advocacy have brought down dictators,
> staved off some of the worst of economic policies aimed at others' profit, and
> kept the population from ever fitting quietly into anyone else's plans for them.[36]

The legacy of Haitian women forming the core of the struggle goes back to Anacaona, a queen of the original Arawak inhabitants of Haiti, who is said to have led the fight against her people's enslavement by the Spanish.[37] The Ligue Feminine d'Action Sociale (Feminine League for Social Action) helped organize for women's rights in Haiti as early as 1934, and provided a civil society example that is self-consciously imitated by current women's rights groups like SOFA (Solidarité Fanm Ayisyen—Haitian Women's Solidarity). Women played significant roles in the pro-democracy resistance to Jean-Claude Duvalier and the opposition to the military governments that followed him.[38] More recently, a women's movement led by organizations like Kay Fanm (Women's House), KOFAVIV (Komisyon Fanm Viktim Por Viktim—Commission of Women Victims for Victims), KONAMAVID (Kodinasyon Nasyonal Mawom Viktim Direct—National Commission of Direct Victims in Hiding), and FAVILEK (Fanm Viktim Leve Kanpe—Women Victims, Get Up, Stand Up) successfully pushed for the adoption of the 2005 law on violence against women and for bolstering the status of the MCDF (Ministére á la Condition Feminine et aux Droits des Femmes—Women's Ministry).[39] Bell compiled a collection of first-person stories in a 2001 book, *Walking on Fire: Haitian Women's Stories of Survival and Resistance*, that chronicles the efforts of Haitian women who were activists in the *tilegliz* (grassroots Christian "little church") movement, union organizers, independent journalists, and the leaders of rural collectives.[40]

When faced with the chaos and fear of the post-earthquake rape crisis, these women and their organizations responded again.

Taped to the wall next to the entrance of the KOFAVIV building are two large hand-lettered signs. One reads, *Mwen pa fè vyolans. E ou?*—"I don't do violence. Do you?"

The other reads, *Viv Egalite Ant Fanm Ak Gason*—"Long Live Equality between Men and Women." Inside, about twenty women are gathered in a semicircle, reviewing the process of reaching out to women in IDP camps, where they provide training in legal rights, pass out whistles for security, and offer a toll-free crisis number for victims of violence. These women are called "agents," and they are the front line for KOFAVIV.

KOFAVIV was founded in 2004 by a group of women who had themselves suffered from rape and other forms of violence during the rule of Haiti's military coup regime, from 1991 to 1994. Judith Blaise Joseph, an apprentice lawyer with KOFAVIV, explains that one of the agents' main charges is "accompaniment"—accompanying victims of rape to medical services, to the psychologist on KOFAVIV's staff, and to the legal services that Joseph and an *avoka* colleague deliver in partnership with BAI. KOFAVIV also provides emergency shelter and safe houses for victims and their families when it is dangerous for them to return to the camps or neighborhoods where their attackers may still roam.

Joseph (no relation to BAI's Mario Joseph) is a broad-shouldered woman, nearly six feet tall and wearing a floral-print green and brown top and a long brown skirt. She smiles often and speaks in Creole—unless she really wants to emphasize a point; then she raises her voice slightly and switches to English for my benefit. Joseph and her *avoka* colleague, who is helping a victim file charges at the prosecutor's office today, train the agents in the principles of the law, and act as the liaison between the victims and the police station. That outreach to the police, which has included invitations to join training sessions and participate in planning meetings, has yielded a startling result. The same police force that used to scorn the women who dared to report a rape is now bringing victims directly to KOFAVIV for help.

Joseph pulls out a *Certificat Medical Pour Agression Sexuelle*, the form for medical documentation of a rape victim's injuries that BAI and KOFAVIV are urging all medical providers to use as a uniform source of evidence for prosecution. Once KOFAVIV's agents shepherd the victim through medical and psychological intervention, Joseph guides them through the legal process. Ideally, a victim should be able to file charges and appear before the prosecutor without the benefit of counsel, because the *avoka* has no ability to ask questions at these stages. But the system is not to be trusted yet, Joseph says. Middlemen and racketeers haunt the legal system in Haiti, using the widespread official corruption as a wedge to take advantage of those without counsel. "We want to be present, because we want them to respect the victim's rights," she says. This legal representation is conducted in tandem with BAI, with whom KOFAVIV is tightly linked. (When KOFAVIV's offices were destroyed in the earthquake, their staff worked—and some of them lived for a time—in BAI's offices, which were damaged but intact.) Both BAI and KOFAVIV reach beyond the confines of legal representation and psychosocial support to provide craft-making and small business skills training for women, along with security programs inside the IDP camps. The need is immense. BAI and KOFAVIV together have represented over two hundred rape victims in legal proceedings, and they struggle to respond to the many others who need help pursuing justice.

The advocates focus on prevention, too. The police training and outreach is a big part of that agenda, along with constant and aggressive street protests and media outreach. BAI's grassroots coordinator, Rose Getchine Lima, works with KOFAVIV and other women's groups such as FAVILEK and KONAMAVID to organize regular sit-ins in front of the Ministry of Justice. On International Women's Day (March 8) in 2012, over one thousand women marched from BAI's offices and from the MINUSTAH base at Fort National to the Women's Ministry and the Parliament building. The women carried signs and sang songs demanding justice for women victims of *kolera* and rape, and were joined by a group of men carrying signs saying *Gason Kore Fanm, Fanm Kore Gason*—Men Support Women, Women Support Men. When the group stopped in front of the Women's Ministry, Judith Joseph was among the speakers calling for more women to be appointed as police officers and judges.

That advocacy has reached beyond Haiti to engage the international community. Working with IJDH, BAI and partner organizations successfully lobbied for a resolution in the US Senate and the US House of Representatives demanding better response to the rape crisis from the Haitian government and the US and international community involved in Haiti.[41] The advocates submitted reports and solicited media attention. They lobbied UN member states to include statements of concern about violence against Haitian women in their 2011 recommendations to the UN Office of the High Commissioner for Human Rights as it conducted its Universal Periodic Review of Haiti's human rights record. Ultimately, twenty-two member states used the process to officially register concerns about gender-based violence and/or discrimination.[42] And, in October 2010, attorneys for BAI and IJDH, joined by other international human rights advocates, filed a formal request for precautionary measures with the IACHR. The request called for the Haitian government and the international community to immediately provide security, lighting, and medical care in the IDP camps.[43]

Hundreds of similar requests are filed each year and only a handful granted, but the IACHR responded to this petition with strong recommendations. The commission told the Haitian government to place security patrols in the camps, train public officials to respond to complaints of sexual violence, ensure medical and psychological care for rape victims, and include grassroots women's groups in planning and implementing these initiatives.[44] Advocates say that the commission's decision is the first to explicitly hold the government of Haiti legally responsible for preventing third-party violence against women, and they continue to update the commission on the progress of government compliance with its recommendations. IJDH and BAI also filed a memorandum with the UN Human Rights Committee, questioning Haiti's compliance with the International Covenant on Civil and Political Rights.[45]

Do all the individual interventions, mass gatherings, and international appeals make a difference? Judith Joseph and other advocates say that they see the results every day. "The events have a big impact on the media, and the government is sensitized by the protest," she says. "Along with the trainings, the protests have made the system respond better, which is causing women to be more comfortable reporting abuse." Most importantly, there appears to be far less abuse to report. In the fifty-plus IDP camps where KOFAVIV had a presence, the number of reported rapes dropped more than 50 percent from 2010 to 2011, and the 2012 trends showed a continued decrease. Women's groups and the Haitian National Police both reported to the UN independent expert on human rights in Haiti that violence against women in the camps dropped in 2011.[46] In Place Pétion at Champs de Mars, an IDP camp located across from the National Palace, BAI and KOFAVIV selected twenty-five men for training to provide twenty-four-hour volunteer security. Wearing T-shirts and badges to identify them, the men were happy to perform the service. "We cannot stand by, allowing this to happen in the heart of our community," Delra, one of the men, told Britain's *Guardian*. "The Haitian police cannot be relied on. And long ago we lost faith in the UN. So we have taken it into our own hands. We send out a strong message that these attacks will not be tolerated and that those using sexual violence are weak, not strong men and will be brought to justice."[47] Before Delra and his colleagues, called "sensitization agents," began their rounds, an average of five or six women and girls were being raped in the camp every week. From the time of the project's formal start in February 2011 until the camp closed over a year later, there were no reported rapes.

One afternoon in Port-au-Prince, I spoke with a young woman with short dread-locks and matching earrings and necklace. The woman used to live in the Place Pétion camp before the security was in place. The woman does not want her name published, but she is willing to share her story. "I survived it, so it is OK to talk about it," she says. Her mother was killed in the earthquake and the family home destroyed, so she and some siblings and cousins sought refuge at the IDP camp at Champs de Mars. One night three months after the earthquake, she was sitting alone outside the tent when two masked men attacked her. There was no security around then. "At night, God was our only security," she says.

The woman fought back and screamed, only to be punched repeatedly in the jaw and head. But she put up enough of a fight and made so much noise that her attackers fled before they could complete the intended sexual assault. Still, the young woman was left physically and mentally battered. She sank into a depression and dropped out of school. "At first, I kept it hidden," she says. "Normally, my mother would have been the one to help me deal with this, but she was no longer with me."

Fortunately, FAVILEK was. A companion women's rights advocacy group to KOFAVIV, FAVILEK was founded by rape victims who had been attacked after the 1991 coup d'état. Like KOFAVIV, FAVILEK provides intervention and support for victims of post-earthquake rapes. Although the young woman went to FAVILEK for her own needs, she found herself called to help others. "Soon, I was not so much focusing on what had happened to me."

Now, the young woman regularly meets victims at the hospital and then accompanies them as they file police reports and then see the lawyers at BAI. When she describes FAVILEK's efforts to sensitize Haitian men and its success in persuading the police to investigate rapes, she allows herself a small smile for the first time in the conversation. She pulls out her laminated FAVILEK identification card, which designates her as a volunteer agent, and puts it on the table in front of me. "I am a *viktim*," she says. "And FAVILEK is an organization that helps victims of violence."

When I ask KOFAVIV's Judith Joseph for an individual example of legal advocacy having an effect, she points to sixteen different cases where rapists have been arrested and jailed, with the cases now in front of the investigating judge. In one KOFAVIV/BAI case, a man who raped a five-year-old girl in an IDP camp was arrested, only to be released by the prosecutor before the victim had been questioned by the prosecutor. The man lived only a few tents away from the victim's family, who feared retribution and a new attack. KOFAVIV and BAI intervened immediately, and the man was rearrested and now awaits trial. In another case that advocates point to, a fifteen-year-old orphan was brutally raped by ten men, and BAI and KOFAVIV helped her get placed with the government child protection services agency, connected to psychological treatment, and returned to school. One of her attackers is now jailed and facing charges. In another recent BAI case, Haitian police responded quickly and strategically to a rape complaint: the police had the victim call her assailant to determine his location, and police went there in plainclothes to successfully arrest him.

More reason for optimism is found in the fact that the Haitian Women's Ministry and the OAS have drafted a new comprehensive law on violence against women that includes provisions for relocation, medical care, and financial assistance to victims of numerous forms of gender-based violence. Women's organizations have been included in consultations about the new law, although a new version has yet to be released.[48] In July 2012, BAI attorneys helped prosecute the first post-earthquake rape cases brought to trial in Haiti. In one of the cases, the victim was a twelve-year-old girl with spinal damage because of earthquake injuries. Both cases resulted in convictions, and both defendants were sentenced to the maximum fifteen-year term. By the end of the summer of 2012, thirteen more rape convictions had been handed down. This success did not happen because of a judicial system suddenly and independently coming to its senses. "These cases worked because grassroots women's groups made them work," Mario Joseph says.

Judith Joseph sees these cases as reason for hope. "The system is not adequate yet, and justice is very slow in Haiti," she says. "But since we are following so many cases in court and organizing protests in the street, things are improving." The lawyer adopts the language of the sworn affidavit to make her point: "By information, it is better now."

Judith Joseph grew up in Port-de-Paix in northwest Haiti, and her mother, a former schoolteacher, now lives in Miami with the rest of Joseph's extended family. Her mother has applied for permission for Joseph to immigrate to the United States too, but Joseph refuses to go. When asked why, she switches to English again and jabs a forefinger into the table. "Because I love Haiti and I love my job," she says. "It is important for me to be here to help the Haitian women."

Life in the post-earthquake IDP camps is dangerous and miserable. But for many camp residents, like those in Grace Village, there is a worse alternative: they could get evicted. Haitian law as applied to forced evictions is clear. Purported landowners who wish to evict tenants or camp residents need to first prove legal title. It is an impossible burden for most to meet, given that only 5 percent of Haitian land titles were recorded before the earthquake, and many of those recorded were obtained by fraud or theft.[49] Even if an alleged property owner could prove title to land where earthquake refugees were staying, he would still have to pursue an order of possession in a court of law, not just push off alleged trespassers. And then, even if all those requirements were met, the Haitian government would be compelled to provide earthquake victims with alternative housing, per principle 7 of the UN Guiding Principles on Internal Displacement.

Yet, once again, Haitian law on paper often does not provide protection in reality. People claiming to own the land on which camps have been erected have been able to evict as many as 230,000 people since the earthquake, usually through sheer intimidation.[50] An International Organization of Migration study in 2011 showed that a third of the persons who had left the IDP camps did so because they were evicted, and more than half of the persons who left the camps still lived in unsafe or unstable housing.[51] At the end of 2012, six thousand new homes had been constructed and eighteen thousand repaired, addressing only a fraction of the need in Port-au-Prince, where 1.5 million persons were displaced by the earthquake.[52] As the International Federation for Human Rights stated in 2012, "It is no exaggeration to suggest that for the majority of these people [former IDP camp residents], their current situation is more precarious than it was before the earthquake."[53]

Recognizing both the consequences of eviction and the limits of litigation strategies—Haitian law has no mechanism to obtain injunctions to stop illegal evictions from occurring—BAI turned to its grassroots coordinators and a broader advocacy strategy. First, BAI held training sessions on legal rights and camp resident solidarity in the IDP camps. As Mario Joseph and Jeena Shah put it in an essay contributed to the book *Tectonic Shifts: Haiti since the Earthquake*, "We aimed to get the people to stop thinking of themselves as beneficiaries of charity but rather as holders of rights; to stop thinking that the varying levels of misery in the camps meant that they were not all seeking the same thing (adequate housing); to stop thinking that their needs must be addressed by unaccountable humanitarian aid actors, but instead by government, which is charged with this duty by the Haitian Constitution."[54]

Success came when BAI-trained leaders of a camp near Toussaint L'Ouverture Airport were faced with a planned eviction. When the alleged landowners sent armed men to force out the camp residents, the men were greeted by a massive sit-in and handed copies of an IACHR directive on the rights of IDP camp residents. The armed men left, and the residents stayed.

At another camp, BAI-trained residents received a notice to come to court to face an eviction claim. They obeyed, but brought along BAI attorneys and a large contingent of camp residents and other camps' leaders, many of whom staged a noisy demonstration outside the courtroom. The judge declined to order the eviction, instead telling the alleged property owner that he would receive possession only if he followed the proper legal procedures. It was a signature example of human rights advocacy on the international stage leading to a ground-level benefit—a success story that came about as much from a change in the camp residents' mindset as the threat of court action. "Ideally, these kinds of statements from the UN or the IACHR shift the paradigm," says IJDH's Nicole Phillips, who has drafted many of the recent petitions to international agencies and helped with the lobbying efforts. "When you are living in these [IDP] camps, and you are told by everyone that you have no rights, it can be very powerful to learn that an international body has ruled that you do have the right to housing and to be free from violence."

In other cases, camp residents held protests in front of the prime minister's office, and residents at risk of eviction attracted international news coverage when they staged a sit-in on a busy downtown Port-au-Prince street.[55] When the Port-au-Prince prosecutor agreed to the camp residents' request to pursue criminal charges against the mayor of Delmas for illegal evictions, BAI lawyers discovered that community members were initially surprised and then empowered. Simultaneously with the local actions, BAI and IJDH filed international complaints and provided source material for media stories publicizing the plight of those at risk of eviction. BAI and IJDH participated in a mid-2012 campaign that combined street demonstrations in Haiti and an online petition directed to President Martelly and US secretary of state Hillary Clinton, among others, calling attention to the estimated four hundred thousand Haitians still homeless after the earthquake.[56] "I'm pretty confident that the public advocacy around evictions has been successful," Concannon says. "There are tens of thousands of people threatened with eviction who have not been evicted. I think at the very least what we've done is to make eviction harder, raised the legal and political price, and slowed it down."

The advocacy on behalf of cholera victims has followed a similar path. While waiting for a ruling on the legal claim filed by BAI and IJDH, Mario Joseph, local grassroots organizations, and victim organizations have organized noisy demonstrations outside MINUSTAH bases, courted international media attention, and taken every opportunity to raise the profile of the suffering and ratchet up the pressure on the UN. As the Haiti Support Group, a BAI/IJDH ally, urged its members in early 2012, "How much further it [the legal claim] goes may depend crucially on much more of the same—publicity and pressure. And that means it depends on us. So on behalf of that distraught mother in the street, and the many thousands of others she represents, take action now and demand justice (read more, learn more, do more)."[57]

New York University law professor Margaret Satterthwaite agrees with this approach. Satterthwaite directs the school's Center for Human Rights and Global Justice and has researched and written on humanitarian intervention and access to water in Haiti. "I think the multilevel approach in the cholera claims, and particularly the grassroots advocacy going on, is crucial here," Satterthwaite says. She adds:

> Because what we are talking about is really changing the terms of a debate. It's not just about whether there is scientific causality you can prove using these microbial studies. It is a question about how do you talk about who is responsible as a moral matter, as a human rights matter.
>
> Whose responsibility was it to make sure that the poorest Haitians did not die as a result of the actions that occurred by the Artibonite in October of 2010? That is definitely a legal question, but it also has to be an issue of "What is the right thing here?" too. And that requires people out in the streets making their voices heard, that includes people talking to elites and moral decision leaders, that includes reframing what the UN is in the world. That means advocates saying that we have to hold the UN to the same standards we are asking them to spread throughout the world in terms of advancing human rights.

The original agenda for a February 2012 visit to Haiti by the UN Security Council seemed designed to avoid any such discussion about the UN's responsibility for the cholera outbreak. But Joseph and grassroots organizations helped organize cholera victim demonstrations that confronted the Security Council delegation, helping spur members of the Haitian Parliament and Haitian journalists to raise the issue with the visitors. The US permanent representative to the UN, Susan Rice, later gave a statement calling for the UN to "redouble its efforts to prevent any further incidents of this kind and to ensure that those responsible are held account-able."[58] The delegation added to their agenda a visit to a cholera treatment site. Three weeks later, UN special envoy to Haiti and former US president Bill Clinton became the first UN official to publicly acknowledge that the outbreak was caused by UN peacekeepers.[59]

The beyond-the-courtroom advocacy approach after the earthquake, working in concert with local grassroots groups, followed a well-established BAI model. The Raboteau prosecution was spurred more by the weekly victim demonstrations and by Joseph and Concannon's media campaign than by any legal arguments. After the 2004 coup, when Joseph found himself representing dozens of political prisoners, a network of the prisoners' families and friends agitated for justice within Haiti. Joseph credits that activism for keeping most of the political prisoners alive and leading to their eventual released from jail.

BAI's and IJDH's use of international pressure to achieve justice in Haiti is another time-honored tactic. When the military coup government of Prime Minister Gérard Latortue arrested and jailed populist priest Father Gérard Jean-Juste for the second time on bogus murder charges, Joseph was unable to secure a Haitian court order to obtain Jean-Juste's release from prison. Concannon and others persuaded Amnesty International to add Jean-Juste to its roster of political prisoners, prompting a flood of letters and calls to Haitian officials.[60] Concannon then reached out to his advocate contacts in the state of Indiana. Informed by Concannon's briefing, the Indiana advocates submitted a petition to their state's senior senator, Richard Lugar, chair of the US Senate's Foreign Relations Committee, asking him to intervene on Jean-Juste's behalf. (Full disclosure: I was one of those Hoosier advocates.) Lugar's staff and then the senator himself met with the activists. Soon after, Lugar sent a letter to Latortue, hand-delivered by State Department officials, calling for Jean-Juste's immediate release. Latortue called Lugar, and then let Jean-Juste go.

"In the end, I don't think the legal work could have made the difference in this case," Concannon says. "They [Haitian officials] were going to ignore the law. They released Gerry because of politics. It turns out the key to his jail cell was in Indiana, not Haiti."

At most stages of its evolution, the advocacy in the United States by IJDH has been largely a product of Concannon's efforts, supplemented by a rotating group of undergraduate and law school interns, volunteers, and entry-level paid staff, some of whom go on to long-term careers in human rights work. More recently, the organization hired a communications coordinator, but the paid staff remains tiny. Concannon sees recruiting volunteers, donors, and advocates as the core of his job, so he was intrigued when his undergraduate alma mater, Middlebury College in Vermont, invited him to speak at a January 2012 symposium launching the school's Center for Social Entrepreneurship. Middlebury had joined the many universities, business schools, and not-for-profit organizations responding to a surge of interest in social entrepreneurship. Global heroes like Nobel Prize winner and microloan pioneer Muhammad Yunus and Teach for America founder Wendy Kopp have inspired a generation of young people to pursue the social entrepreneurship vision of innovation and service.

Concannon was surprised by the invitation, because he did not think of IJDH's and BAI's work as fitting into some advocates' definition of social entrepreneurship. The first evening of the symposium did nothing to change his view. The keynote speaker was Bill Drayton, founder and CEO of the organization Ashoka and widely considered to be the originator of the term "social entrepreneur" and the trend that grew around it. Drayton's organization defines social entrepreneurship in contrast to the effort to achieve a governmental or political solution to injustice and suffering. Ashoka's website answers the question "What Is a Social Entrepreneur?" in part by stating, "Rather than leaving societal needs to the government or business sectors, social entrepreneurs find what is not working and solve the problem by changing the system."[61] Drayton's speech at Middlebury followed along the same lines, ignoring political struggles and emphasizing a go-it-alone philosophy. To Concannon, it sounded like the same perspective that has led to Haiti having thousands of NGOs and no functioning government.

Around the same time as the Middlebury conference, *New York Times* columnist David Brooks took the social entrepreneurship model to task on this very point. Brooks praised the idealism and energy of "wonderful" young people pursuing this vision: "Often they are bursting with enthusiasm for some social entrepreneurship project: making a cheap water purification system, starting a company that will empower Rwandan women by selling their crafts in boutiques around the world." But Brooks sharply criticized what he viewed as social entrepreneurs' avoidance of politics and government when pursuing change. "That's a delusion," he wrote. "You can cram all the non-governmental organizations you want in a country, but if there is no rule of law and if the ruling class is predatory, then your achievements won't add up to much. . . . Yet one rarely hears social entrepreneurs talk about professional policing, honest courts, or strict standards of behavior; it is more uplifting to talk about microloans and sustainable agriculture."[62]

Brooks's piece—and its somewhat condescending tone—produced a torrent of replies in defense of social entrepreneurs. Some rebuttals unwittingly underscored Brooks's argument. In an article posted on the social entrepreneurship news site *Dowser*, J. Gregory Dees, a professor in the Fuqua School of Business at Duke University, and creator of the first social entrepreneurship course in the United States, cited several examples of anticorruption NGOs. But Dees also could not help but champion the fact that these and other private organizations performed "functions that obviously could not be left to government alone," and highlighted government's limitations caused by bureaucratic and political constraints.[63] This version of social entrepreneurship failed to resonate with Concannon. After all, his organizations' mission is to compel government to live up to its obligations to protect individual rights and provide essential services.

But the second day of the Middlebury symposium revealed a different brand of social entrepreneurship. Concannon participated in a workshop where students were critical of the notion that recent college graduates should be founding their own NGOs en masse. The clear consensus of the group was that the struggles of the poor are inextricably intertwined with local and international politics. The second evening's keynote speaker, Jacqueline Novogratz of the Acumen Fund, cautioned against the global proliferation of NGOs and emphasized the need to steer clear of arrogance and individualism. Concannon learned that the social entrepreneurship movement claims as its own several organizations that partner with governments and push for the rule of law and functioning, transparent justice systems. As Sally Osberg, CEO of the social entrepreneurship–supporting Skoll Foundation, wrote in response to David Brooks's column, "They [social entrepreneurs] know that social justice depends on citizens capable of claiming their rights—and governments capable of delivering."[64]

That sounds like us, Concannon realized. Seizing the opportunity to include IJDH and BAI in a movement brimming with youthful energy and commitment, and attracting philanthropic dollars to support it, Concannon began working on ways to describe the organizations in social entrepreneurship terms. He found it easy to do. "I would argue that social entrepreneurship's emphasis on sustainability requires significant attention to government solutions, which is of course our emphasis at IJDH," he says. Concannon began telling audiences about the global South-North collaboration at the heart of BAI and IJDH, their multilevel approach to advocacy in both grassroots and international arenas, and the leveraging strategies involved in using individual lawsuits to instigate systemic change. His arguments found a welcome reception. After all, even the Ashoka website lists as historic examples of noted social entrepreneurs unabashed government-focused activists like Susan B. Anthony and John Muir.[65]

———

In pursuing a strategy that combines litigation with populist pressure, BAI attorneys say that they draw inspiration from a famous South African campaign to gain access to HIV treatment for pregnant mothers. The 2002 decision by South Africa's Constitutional Court in the case of *Ministry of Health and Others v. Treatment Action Campaign and Others (No. 2)* was the culmination of years of activism and agitation. In fact, the plaintiff, Treatment Action Campaign (TAC), had turned to litigation only after first pursuing a solution through civil disobedience, community education, meetings with drug manufacturers, and publicizing the stories of mothers who were denied access to the treatment that likely would have saved their children's lives. That pressure continued while the suit was pending, with a series of marches, rallies, and workshops leading to a national treatment summit and a courthouse vigil before an interim hearing on the case. When the case reached the Constitutional Court, rallies and marches were held throughout the country, and activists wearing "HIV-Positive" T-shirts filled the courtroom.[66]

The decision by the Constitutional Court held that the government of South Africa had a positive obligation to implement the country's constitutional guarantee of access to health services—a part of a broad set of rights similar to those contained in Haiti's constitution. The government breached that obligation, the court ruled, when it failed to develop a comprehensive antenatal HIV treatment program. The sweeping decision made the TAC case one of the most celebrated human rights decisions in history, and one that has its roots in activism outside the boundaries of formal litigation. When the South African government dragged its feet in complying with the court order, TAC staged a twenty-thousand-person march on the opening of Parliament in 2003, launched a campaign of sit-ins and voluntary arrests, and filed charges of culpable homicide against two government officials. The South African cabinet responded, finally committing the government to provide the HIV treatment previously ordered by the court.

Amy Kapczynski and Jonathan Berger wrote in their history of the case, "[The] story is less about a judgment or a doctrine than it is about a movement. . . . TAC did the political and technical work to make the Constitutional Court's judgment seem both legally obvious and morally necessary."[67] There are other recent precedents for successfully combining litigation with a broader campaign for social justice, including the Right to Food Campaign in India and coordinated challenges in Nigeria to evictions and displacement of communities by corporations and the government.[68]

Joseph and Concannon call their similar approach "victim-centered."[69] The term corresponds to the *viktim* label adopted by many Haitian grassroots organizations, which can sound dated to advocates outside the country. "After living in Haiti, it is curious to me that the word 'victim' is considered a pejorative in the US," Concannon says. "In Haiti, they use it simply to describe a situation where a group needs help enforcing its rights because someone has done them harm. The word *viktim* is used to explain that these aren't people who have been bad or lazy or have some intrinsic problem. There is a lot of pride in victim's organizations in Haiti, and it is certainly not a pejorative term there. In the United States, "victim" is pejorative precisely because we so frequently blame victims for having their rights violated.

BAI's partnership with organizations like KOFAVIV, the Duvalier survivors group, and cholera victims is the foundation of the victim-centered approach. The goal is for the relationships to mutually support the organizations and the legal advocacy. BAI lawyers prefer the term "legal empowerment" over "legal aid," and are very comfortable labeling all their work as political in nature. Invoking the TAC campaign as an example, they say that their lawsuits provide a platform for community organizing while the activism helps the litigation be taken seriously in a system where quiet cases can be ignored or even dropped. As BAI lawyers Meena Jagannath, Nicole Phillips, and Jeena Shah put it in a 2012 law review article, "The victim-centered approach to human rights lawyering strives to valorize the struggles of the poor and marginalized communities while arming them with the language of rights to bring their voices into political dialogue."[70]

The Haitian state of affairs has demanded this approach, Concannon says, pointing to a legal system long characterized by an unwillingness or lack of capacity to place limits on the actions of the powerful and wealthy. So BAI turns to the *partie civile* procedure to allow the poor and victimized to stick their collective foot in the courthouse door. Once inside, the advocates adopt a carrot-and-stick approach to improving the Haitian justice system. BAI and IJDH provide governmental officials with technical assistance, such as the draft questions and technology enhancements offered to the Duvalier investigators or the training offered to Haitian police in responding to rape complaints. The lawyers also provide more mundane material support for an often cash-strapped system. As recently as 2011, Joseph provided gas money to police who needed to drive to arrest a rape suspect. But they also push the government hard. The demonstrations and constant outreach to media and the international community provide the "stick" to prod a reluctant system to protect human rights. Beyond short-term gains for the individual and the cause, the advocacy secures for the poor a recognized role in the political discourse and legal system going forward.

It is a beautiful March morning at the BAI offices in downtown Port-au-Prince. On the front porch of the building, an open-air area rebuilt after earthquake damage, five students from Drexel University's law school in Philadelphia sit in front of their laptops, cardboard boxes of documents at their sides. They are spending their spring break gathering and inputting data on the thousands of cholera claims made by BAI clients. Fordham Law students just left the building, and are on their way to make observations and collect statements at IDP camps that have not received promised services of water and toilets. A contingent from Duke Law will be here next week. Behind the building, about twenty women from a group living just outside the slum of Cité Soleil hold a press conference, calling for more women to be appointed to government office. "*Ti machan* [women street merchants] and women farmers are the engine of Haiti's development, so they should be a part of the decision-making," one of the group leaders tells a TV camera and a reporter with a tape recorder.

There are several Haitian lawyers and clerks in action here as well (not including Mario Joseph and a colleague, who are in Geneva for the UN Human Rights Council's review of Haiti). Nick Stratton, an American intern working on BAI's communications, steps away from the Drexel students to tell a visitor about video of a recent cholera protest he has uploaded to YouTube. A man walks out of an office in the back of the building, carrying a stack of newspapers, and hands out several, pointing out the English-language articles to the Americans. The newspaper is *Haïti Liberté*, distributed in the United States, Canada, and Haiti, with its Haitian headquarters here at BAI. This week's headline story is "*Qui Est Laurent Lamothe?*," an examination of some questionable business dealings by Lamothe, the prime minister-designate. (Lamothe was officially named prime minister in May 2012.) In 2011, *Haïti Liberté*, in partnership with US magazine the *Nation* and the transparency-advocacy group WikiLeaks, drew from thousands of diplomatic cables from US embassies around the world for a series of damning articles about US policies toward Haiti.

The man distributing the papers is Yves Pierre-Louis, recognizable with his gray-flecked beard and plaid shirt as one of the people in the front lines of several recent demonstrations in and around Port-au-Prince. The Haitian editor of *Haïti Liberté*, Pierre-Louis studied law before finding his calling in advocacy journalism. "It is because I have a political view that I am a journalist," he says. "The newspaper and I both fight against oppression and violence."

To Pierre-Louis, the Haitian women's group, and the US law students, it makes perfect sense for BAI to be hosting this mix of investigative journalism, community organizing, and international partnerships. Pierre-Louis points to President Martelly's platform of "Four E's"—*Education, Emploi, Environnement,* and *État de Droit* (Education, Employment, the Environment, and Rule of Law)—and insists they would not exist but for the people of Haiti demanding the president take action. "Yes, law exists on paper in Haiti," Pierre-Louis says. "But corruption is so high that poor people cannot afford justice. So we have to hold demonstrations and protests to force the judge to reach fair results and the president to respect the rights of the poor.

"The government claims there is a state of law. We are fighting hard to make that claim a reality."

7

The Donkey
and the Horse

Haiti and the United States

On a January night in 2009, Rob Broggi, a hedge fund manager and board member of the ONEXONE Foundation, attended a forum on Haiti at the John F. Kennedy Library in Boston. The agenda featured a panel discussion that included actor and activist Matt Damon, Broggi's former college roommate. Also on the panel were Paul Farmer and Brian Concannon, whom Broggi had never met.

That night, Concannon delivered a detailed indictment of US policy toward Haiti. "And I didn't believe a word of it," Broggi says. "I thought Brian in particular was a sort of left-wing radical, and he was exaggerating a lot of these points, especially relative to the US State Department's role in a lot of schemes, which clearly in his opinion served the United States' interests at the great expense of the Haitian people."

Broggi decided to begin his own research on Haiti's history and current situation. "The more I learned about it, the more I learned that Brian was exactly right," he says now. "If anything, he and Paul were being too kind about the significant injustices that have been borne by the Haitian people." Broggi called Concannon, introduced himself, and soon after joined Farmer on the IJDH board of directors.

In a classroom at Drexel Law School in Philadelphia in the fall of 2011, Brian Concannon describes to the assembled students and faculty the grim situation in Haiti. He talks about the tragic loss of life in the earthquake, the massive destruction of Port-au-Prince, and the post-earthquake homelessness, hunger, and violence against women. He discusses the devastating impact of the cholera epidemic.

Concannon's dark eyes, set off by his graying, receding hair and a close-cropped beard, signal intensity. He is dressed in a sober charcoal suit. The subject he discusses is a serious one; he treats it as such, and pulls his audience along with him.

Concannon then makes his case that Haiti's only chance to recover from this desperate state of affairs is by inculcating the rule of law. "The people of Haiti are not poor because they don't work hard," he says. "The people of Haiti are poor because they can't enforce their rights." He rattles off a list of fundamental rights Americans take for granted: the right to enforce a contract, the right to be treated fairly as a citizen complaining of official misconduct, the right to possess and leverage clear title to property. All are largely absent in Haiti, he says. Concannon tells the group that the enforcement of basic human rights must occur if the Haitian people are to escape an endless cycle of disaster and struggle.

To illustrate this statement, Concannon shows the Drexel audience a PowerPoint slide comparing in stark relief the effects of a 2010 earthquake in Chile with the disaster that had occurred a month earlier in Haiti. Although the Chilean earthquake was 500 times stronger than Haiti's, Haiti suffered 230 times more mortality.[1] Concannon explains how enforced building and zoning codes could have saved tens of thousands of Haitian lives, and how rebuilding and reinvestment in Haiti is blocked by the inability of landowners to prove legal title. He walks through the responses to the crisis by the BAI and IJDH—the lawsuits and demonstrations to stop mass evictions, the groundbreaking cholera claims, and the international advocacy and ground-level push on behalf of women left vulnerable by the weakness of the Haitian state.

Born and raised by Irish American parents in a Boston suburb, Concannon seems an unlikely champion for the people of Haiti. But commitment to serving the poor is a family tradition. Concannon's late father, Brian Sr., was a personal injury lawyer who enjoyed taking on the cause of the underdog. "Dad was a gregarious guy; he was fairly intellectual, well-read, the kind of person who liked to spout off Greek and Latin. Mom was more intense and focused on social change," Concannon says.[2] RoseAnne Concannon taught high school English before going to law school after her kids were grown; she became a family law attorney representing victims of domestic violence. Concannon is the second of five children, and all the siblings are either social workers or public interest lawyers. The original Concannon law office furniture has been handed down to the IJDH offices in Boston.

After graduating from Georgetown Law Center in 1989, Concannon practiced law for a few years with the Boston firm of Mintz Levin—work he found to be "morally neutral." Neutrality was not in Concannon's nature, says his Georgetown classmate Nancy Reimer. "We all went to law school thinking we would save the world somehow," Reimer says. "But Brian had that idealism and then some. You knew that a corporate law firm was not his long-term future." Sure enough, Concannon eventually quit the firm. He spent several months considering whether to dedicate himself to environmental advocacy or human rights law, and then began working for the UN in 1995. Concannon had studied French at Middlebury College, and was intrigued by the idea of working in Francophone Africa. Instead, he was assigned to Haiti as a human rights observer. Immediately, he started reading everything about Haiti that he could get his hands on.

The book that made the most profound impression on Concannon was Paul Farmer's *The Uses of Haiti*, first published in 1994. In the book, Farmer, an anthropologist as well as a physician, explains the meaning of the title: "Haiti, like other small and dependent nations in the Southern Hemisphere, has long existed to serve the wealthy—if not the wealthy of Haiti, then that of Europe and North America. Haiti exists to provide its clients with tropical produce, raw materials, or cheap labor. Outside of their country, Haitians are useful for cutting cane, cleaning buildings, or driving cabs. Of all the uses of Haiti, these have been the most constant."[3]

Indeed, exploitation has been the sad and recurring theme of Haitian history since Christopher Columbus arrived in 1492 at the island called *Ayiti*, "land of mountains," by the Taino natives living there. The Arawak-speaking people on the island Columbus renamed Hispaniola were quickly put to work building Spanish forts and cultivating sugar cane for export. European-imported disease, violence, and hard labor caused the natives to die at such a startling rate that the Taino population dwindled to nearly zero in just a few decades. But the appetites of colonial powers did not diminish accordingly.[4]

By the seventeenth century, the French had colonized the western third of the island of Hispaniola, and called their claimed territory Saint-Domingue. To replace the labor of the now-extinct natives, enslaved Africans were brought to Saint-Domingue in bondage. As many as a million slaves were transported to the island, with brutal working conditions and abuse killing one-third of them in the first few years after their arrival. The toil of these slaves, who made up nine-tenths of the colony's population, transformed Saint-Domingue into the world's dominant supplier of sugar and one of the globe's top exporters of coffee, cotton, and indigo. By the mid-1700s, the colony was producing more wealth than the thirteen North American colonies combined.

Then, in August 1791, Saint-Domingue exploded. Legend has it that the Haitian revolution was launched during a dramatic religious ceremony presided over by a slave named Boukman at Bois Caïman in the northern part of the island. At that ceremony, Boukman is said to have announced, "God who is so good orders us to vengeance / He will direct our hands, give us help / Throw away the image of the God of whites who thirsts for our tears / Listen to the liberty that speaks in all our hearts."[5] Tens of thousands of slaves began a massive revolt, destroying plantations and killing white masters. The whites retaliated for the attack by killing many Africans for every white killed, a pattern that would continue in the conflicts to come. Boukman was soon captured and beheaded by the French, but the resistance continued. Many of the slaves had been soldiers in Africa before their capture, and they deftly assembled into small mobile units that launched deadly guerilla attacks against the slaveowners. Former slaves like Toussaint L'Ouverture (who brought his former white masters to safety before joining the rebels) joined the uprising and forged an alliance with the Spanish, who provided weapons in the hopes of gaining control of the French colony themselves. Great Britain was making moves to gain power over Saint-Domingue, too, seeking the allegiance of the plantation owners. Facing the potential loss of its colony to its European rivals and acknowledging the slaves' dominant numbers, the French made the decision to abolish slavery in order to secure the allegiance of the slave insurgents.[6]

L'Ouverture, now carrying the title of French general and later governor, took control of the colony. But after Napoleon Bonaparte seized power in France in 1799, he sent a military expedition, led by his brother-in-law Victor Emmanuel Leclerc, to restore direct French rule of Saint-Domingue. Leclerc's mission, in Napoleon's words, was to "rid us of the gilded negroes." L'Ouverture was captured and transported to France. As he boarded the ship, L'Ouverture issued a famous warning to his captors. In his excellent one-volume narrative, *Haiti: The Aftershocks of History*, Laurent Dubois says the most accurate rendition of L'Ouverture's declaration is "In overthrowing me you have cut down in Saint Domingue only the trunk of the tree of liberty of the blacks; it will spring up again from the roots, for they are deep and numerous."[7]

L'Ouverture died in a French prison. But, as he predicted, the resistance carried on. Initially, many of the leaders of the slave rebellion, including L'Ouverture's lieutenant, Jean-Jacques Dessalines, agreed to join the French side. However, the defection of their leaders did not cause the former slaves to abandon their struggle, and they instead created small battle groups and headed to the mountains to launch attacks. Eventually, their leaders rejoined them. At a gathering of rebel generals in May 1803, Dessalines symbolically separated the former slaves from France once and for all, tearing the white bar out of the French tricolor flag and stitching together the red and blue to create the flag of a new nation. The French were driven off the island, and on January 1, 1804, the Republic of Haiti became the first—and still the only—nation to be created by a successful slave rebellion. Most versions of the new red-and-blue Haitian flag contained the words *Liberté ou la mort*—liberty or death. After a bloody thirteen-year struggle for freedom, during which an estimated 150,000 ex-slaves died, there was no doubting the people of Haiti's commitment to that principle.

But the glorious dream of Saint-Domingue's former slaves was a nightmare for the world powers that had built their empires and economies on a structure of slavery and colonization. Although Haiti joined the United States of America as the hemisphere's only other republic, the United States, barely a quarter-century removed from its own successful rebellion, was far from welcoming. The United States had been a dedicated trading partner with the French via Saint-Domingue, and had sent troops and money to defend the colony's white slaveowners from the revolt. George Washington had said that it was "lamentable to see such a spirit of revolution among the blacks" of Saint-Domingue.[8] Thomas Jefferson wrote of Haiti's slave rebellion, "If this combustion can be introduced among us under any veil, we have to fear it."[9] Beginning with Jefferson's presidency, the United States refused to recognize Haiti's independence. Senator Robert Hayne of South Carolina in 1824 explained the stance that was the official US position for the first half-century of Haiti's existence: "Our policy, with regard to Hayti [*sic*], is plain: We can never acknowledge her independence." He considered the topic one of several that "the peace and safety of a large portion of our Union forbids us even to discuss."[10]

Viewed through the eyes of committed slave-owners and those who relied on an economy built on human bondage, the fear was quite justified. Haiti declared itself a refuge for escaped slaves and proudly served as a model for subsequent campaigns to end slavery and colonialism, including hosting Simón Bolívar and other Latin American revolutionaries as they planned their rebellions. The Haitian legacy of successful guerrilla resistance to slavery also inspired many US slaves and abolitionists, including Gabriel Prosser, who led a slave revolt in Virginia in 1800, and likely Nat Turner, who led his own rebellion in 1831.[11] John Brown was a student of the tactics of the Haitian Revolution, and Brown invoked the memory and strategies of Toussaint L'Ouverture before his raid on Harper's Ferry. When Brown was hanged, flags in Haiti flew at half-mast.[12] A major thoroughfare in Port-au-Prince is still named John Brown Avenue.

But the tension over slavery, and even an official French and American embargo of Haiti, did not prevent US and European merchants from trading with Haiti in the nineteenth century. The proximity of the United States led to increasing American involvement in the Haitian economy. The balance of trading power between Haiti and the wealthier nations was far from equal, however. France refused to relinquish its colonial claim on Haiti and threatened blockade and war until it successfully extracted from Haitian president Jean-Pierre Boyer in 1825 a promise to pay reparations for the French property seized in the rebellion.[13] The United States, along with Germany, France, and Britain, routinely engaged in "gunboat diplomacy" to collect on debts allegedly owed by Haitians. For example, in December 1914, US marines docked their warship in Port-au-Prince, disembarked, and entered the Banque National d'Haiti, where they took a half-million dollars in gold (worth $11 million today). The marines reboarded their ship and brought the gold to New York.[14]

——————

Even expropriations like these were subtle compared to the US Marine invasion of Haiti in July 1915. In the preceding years, the United States had occupied Cuba and Puerto Rico, sent marines twice to the Dominican Republic, and taken over construction of the Panama Canal. Soon enough, Haiti too was under control of the United States' heavy hand in the Caribbean.[15] But Haiti was different, according to Woodrow Wilson's secretary of state, Robert Lansing: "The experience of Liberia and Haiti shows that the African race are devoid of any capacity for political organization and lack genius for government. Unfortunately there is in them an inherent tendency to revert to savagery and to cast aside the shackles of civilization which are irksome to their physical nature."[16] (An even less nuanced evaluation of Haiti was provided by Lansing's predecessor as secretary of state, William Jennings Bryan, who was stunned by revelations contained in a briefing on the country about which he knew little. "Think of it," Bryan said. "Niggers speaking French!")[17] Certainly there was political turmoil in Haiti, none of it helped by foreign powers raiding the county's coffers. But consider the turmoil in Lansing's own United States, where three presidents had been assassinated in the preceding half-century, lynchings were commonplace in the South, and preparations were being made for entry into the massive, senseless carnage of the First World War. Yet Lansing's racist message was largely well received in the US media, where *National Geographic* applauded the marines for squelching the sovereignty of Haitians, whom the magazine called the "unthinking black animals of the interior."[18]

Shortly after the invasion, the US forces declared martial law in Haiti, seized control of the Haitian treasury and customs houses, and arrested the editors of a newspaper critical of the American actions. Another early agenda item for the American occupiers was smoothing the path for US corporations seeking to take advantage of Haiti's natural resources. Standing in their way was an iconic clause of the Haitian Constitution, dating back to Jean-Jacques Dessalines, that prohibited foreign ownership of property. Both a symbolic and concrete repudiation of the oppressive days of French ownership of Haitian plantations—and people—the ban carried such importance to the Haitian citizenry that it had been referred to as the "Holy Grail" of the country's independence.[19] Predictably, Haiti's elected senators and deputies refused to go along with US wishes to strike down the ban. So the Americans simply dissolved the Haitian Parliament—at gunpoint. (Smedley Darlington Butler, the marine officer who led the armed contingent ordering the Haitian legislators to disperse, referred to Haitian leaders as "shaved apes . . . just plain low nigger."[20] However, Butler also later expressed some misgivings about his role, saying that he had been "a gangster for capitalism" in making "Haiti and Cuba a decent place for the National City Bank boys to collect revenue in."[21]) The Haitian Parliament would remain silenced for the next dozen years.

In its place, the marines and the US-created Haitian army oversaw a referendum on the new constitution that the parliament had refused to ratify. Opponents of the new constitution were arrested before the election, and, under the watchful eyes of the marines and Haitian army soldiers, Haitians coming to the polling places were offered only a white ballot marked "Oui." Few dared to make a special request for a pink ballot marked "Non." The measure passed, 98,294 to 769.[22] Quickly, North American firms snatched up a quarter-million acres of prime Haitian real estate for plantations of sugar, bananas, and rubber. Peasants were driven from their homes and often compelled to reenact Haiti's despised past by working for foreign occupiers, sometimes as forced labor and always for very limited compensation. This was a tragic turn for Haitians, but it was a gold rush for foreign investors, as the New York daily *Financial America* said in November 1926: "The run-of-the-mill Haitian is handy, easily directed, and gives back a hard day's labor for 20 cents, while in Panama the same day's work cost $3."[23]

The de jure seizure of the Haitian economy by the United States was readily accomplished, but maintaining de facto control of the country would prove to be a bloodier task. Marines responded to resistance by rural Haitian militias known as Cacos by burning entire villages considered friendly to the rebels. Marines also turned to the new but decidedly imprecise tactic of aerial bombing, and summarily executed captives suspected of being involved in the resistance. In 1919, a marine general prepared a confidential report on the Haiti mission, admitting that "practically indiscriminate killing of the natives has been going on for some time."[24] When the Caco leader Charlemagne Péralte, formerly a Haitian army commander, was assassinated by a marine, Péralte's body was brought by train to the town of Le Cap. There, the corpse was stripped bare and tied to a door of the local police station, where photographs were taken and residents were brought to view the body. US airplanes then dropped photos of Péralte's body in rural areas of Haiti considered to be supportive of the Cacos movement.[25] (When Jean-Claude Duvalier was forced out of the country in 1986, a crowd of Haitians tore down a statue of Christopher Columbus from its base in Port-au-Prince, threw it into the sea, and renamed the area where the statue had stood after Charlemagne Péralte.)

The rural resistance was followed by student strikes and popular demonstrations against the occupation. As the occupation continued, the Haitians forged alliances with international organizations, including the NAACP, which condemned the US role in Haiti. It took nearly two decades, but eventually the Haitian opposition to the US occupation grew too large to control. The marines' departure in 1934 was hailed as Haiti's "second independence."[26] But the scars of the era lingered, as did US influence in Haiti.

Much as Adolph Hitler manipulated German resentment after the national humiliation of World War I, the physician-turned-politician François "Papa Doc" Duvalier skillfully exploited simmering Haitian bitterness over US domination. Duvalier was among many Haitians who noted the Americans' reliable practice of elevating light-skinned Haitians to positions of prominence, including all four presidents installed by the United States. The self-described *noiriste* Duvalier pledged his support to the blacker masses of Haiti. But the tactically nimble Duvalier also adopted an anti-communist stance that earned him the endorsement of the US embassy in his first presidential election, in 1956. Thus began a three-decade, two-generation reign of Duvalier terror over Haiti, bolstered by American guns and money.[27]

Within two years of that election, the US Marines returned to Haiti, this time to assist the Haitian army in pushing back a rebel challenge to Duvalier's increasingly repressive rule. According to Colonel Robert Debs Heinl Jr., who commanded the mission, a Marine contingent sent to Haiti in 1959 was told by the State Department that "the most important way you can support our objectives in Haiti is to help keep Duvalier in power."[28] In ensuing years, the United States provided millions of dollars in financial support to Duvalier, with the $13.5 million delivered by the United States in 1961 (the equivalent of $104 million in 2013 dollars) accounting for more than 50 percent of the government of Haiti's budget. The United States provided machine guns and rifles to both the Haitian military and the terrorizing *tontons makouts*, at least until Duvalier's blatant election fraud and political violence annoyed the Kennedy administration enough to inspire a cutoff in military aid in 1961. But, just a year later, Cold War realpolitik won out over human rights concerns, and the US-to-Haiti money flow was regenerated in return for Duvalier casting the deciding vote to expel Cuba from the OAS. Later, Richard Nixon sent New York governor Nelson Rockefeller to Port-au-Prince for a high-profile meeting with Duvalier, giving the dictator international credibility, after which the United States sent another $1 million in arms to Haiti, in 1971.[29]

When François Duvalier died that same year, the United States sent warships to block any potential invasion of Haiti by exiles who could have interfered with nineteen-year-old Jean-Claude Duvalier's ascension to power. The younger Duvalier immediately made a public pledge to be a bulwark against Communism, and Haiti continued to receive hundreds of millions of dollars in US aid—an estimated $467 million from 1972 to 1981 alone.[30] Jean-Claude Duvalier was never considered to possess the Machiavellian political mind his father had, but he proved nimble enough to adjust to his American patrons' changing perspectives on the relative importance of human rights in Haiti. During the Jimmy Carter administration, Duvalier briefly allowed opposition parties to form and an independent media to exist, only to brutally shut them down when Ronald Reagan was elected. The importance of the US role in propping up the Duvaliers was underscored when some of that support was finally pulled away. Unnerved by growing protests, strikes, and deadly reprisals by Duvalier's *makouts* on demonstrators, the United States announced on January 31, 1986, that it would be reducing its $56 million aid package to Haiti. A week later, Duvalier and his family fled Haiti—on a US cargo plane.[31]

Yet the end of the Duvalier era did not signal the end of US involvement in Haiti any more than the end of the Marine occupation had. The military junta that quickly replaced Duvalier used US-donated antiriot equipment and training to violently resist popular demonstrations for democracy. The United States, wielding the power of that aid and the invoice for a substantial debt racked up by the Duvaliers, was able to convince the military government to capitulate in one area where even the Duvaliers had refused to budge. General Henri Namphy cut Haiti's import tariffs and reduced government support to local farmers, thus opening the Haitian market for imports of government-subsidized food from the United States. The post-Duvalier military government killed thousands of Haitians in a vicious backlash against calls for democratic elections, but Namphy's decision on economic policy may have been an even more deadly blow inflicted on the Haitian people.[32]

The tariff and budget decisions by Haiti's post-Duvalier government reminded Haitians of a lesson they had learned well in the previous century: the eviction of an oppressive power from their shores does not mean that the economic price for the repression leaves with it. When France in 1825 was able to force Haiti to agree to compensate the French for property lost in the revolution to the sum of 150 million francs (by comparison, the Louisiana Purchase price was 80 million francs), the debt crippled the Haitian economy. As Mark Danner wrote in a *New York Times* essay days after the January 2010 earthquake, "The new nation, its fields burned, its plantation manors pillaged, its towns devastated by apocalyptic war, was crushed by the burden of these astronomical reparations, payments that, in one form or another, strangled its economy for more than a century."[33] Indeed, just two decades after the country's independence, a vicious cycle was set in motion, and Haiti assumed the status of a perpetual debtor nation. Money that should have gone to building much-needed roads and schools and sewage systems in Haiti was instead sent off to France. In 2003, the government of Haiti calculated that the debt, with its original price being about $3 billion in modern currency, had ultimately cost the country $21 billion.[34] These reparations to France, and subsequent loans taken out to pay for them, snowballed until Haiti was in a state of financial disarray that has haunted the country from the early nineteenth century to today. The year before the United States' 1915 invasion, Haiti's government was spending 80 percent of its revenue on debt service.[35] And, as recently as 2006, Haiti was spending twice as much on debt repayment—much of it racked up by the thieving Duvaliers—as it was on desperately needed health services.[36]

When Haiti needed aid to meet the subsistence needs of its people, it was presented by its creditors with a series of disadvantageous offers that the country's leaders were in no position to refuse. For example, under Jean-Claude Duvalier, USAID launched a campaign to transform Haiti into the "Taiwan of the Caribbean"—that is, the supplier of the cheapest export-assembly labor in the Western Hemisphere.[37] As a 2003 report by the American Center for International Labor Solidarity put it, "Under this model, workers are seen as primarily a production cost."[38] And that cost was remarkably low. Wages were held down by enormous unemployment, the absence of unions, and little prospect of worker activism under a repressive regime. Duvalier was sufficiently politically and financially indebted to the United States to agree to a neoliberal economic program eliminating nearly every obstacle to free trade and providing tax exemptions for profits and tariff exemptions for the importing of raw materials and machinery.

By 1984, Haiti was the ninth-largest supplier of goods to the United States, mostly of assembled products like baseballs, clothing, and toys.[39] One of the businesses to take advantage of the setting was Hemo-Caribbean and Company, which purchased plasma from impoverished Haitians to be frozen and shipped to US laboratories. At the height of its operation, the scheme sent five tons of plasma out of Haiti each month. When the arrangement received some criticism in the international media as a ghoulish enterprise, the biochemist in charge of the operation responded, "If the Haitians don't sell their blood, what do you want them to do with it?"[40]

The neoliberal process of keeping wages and social supports minimal and tariffs and taxes almost nonexistent was part of a process called "structural adjustment" that was dictated by Haiti's international creditors like the International Monetary Fund (IMF).[41] By the time Duvalier was forced out in 1986, there were three hundred US corporations working in Haiti.[42] Those companies, and their consumers, may have benefited from the arrangement, but the people of Haiti saw little positive impact. As Haiti-born Wesleyan University professor Alex Dupuy has written, a host country does not benefit from an industry where raw materials are imported in and the assembled products are shipped out.[43] The coveted "multiplier effect," generated when goods are both produced and purchased locally, is absent from this export-only model. Combined with poverty wages that provided little purchasing power to workers struggling to make ends meet, this meant that all of the bustling export-assembly activity did not move the economic needle. Even the World Bank, a champion of the strategy to build Haiti as an export-assembly hub, admitted in 1978 that the sector had provided little positive effect on the country's economy. Duvalier conceded the same point three years later.[44]

Unfortunately, this sad episode of Haiti's economic history appears poised to repeat itself. In 2009, Paul Collier, an Oxford professor of economics and a former director of the World Bank's Development Research Group, prepared a report on Haiti at the request of UN secretary-general Ban Ki-moon. The key to Haiti's economic recovery, Collier concluded, would be the revival of the Haitian garment industry and its potential to create hundreds of thousands of Haitian jobs. Remarkably, Collier seemed unconcerned that those jobs were destined to pay sub-poverty wages. In fact, it was the existence of rock-bottom wages and desperate Haitians willing to work for them that Collier saw as providing the key to Haiti's future. "Due to its poverty and relatively unregulated labour market, Haiti has labour costs that are fully competitive with China, which is the global benchmark," he wrote.[45]

The US Congressional Research Service echoed that analysis in a 2010 report, which warned that a recent increase in the Haitian minimum wage could reduce that competitiveness.[46] The increase the CRS report characterized as "large" raised the Haitian minimum wage for textile workers to about $3 per day. A 2011 survey of twenty-seven Haitian garment factories showed that a majority of them paid workers even less than the law required.[47]

Yet the US State Department, the IDB, and the Martelly government continue to see bright prospects for Haiti in this low-wage blueprint. To supplement the many

.trade incentives and duty exemptions included in the Hemispheric Opportunity through Partnership Encouragement Act of 2008 (HOPE II) and the Haiti Economic Lift Program (HELP) Act of 2010, they pulled together over $200 million in post-earthquake subsidies to create an industrial park in northeast Haiti.[48] The site chosen for Caracol Industrial Park seems less than ideal, since it is located in Haiti's first-ever marine protected area and hundreds of farmers had to be evicted to make room for the construction. Questions were also raised about the likely economic benefit of the project. The park's anchor tenant, Sae-A Trading, a South Korean clothing manufacturer and supplier to American retailers like Walmart and Gap Inc., has a troubled labor history in Central America. Predictably, the company's promised jobs in Haiti are set to provide extremely low pay, with March 2013 reports that Haitians working at the park were taking home only US$1.36 per day after paying for their transportation and food.[49] Even José Agustín Aguerre, the IDB's Haiti department manager, gave the idea a less-than-ringing endorsement, telling the *New York Times* as the park opened, "Yes, it's low-paying, yes, it's unstable, yes, maybe tomorrow there will a better opportunity for firms elsewhere and they will just leave. But everyone thought this was a risk worth taking."[50]

David is not so sure. (His name has been changed to protect him from possible retaliation.)[51] I spoke to him one late afternoon in front of an arched entrance labeled "Parc Industriale Metropolitain." Behind us, thousands of Haitians streamed toward the traffic-choked streets of Port-au-Prince. The industrial park houses a huge expanse of garment assembly plants near the airport, and it was time for a shift change. David, a thin thirty-two-year-old man wearing a short-sleeve dress shirt and dark slacks, works here at a company called Interamerican Woven. At his factory, David is part of a team of several thousand that puts together pants for export to the United States.

While a lot of high-powered people think David's job represents the answer to Haiti's many problems, it certainly has not raised him out of poverty. David's wages do not reflect that Interamerican Woven, like the other companies in this complex, benefits from very favorable trade agreements and other subsidies to buttress the Haitian garment assembly industry. Gesturing in the direction of the workers leaving the industrial park, David says that most of them earn about two hundred Haitian gourdes per day and work nine-hour days six days each week. David earns 250 gourdes per day. The typical exchange rate is forty Haitian gourdes for one US dollar, so these workers take home about $5 or $6 each day.

The initial daily expense for the Haitian garment worker is transportation, David explains. He lives relatively close to the industrial park, and considers himself fortunate to pay only forty gourdes per day for his ride to work in a *tap-tap*—one of the colorful, overcrowded vans and covered pickups that serve as the chief mode of transportation in Port-au-Prince. But some of David's colleagues live further away, with many paying sixty gourdes each day just to get to and from work.

Buying a simple breakfast of plain spaghetti and juice, plus rice and beans for lunch, costs another hundred gourdes or so. That means these workers head home after clearing only forty gourdes for each day's work—about one US dollar—and they have not yet paid for dinner or housing. David's real-time cost-of-living analysis is backed up by others I talked to in Haiti. In 2011, the AFL-CIO–supported Solidarity Center conducted a study estimating the living wage for apparel workers in Port-au-Prince. Factoring in the costs of necessities like food, housing, cooking fuel, and child care, the Solidarity Center estimated a living wage for an adult with two dependents to be 1,152 gourdes—about $29—per day.[52]

The conditions at the garment assembly factories are rough. David says his workplace at Interamerican Woven is brutally hot—a literal sweatshop—with little ventilation and limited potable water. An October 2012 report, produced by the International Labour Organization (ILO) and International Finance Corporation as part of the Hope II legislation, confirms this. The report says the company and several other garment assembly companies were regularly out of compliance with minimum wage, overtime, and social insurance requirements, as well as failing to meet baseline requirements for workplace conditions like acceptable temperatures and clean drinking water.[53] A subsequent study by the Workers' Rights Consortium, published in October 2013, found that Haitian workers at these factories, who make clothes for sale by North American name brands like Gap, Gildan, Kohl's, Levi's, Russell, Target, VF, and Walmart, were being deprived of nearly a third of the wages they are legally due. Some of those factories named as sites of this wage theft include those at the generously subsidized Caracol Industrial Park.[54]

Jackson (also not his real name) works for one of the companies, Global Manufacturers and Contractors (GMC), which was identified in these reports. He is among two-thousand-plus workers assembling the T-shirts of name brands like Hanes and Champion. Jackson and his wife have two young children. To make ends meet, both parents work six days per week, with Jackson's wife skipping church on Sundays to take on an extra part-time job. Even with that extra income and some scholarship support for their children's schooling, the family runs out of money before each paycheck. In order to pay rent and keep food on the table, they engage in a regular practice of borrowing from family and friends.

Jackson is not accepting the situation passively. He is an active member and the general secretary of SYNOTHAG, a *syndicat* of workers advocating for better wages and conditions. Company management pushes against the union, he says, harassing its members whenever possible. Investigations by the ILO have confirmed widespread violations of union rights in the Haitian apparel industry.[55] "The people fired for being part of the union make a list this long," Jackson says, holding his hands two feet apart. "They find a different reason to let them go, but they are tagged because they are part of the *syndicat*."

Jackson is undeterred. The salaries are unfair, and the companies could easily pay them better, he says. If that means a little less profit for the owners, that is a reasonable cost for justice. His position is backed up by economic analysis by the World Bank's International Finance Corporation, which analyzed the competitiveness of the Haitian garment assembly industry in 2011. The report concluded that the preferential market access to the United States provided by HOPE II and HELP, and comparatively low sea freight costs, provide a distinct market advantage to these companies.[56] "The argument that factories in Haiti can't raise wages is bogus, as they have some of the most competitive costs in the world already," says Jake Johnston, a research associate for the Center on Economic and Policy Research. "A slight raise in wages won't kill the industry."

The T-shirts Jackson makes for GMC are shipped to *Etazini*—the United States—so I ask him if he has any message for Americans. He thinks for a moment, then replies: "*Wi*. I appeal to their conscience, and hope they ask questions about what they are buying. We make T-shirts for cents, they buy them for dollars," he says. "That is the reason we come together to support each other; to fight for fairness."[57]

The migration of Haitian people from the countryside to compete for low-wage jobs in Port-au-Prince is a phenomenon created by the late twentieth-century structural adjustment mandates on Haiti, especially the disastrous agricultural policies dictated by the United States and other international creditors.[58] Although trade imbalance has been a staple of the Haitian economy for centuries, the Haitian people had nurtured a successful agricultural sector dating back to the revolution. Separate from the often-dysfunctional government, rural Haitians adhered to the *lakou* system of property management, which successfully divided former plantations into small plots, respected a process of joint decision-making, and yielded crops that supported the extended families living there. Following what Haitian sociologist Jean Casmir calls a "counter-plantation" system, Haiti had for generations met its own food needs and exported to other countries.[59]

Then, beginning in the 1970s and 1980s, the IMF, with the United States as its largest shareholder and dominant voice, forced Haiti to dramatically reduce tariffs on imported staples. The Haitian tariff on rice, for example, was dropped from 50 percent to the current rate of 3 percent, far below the regional average of 20 percent.[60] The result is that Haitian farmers can no longer compete with food imports from the United States or other countries where food crops are highly subsidized by their governments. As Haitian women's rights activist Yolette Etienne says, "You who used to grow your own plantains, who didn't need to buy plantains, are told, 'You don't have to grow plantains because we make enough for you to buy them from us when you need them.' But where do you get the money to buy these plantains from overseas?"[61]

Today, Haiti imports more than half its food. Eighty percent of rice consumed in Haiti is imported, and the one-time sugar capital of the world actually imports sugar as well. Haitian farmers who can't sell their crops stop growing them, which means that there is no local alternative when international prices spike or economic fortunes drop. In April 2008, the price of rice doubled, sending thousands of Haitians into the street for the so-called Clorox food riots, the name inspired by hunger so painful it felt as if bleach were eating away at one's stomach. Those Haitian hunger pains can be traced directly back to US and global trade policies.[62] "If governments that preached trade liberalization in Geneva would practice it—and that includes reducing domestic support measures that affect trade—if everything was on a level playing field, that would be very helpful to Haiti," Marc Cohen, a senior researcher on humanitarian policy and climate change at Oxfam America, told *Foreign Policy* magazine in 2013.[63] Little wonder the IMF rice tariff edict is referred to in Haiti as the *plan lanmo*—Creole for "death plan."[64]

The collapse of the Haitian agricultural system has had predictably grim ripple effects. Wood and charcoal are the chief fuel sources in Haiti, and thus survive as two of the few remaining cash crops, leading to dramatic deforestation. In 1923, in the middle of the US occupation, 60 percent of Haiti was covered by forest; in 2006, the number was less than 2 percent.[65] The deforestation in turn leaves Haiti vulnerable to flooding and landslides in the wake of heavy storms. In 2004, for example, Tropical Storm Jeanne caused major flooding in Haiti and three thousand people were killed. By comparison, Jeanne was a full hurricane when it hit Puerto Rico, Barbados, the Dominican Republic, and the United States, but only thirty-four people were killed in all those countries combined.[66] Concannon describes the effect and its economic origins this way:

> [People point to] the mountain farmers who cut down the trees that in other countries slow the rain down. But the farmers would not cut the trees if they had a choice—they know better than the experts what happens when rain hits a deforested slope, because it rushes away with the topsoil that is needed for next year's crop and is many farmers' only legacy for their children. But legacies and next year's crop mean nothing when the children are dying now, so the farmer cuts and sells the tree to buy today's medicine and food.[67]

Hundreds of thousands of Haitians have migrated away from this denuded countryside where they can no longer earn a living. Some head overseas (19 percent of Haiti's GDP is made up of remittances from emigrants living abroad), but most go to Port-au-Prince. The city that had 150,000 residents in 1950 now has three million people living in it, crammed into poorly constructed and poorly planned hillside structures, many of which collapsed in the earthquake.[68]

Haiti is a country where the international community is used to having its way. The billions of dollars Haiti owed to international creditors gave those creditors the leverage to dictate many internal policies. The international community has assumed duties like peacekeeping that would traditionally be performed by the state, and thousands of foreign-funded entities in the "Republic of NGOs" influence policy and command resources. As a result, the Haitian government rarely has been in a position to argue with outsiders' views of what is best for Haiti, whether it be paying reparations to France, submitting to US occupation, or adopting neoliberal economic policies. The Haitian proverb *Sak vide pa kanpe*—an empty sack cannot stand up—has often been applied to describe Haiti's government. Haiti's first democratically elected president, Jean-Bertrand Aristide, tried to assert a different vision for Haiti's economy. But the United States and the international community pushed back—hard.

Aristide was elected in November 1990 by a landslide total of over 67 percent of the vote, easily defeating neoliberal economist and former World Bank official Marc Bazin. The victory was the crowning triumph of the Haitian pro-democracy struggle that had ousted Jean-Claude Duvalier in 1986. The movement grew out of small community organizations (*organisations populaires*) and church groups (*tilegliz*). These groups were inspired in part by the passionate sermons and radio addresses of Catholic priests, especially Aristide, who were proponents of liberation theology and its preferential option for the poor. The *makouts* and the succession of military rulers who replaced the Duvaliers responded to the pro-democracy movement violently, but their brutality only seemed to build the momentum for change. The crackdown raised the profile of reformers like Aristide, who somehow survived four assassination attempts. The 1990 election victory by the Aristide-led Fanmi Lavalas party (the name refers to the many drops of water that together make a mighty flood) was an historic victory for the majority poor of Haiti who sought to move, in Aristide's words, "from misery to poverty with dignity."[69] Pursuing that agenda, the newly elected Aristide tried to reverse neoliberal policies. He raised the minimum wages of workers in the assembly industries, increased tax collections from the wealthy, and adopted policies to protect Haitian farmers from the effects of subsidized food imports.

Aristide was met by fierce resistance from the United States, which helped fund an organized political opposition through USAID dollars. Among its targets was the minimum wage increase, which a USAID-funded study said "would reduce the overall competitiveness of Haiti."[70] As one US official told the *Boston Globe* later, "Aristide—slum priest, grassroots activist, exponent of liberation theology—represents everything the CIA [Central Intelligence Agency], DOD [Department of Defense], and FBI think they have been trying to protect this country from for 50 years."[71] Less than a year after his election, Aristide was overthrown by Haitian army officers, many of whom had been trained at the Georgia-based US Department of Defense School of the Americas (since renamed the Western Hemisphere Institute for Security Cooperation) and/or were on the payroll of the CIA. The CIA's chief Latin American analyst testified to Congress that the coup general Raul Cédras was part of "the most promising group of Haitian leaders to emerge since the Duvalier dictatorship was overthrown."[72]

Despite this reassurance, the coup government proved to be brutal even by Haiti's standards, killing thousands—including the Raboteau massacre victims—and causing mass migration. Within six months of the coup, the US Coast Guard had intercepted more than thirty-eight thousand Haitians fleeing the country.[73] The growing refugee crisis in the United States was accompanied by a movement in support of the Haitian democracy that was informed and inspired by Haitian activists smuggling themselves and information out of their besieged country. Highlights of the movement included a street-clogging demonstration of more than sixty thousand protesters in New York City in October 1991 and a high-profile hunger strike by the activist Randall Robinson.[74] In response, the Clinton administration helped Aristide return to Haiti in 1994, but only after first extracting promises to cut government programs for the poor and to lower food tariffs.[75] In 2010, President Clinton, currently the UN special envoy to Haiti, expressed regret for that mandate: "It may have been good for some of my farmers in Arkansas, but it has not worked. It was a mistake. . . . I did that. I have to live every day with the consequences of the lost capacity to produce a rice crop in Haiti to feed those people, because of what I did."[76]

Even with the concessions that enabled his return, Aristide continued to pursue policies, including a minimum wage increase, that the US government felt were interfering with its economic priorities. Aristide "wasn't going to be beholden to the United States, and so he was going to be in trouble," US senator Christopher Dodd would say later. "We had interests and ties with some of the very strong financial interests in the country, and Aristide was threatening them."[77]

In 1996, Congress passed the Dole Amendment, banning USAID from giving funds to the Haitian government, with some humanitarian and electoral exceptions. Then, in 2000, the United States broadened its efforts, using its influence to impose a total international aid embargo on the Haitian government.[78] The justification provided for the embargo, which cut the Aristide government's already-limited spending power in half, was to force a change in disputed 2000 legislative elections. The dispute was a relatively minor one: an accepted Haitian vote calculation system was deemed incorrect by the OAS, which also characterized the elections as "a great success for the Haitian population" and conceded that the majority of the election outcomes would not change under a different calculation.[79] But the United States, which had bankrolled and armed the Duvaliers, now rose up in righteous anger at alleged injustice in a left-leaning Haitian government. The irony was not lost on Amy Wilentz, author of *The Rainy Season*: "During the four regimes that preceded Aristide, international human rights advocates and democratic observers had begged the State Department to consider helping the democratic opposition in Haiti. But no steps were taken by the United States to strengthen anything but the executive and the military until Aristide won the presidency. Then, all of a sudden, the United States began to think about how it could help those Haitians eager to limit the power of the executive."[80]

Perhaps the most damaging anti-Aristide action was the US decision to block an earmarked $146 million loan to Haiti from the IDB. The money was set to be used for programs that included improvements to the water infrastructure system, whose deficiencies proved so deadly in the 2010 cholera outbreak.[81] As Dr. Evan Lyon of Haiti-based Partners in Health said, "[It is] reasonable to draw a straight line from these loans being slowed down and cut off to the epidemic that emerged."[82] By early 2004, Haiti was in crisis. The embargo and the loan blockade had tightened a noose around the Haitian economy, and USAID-supported politicians and radio stations were increasing their criticism of Aristide.

Former Haitian military officers, trained in the Dominican Republic and bearing new US automatic rifles and grenade launchers, began marching through rural Haiti, destroying police stations and a power plant. (The rebel leader, Guy Philippe, would later claim he was in daily contact not just with the US-backed opponents of Aristide but with US officials directly.)[83] In February 2004, just a few weeks after Haiti celebrated the bicentennial of its independence, Aristide left the country, escorted by US Army Special Forces. The Bush administration said that the US military was helping the president flee to safety. Aristide and other witnesses say that it was a kidnapping.[84]

The day Aristide left Haiti, US president George W. Bush told reporters, "It's the beginning of a new chapter in the country's history," and sent marines back to Haiti to help quell the reaction to Aristide's departure.[85] US State Department spokesperson Richard Boucher said, "We call on all Haitians to respect this peaceful and constitutional succession."[86] The new government wasted no time in reversing the Aristide pro-poor economic policies that had frustrated the Bush administration: the new prime minister, Gérard Latortue, quickly ordered a three-year tax exemption for Haiti's largest industries and merchants. Then, during the two years following the 2004 coup, three thousand Haitians were killed (including Jimmy Charles) and thousands more Aristide supporters jailed (including Father Gérard Jean-Juste).[87]

When he initially found it impossible to believe any version of Haiti's history where the United States has so reliably played the role of the villain, Rob Broggi recognized he was not alone: "I think the typical American reaction is this: Why would the United States, after giving Haiti all this money over all these years, care about a little country with eight million people and why would they care to exploit that? There's nothing there to exploit. You know, the US gives them money, we help them, and they just can't get their own act together."

As Paul Farmer wrote in his 2011 book, *Haiti after the Earthquake*, "Haiti has a terrible reputation internationally for dozens of reasons, most of them wrong."[88] But some of the perception that Haiti is sabotaging itself is accurate. The United States has indeed provided many aid dollars to Haiti, and Haitian leaders bear their own share of responsibility for the country's dismal condition. Not coincidentally, almost all those leaders come from the country's tiny but very rich elite, where 1 percent of the population owns 50 percent of Haiti's wealth. The plantation system is gone, but it has been replaced with an economy with similar characteristics: subsistence farmers are marginalized and export benefits accrue almost solely to the wealthy.

Remarkably, Haiti leads the Americas in the number of millionaires per capita while at the same time housing the poorest people in the region.[89] As British philosopher Peter Hallward put it in his 2007 book, *Damming the Flood: Haiti and the Politics of Containment*, "This then is the first basic fact of Haitian political life. The country is dominated by a small and well-integrated group of privileged families, surrounded by millions of impoverished people. . . . The elite owes its privileges to exploitation and violence—the violence of radical inequality and destitution, backed up when necessary by the violence of an army or the equivalent of an army—that allows it to retain them."[90]

The pattern of internal political violence in Haiti is startling, beginning in 1806 with the assassination of Jean-Jacques Dessalines, who had crowned himself emperor of Haiti after independence. The country has now endured a full thirty-two coups d'état and a near-constant state of military dominance over civilians.[91] The government of Haiti made disastrous choices in loans and alliances, and has never been able to develop an economy that is independent of foreign powers, particularly the United States.

Yet Haiti's own missteps do not change the fact that the United States has had an enduring and often malevolent effect on the lives of the Haitian people. Part of the answer to Broggi's hypothetical questioning of why the United States should bother with Haiti is that Haiti provided a Caribbean bulwark during the Cold War. A desire to offset the influence of Fidel Castro's Cuba and prevent a Communist stronghold from emerging so close to US shores certainly helped spur American support for the reliably anticommunist Duvaliers. Arguably, this support was granted not in spite of the Duvaliers' murderous repression, but because of it: the two Docs' iron fists of political violence created the economic and governmental stability the United States craved from its neighbors.[92]

But US involvement in Haiti both preceded and survived the Cold War, with a common theme that is less about national security than about exploiting Haiti's once-abundant natural resources and still-abundant supply of cheap labor. Some of that phenomenon is attributable to the effects of free-market capitalism stripped bare to a core that consists of the relentless search for low-cost labor. But much of the exploitation of Haiti has been enabled by a form of socialism for the wealthy, as the United States uses a combination of government subsidies and loan-shark pressure to rig competition in favor of US agribusiness over Haitian farmers. Policies that make rural life in Haiti unsustainable have the added benefit of pushing Haitians off the land to compete—alongside David and Jackson—for export-oriented jobs that pay miniscule wages. In 2005, a CIBC World Markets analyst noted approvingly that clothing manufacturer Gildan's labor costs in Haiti were actually lower than labor costs in China.[93] When Haitians leave the countryside to compete for low-wage jobs assembling goods for corporations who are exempted from paying taxes on that labor, the corporations then sell the products at cheap prices in the United States.

American consumers and shareholders win, and Haitians lose. As the Creole proverb says, *Bourik travay pou chwal galonnen*—the donkey works so that the horse can run free.

In *The Uses of Haiti*, Farmer writes that the United States has a "chronic allergy" to Haitian democracy, because a democratically elected Haitian government inevitably will push back against this unequal donkey/horse relationship.[94] Brian Concannon agrees, but he sees a broader historical pattern that suggests a fear by the US government that Haitian attitudes are potentially contagious across borders:

> My conclusion is that Haiti has always been punished by the US because it is a bad example of something. And usually Haiti is a bad example of the gap between what we practice and what we preach. In 1804, the problem was that Haiti was really free—was implementing the ideals we set out in the Declaration of Independence. We weren't, so we could not accept a country that was actually carrying out those ideals. I think the problem now is that Haitians insist on having a popular democracy and a government that carries out policies the people want. It is a poor country and people want progressive redistributive policies that develop the state's role, support agriculture, build schools, and develop the public health system. We certainly have more things like that than Haiti does, but the trend in our country is to cut back those things. So we don't have a strong tolerance for Haitians insisting they go in a different direction.

Concannon's view was more hopeful when he arrived in Haiti in 1995. "My first impression of Haiti was to be struck by the poverty and material deprivation, of course, but I arrived shortly after the restoration of Haiti's first democratically elected government, and there was an exciting sense of hope and determination among the Haitian people." Now that they were no longer being tormented by the military government that had ousted Aristide, the Haitian people told Concannon, what they really needed was action to prosecute past human rights abusers and efforts to secure their social and economic rights. "Nothing against the UN, but these tasks of democratic transition were not in the UN's portfolio," Concannon says. He continues:

> The mission I joined was originally deployed during the coup, and was supposed to observe and report, and did some important reporting. But when democracy was restored, the mission did not do a democratic transition. I think that was partly because of the inertia of a big organization, and partly because the US did not want to do what was necessary. For example, we had our territory and we would drive around the territory, visit a couple of towns every day and talk to judges and prosecutors and civic leaders, priests, everybody, and try to get an idea of what was going on.

We would ask, "Are you getting attacked by the military?," and they would say no. The military has been abolished. Is the paramilitary getting you? No. They would all say, we need economic and social rights. We would say that is not our mission, our mission is civil and political rights. They would say OK, you can help with civil and political rights by prosecuting the people [in the coup government] who were killing us last year. And we would say we don't do that because the UN does not get involved. So basically they give you this, "What good are you?" And we'd say, "Oh, we'll file a report."

At that time, filing a report was not making any concrete improvements in the lives of Haitians. So, after a while it became clear the mission wasn't going to switch fast enough to be relevant. And it just got harder and harder to take people's time, get all their information, and tell them I wasn't going to do anything concrete to act on that information.

So Concannon switched roles to join the fledgling BAI, created to push the investigation and prosecution of human rights abuses. After teaming with Mario Joseph to win the Raboteau verdict, the lesson Concannon took away from that success was that BAI could indeed get justice for its Haitian clients, but only if it added to its lawyers' toolbox of briefs and motions the implements of community organizing and international-level advocacy. "Human rights progress does not come from litigation alone," Concannon says. This is true not just in struggling nations like Haiti, Concannon says, pointing to the historic sea change in US Supreme Court rulings. In less than sixty years, the court moved from the infamous 1896 *Plessy v. Ferguson* decision upholding the racial segregation doctrine of "separate but equal" to the doctrine's unanimous 1954 repudiation in the landmark case *Brown v. Board of Education*. "The difference between the two decisions is not that the Fourteenth Amendment changed or the justices of the Supreme Court got so much smarter in those six decades," Concannon says. "The difference is that years of determined activism had changed the country for the better."

Concannon, who is fluent in Creole, spent nine years in Haiti working for BAI. Phil Huffman, Concannon's friend and rugby teammate during their years at Middlebury College, visited him there several times. "I was struck by Brian's deep connections to the Haitian people and his close and trusting relationships with his Haitian colleagues," says Huffman, who is the director of conservation programs for the Vermont chapter of the Nature Conservancy. "I learned that this is really the essence of Brian's work—to honor the Haitian people's dignity and to immerse himself in the cause of trying to improve their circumstances and combat some of the injustices they have faced for so long."

Concannon's and BAI's experience changed dramatically after the 2004 coup d'état. After the coup, the generals convicted in the Raboteau massacre were released from prison, and the judge in the case was attacked by unknown assailants. One of BAI's clients was killed, and others had their homes burned down. Concannon and others involved in the BAI efforts were devastated. "Ten years of many people's very hard work building democracy in a country that had never known it, ten years of building schools and training lawyers and building a public health system—all of that went down the drain," Concannon says, frustration still evident in his voice nearly a decade later.

Like many others, Concannon places much of the blame for the coup on the US government. "That showed me my place to best help the people of Haiti was not in Port-au-Prince but back here in the States, making the US safe for democracy in Haiti," he says. "We at IJDH are certainly not anti-American. We are only asking the US to stand up and support for Haitians the same ideals of democracy and human rights that are the founding principles of our country. A lot of bad things happen throughout the world in our name—things that Americans, if they really knew, would not accept. And I think that there have been more unjust US policies imposed on Haiti than on any other country."

When asked now if he could choose to do his work today in Haiti or the United States, Concannon does not hesitate:

No question, the US. I liked living in Haiti. But in 2004, when the coup happened and ten years of very hard work building democracy was flushed down the drain at the whim of our president, it was very clear to me that my place wasn't in Haiti. Because I could spend the rest of my life working to build things in Haiti only to see the US knock it down. So my place is in the US, using the lessons and the information and the relationships I obtained in Haiti.

Concannon also acknowledges that fundraising to support BAI's operations is easier to do in the wealthier United States. So is the task of networking with other human rights advocates. "Part of making the United States safe for democracy in Haiti is policy-making, but it is also networking with NGOs, legal groups, and others that can support Haiti," he says. He adds:

Around 2000, when I was still in Haiti, I started going to human rights conferences. When I said I was working in Haiti, they would look at me like I was from a country that had disappeared. A half-dozen years before, everyone knew about Haiti and most folks working on human rights were involved in Haiti efforts because there was a dictatorship then. But then Haiti kind of fell off the map for them. When the coup happened in 2004, it was obviously extremely important that the human rights community get engaged to try to stop it. But they weren't connected to Haiti, and they largely did not respond.[95]

That is not going to happen again on my watch. There are now law school clinics, human rights groups, solidarity groups, and a great network of organizations working on Haiti that understand the need to influence what is going on inside Haiti and in the international community's engagement with Haiti.

Although Concannon has gathered numerous volunteers and a somewhat lesser number of paid staff around him at IJDH, most observers point to him as the indispensable component of the US-based advocacy. Ira Kurzban says Concannon's organizational and analytical skills are the foundation of the effort. "Brian is not just great at gathering skilled and dedicated people around the cause and motivating them to do good work, he is really at the core a brilliant strategist and an outstanding lawyer. Clearly, he could be working in a large law firm making a lot of money, or holding a high-level job in a presidential administration. We are lucky, and the people of Haiti are lucky, that he has instead committed his life to human rights work in the poorest country in the hemisphere." Congresswoman Maxine Waters, former Congressional Black Caucus chair and one of Haiti's leading advocates in US politics, has said often that Concannon and IJDH are the best sources for information on Haiti.[96]

He has not lived full time in Haiti since 2004, but Concannon still has his fans there, as his IJDH colleague Nicole Phillips discovered. During one of her extended stays in Port-au-Prince in 2010, she shared with some of the activists with the Haitian women's rights group FAVILEK the news that Concannon was going to be visiting soon. His second child was born less than two weeks after the earthquake, so he had not traveled to Haiti in several months. Phillips realized the women of FAVILEK knew Concannon from his years living in Haiti, but she was not prepared for the reaction to the news of his upcoming visit. "They all swooned, like he was a movie star or something," she recalls. One of the women put both hands on her chest and said, "Oh Brian, he is my heart!" Haitians see well-meaning *blan* (foreigners) come and go, Phillips explains, and she has never seen a non-Haitian embraced in the way Concannon is. "Brian has committed to them so completely, in learning the language, in living there for so many years, and in staying with the cause long-term, and it has earned him this amazing amount of affection and loyalty," Phillips says.

Concannon is uncomfortable with the personal praise, but he acknowledges that his credibility on Haiti human rights issues derives in significant part from his experience in Haiti and his enduring relationships there. "Maybe someone who was a quicker study than me wouldn't have needed nine years in Haiti to learn what I did. But it certainly would have been impossible for me to do my job effectively without having spent substantial time there and having established a strong relationship with Mario. We built that relationship by working through a lot of crises over the course of the years."

———————

Even after the 2004 coup d'état, some of those Haitian crises continued to be spurred by US actions. Diplomatic cables obtained by the group WikiLeaks and published by *Haïti Liberté* and the *Nation* show that US officials worked hard after the coup to keep the democratically elected Aristide from returning to Haiti, even while the military officials who ousted him were taking bloody vengeance on his supporters.[97] The cables revealed that when Dominican Republic president Leonel Fernández called for Aristide's return in late 2004, he was sharply admonished by the US ambassador to the Dominican Republic. The US ambassador alleged that Aristide was involved in drug trafficking—an allegation never brought to any court and fiercely denied by Aristide's supporters.[98] As recently as 2011, President Obama urged South African president Jacob Zuma and UN secretary-general Ban Ki-moon to block Aristide's return to Haiti from exile in South Africa.[99] Aristide finally returned to Haiti in March 2011.

These same diplomatic cables also showed how the United States actively opposed Haitian leaders' efforts to improve the economic situation in their country anytime the proposals conflicted with US government or business interests. In 2006, Haitian president René Préval signed a deal to join Venezuela's PetroCaribe alliance, in which Haiti would pay only 60 percent of the cost of purchased oil to Venezuela up front, with the remainder payable over twenty-five years at 1 percent interest. It was an undeniably favorable deal for cash-strapped Haiti. But the plan angered the United States, which was at odds with Venezuelan president Hugo Chavez. Predictably, rival oil producers like ExxonMobil and Chevron were also opposed to Haiti's deal with PetroCaribe. The cables obtained by WikiLeaks showed that the oil companies' representatives and then-US ambassador to Haiti Jane Sanderson met behind closed doors and coordinated resistance to the deal.[100]

The cables contained significant correspondence showing the US State Department also assisted contractors for Fruit of the Loom, Hanes, and Levi's in their campaign to resist a unanimous Haitian Parliament decision in June 2009 to raise the minimum wage. The increase, approved by legislators after a series of worker strikes and demonstrations, would have compelled the contractors to pay 62 cents per hour, or about $5 per day, to Haitians sewing clothing for sale overseas. (Recall that a living wage for a worker living in Port-au-Prince has been estimated to be $29/day.) But the cables show US deputy chief of mission David E. Lindwall saying that even the $5/day wage "did not take economic reality into account."[101] In the end, a unanimous Haitian Parliament decision backed by overwhelming public support was no match for the opposition by the contractors and the US government. President Préval and the legislators dropped the textile industry minimum wage to about $3/day. Haitian workers continue to be the lowest paid in the hemisphere.

The US response to the January 2010 Haitian earthquake was in many respects generous and lifesaving. But, as is more fully discussed in Chapter 5 of this book, some of the US actions served as *abse sou klou*—making a bad situation worse, or literally "an abscess on an open wound." Perhaps no US effort post-earthquake was more damaging than its role in the Haitian presidential and legislative elections of November 2010. Haiti's Provisional Electoral Council (CEP), controlled by outgoing president Préval, decided to exclude more than a dozen political parties from the election, including the most popular party, Fanmi Lavalas. It was a decision tantamount to the Republican Party in the United States conveniently excluding the

Democratic Party from elections, and US officials knew it. Republican US senator Richard Lugar and the Democrat-dominated Congressional Black Caucus publicly questioned the chances for a fair election under these terms.[102] Behind-the-scenes communication also showed that US officials were well aware of the blatant unfairness of the election plans. The CEP decision had "emasculated the opposition," said the European Union and Canadian ambassadors, as reported in one of the US diplomatic cables obtained by WikiLeaks.[103] US ambassador to Haiti Kenneth Merten explicitly states in one of the cables that he was aware that President Préval was manipulating the elections. But Ambassador Merten also reports the consensus from a meeting with fellow ambassadors to Haiti from Brazil, Canada, and Spain, which was that "the international community has too much invested in Haiti's democracy to walk away from the upcoming elections, despite its [sic] imperfections."[104]

Of course, protecting an investment in "democracy" by holding unfair elections is an oxymoron, as was amply demonstrated on Haiti's election day. Under the watch of UN peacekeepers, an astonishing level of fraud and exclusion occurred. Thousands of citizens were prevented from voting because they had lost their identification cards and/or were left homeless by the earthquake. Voter intimidation and ballot box stuffing were reported, and nearly one in four votes cast was disqualified or never received by the already-tarnished CEP. The uncounted ballots and the low turnout meant that fewer than one in five registered Haitians voters had his or her votes counted in the election, according to post-election analysis by the Washington-based Center for Economic and Policy Research. The problems were so manifest that twelve presidential candidates led their supporters to the streets to protest the elections. Then two of the candidates—Mirlande Manigat and Michel Martelly—dropped their protests after being informed that a US-pushed reconsideration put them in a second-round runoff, which Martelly won. Participation in the first election was the lowest for any election in the Western Hemisphere in over sixty years. Participation in the second round was even lower.[105]

The United States had de facto control over the fiasco, and could have put a halt to it, Concannon insists. "In the WikiLeaks documents, they [US officials] said, 'Yes, President Préval is manipulating the elections,' and they conceded all the problems in the elections we at IJDH were screaming about and they were publicly denying at the time," Concannon says. "But they conclude we have to go with this election because Préval is our guy. So it is more important to them that the government running Haiti takes orders from the US than that they actually represent the Haitian people."

Coupled with the United States' complicit silence in the Martelly administration's failure to prosecute Jean-Claude Duvalier, the bogus 2010 and 2011 elections provided a post-earthquake American stamp of approval for the perpetuation of the Haitian legacy of corruption at the highest levels of government. (Transparency International's Corruption Perceptions Index ranked Haiti 165th out of 174 countries in 2012.)[106] Even though Duvalier remains free, there have been published reports that Aristide may be indicted by the United States on unspecified corruption charges.[107] If the indictment occurs, Aristide supporters like Ira Kurzban say that it would be just the latest installment of an effort to keep Haiti's most progressive—and arguably most popular—leader out of the political picture.

Kurzban has been by Aristide's side throughout Aristide's up-and-down political career, including escorting Aristide into exile, first to the Central African Republic and then to South Africa. It is a roller-coaster ride that Kurzban insists is being conducted largely by US officials. "Remember that Aristide is the one who approved me setting up BAI in the first place, because he understands the importance of the rule of law. That is the irony of all this, and why the US government dislikes him is still a mystery to me. As I always say, he is no Fidel!" To Kurzban, the Martelly administration—with the cooperation of US intelligence services, if not the US State Department—is headed toward a Duvalierist state of affairs, complete with a Haitian army responding to the orders of a Haitian president and the country's donors. "As some people say, Haiti is returning to 1934, when the United States left Haiti but left behind a US-created Haitian army."

Yet popular US discourse usually attributes Haiti's troubles to its culture, or to some character flaw lying within the people who have suffered so much. After the earthquake, US television reporters spent more time speculating about imminent waves of looting—which never occurred—than on the remarkable solidarity of Haitians and the organized aid they pulled together before the international community ever arrived on the scene. One CNN reporter questioned whether the devastation even bothered the Haitian children she saw after the quake.[108] Another CNN reporter asked a woman, "Why don't you Haitians cry?"[109] *New York Times* columnist David Brooks wrote a post-earthquake column entitled "The Underlying Tragedy" that blamed Haiti for having "progress-resistant cultural influences" like poor child-rearing and Vodou.[110] The day after the earthquake, televangelist Pat Robertson attributed the disaster to what he referred to as Haiti's "pact to the devil."[111] The Billy and Franklin Graham NGO Samaritan's Purse, the recipient of USAID funds for its work in Haiti, has trumpeted its work promoting Christianity and combating Vodou in Haiti, describing the Haitians' need to "take back their country from voodoo, despair, and sin."[112]

This was not a new perspective from powerful Americans. US marine brigadier general Ivan W. Miller said during the early twentieth-century occupation by the United States that the Haitians "had no conception of kindness or helping people."[113] John Russell, the high commissioner of that occupation, wrote, "The Haitian mentality only recognizes force, and appeal to reason and logic is unthinkable."[114] Writing in the *Atlantic Monthly* in 1993, USAID official Lawrence Harrison (whom the *Times*' Brooks cited in his 2010 column) said, "I believe that culture is the only possible explanation for Haiti's unending tragedy."[115]

The notion that Haitians have themselves to blame for their misery is more subtly, but perhaps just as damningly, suggested in the work of the respected author and geographer Jared Diamond. In his 2005 book, *Collapse: How Societies Choose to Fail*, Diamond put forward the argument that culture (Diamond uses the terms "attitudes" and "self-defined identity") is in part to blame for Haiti's struggles compared to its Hispaniola neighbor the Dominican Republic.[116] In an August 2012 column in the *New York Times*, Diamond made the comparison again: "Just as a happy marriage depends on many different factors, so do national wealth and power. That is not to deny culture's significance. Some countries have political institutions and cultural practices—honest government, rule of law, opportunities to accumulate money—that reward hard work. Others don't. Familiar examples are the contrasts between neighboring countries sharing similar environments but with very different institutions. (Think of South Korea versus North Korea, or Haiti versus the Dominican Republic.)"[117]

Diamond's attribution of Haiti's struggles in part to government transparency and the missing rule of law is on the mark, as was his discussion in *Collapse* of the effects of the outside powers' fear of Haiti as "a Creole-speaking African society."[118] But Diamond's reference to Haitian's allegedly unproductive attitudes and his facile reference to "culture's significance" feeds into a blame-the-victim conclusion. Like Diamond's more lengthy analysis in *Collapse*, his column's suggestion that the Dominican Republic and Haiti were and are on even playing fields ignores critical historical facts. *Collapse* never mentions the uniquely harmful effects on Haiti of France's reparations collections, the US and international support of the Duvaliers and then the rebels who twice overthrew Aristide, and the international neoliberal and protectionist policies that continue to handcuff the Haitian people.

Haitian American anthropologist Gina Athena Ulysse calls the practice of blaming the Haitian culture for the country's struggles the "sub-humanity" perspective: if we do not see Haitians as fully human, it is easier for Americans and the international community to accept Haitians' suffering and to approve of heavy-handed breaches of the country's sovereignty. "It stems from the dominant idea in popular imagination that Haitians are irrational, devil-worshipping, progress-resistant, uneducated, accursed black natives overpopulating their God-forsaken island," Ulysse writes.[119]

Little wonder that Paul Farmer says in *Uses of Haiti*, "From the point of view of the Haitian poor, the US foreign policy towards Haiti has never been well-intentioned."[120] Or, as the Haitian proverb says, "Those who give the blows forget, those who bear the scars remember." Randall Robinson—human rights activist, founder of the African American organization TransAfrica, and author of *An Unbroken Agony: Haiti, from the Revolution to the Kidnapping of a President*—is less subtle: "Shadowed by a long past of cruel experiences, contemporary Haitians have ample reason to believe that where the world's white nations are concerned, notions of democracy and other abstract decencies weigh little against the ageless and seductive traditions of color, prejudice, and greed. The leaders of the white world simply do not accord to constitutions and laws of black countries the near-sanctity they accord to their own."[121]

After his talk at Drexel Law, Concannon rushes a few miles across town to a conference of US human rights lawyers. In a meeting where Concannon is one of only two lawyers wearing a suit and tie, he intently listens to various comments, taking notes on a legal pad. It is a friendly crowd for IJDH, and Concannon pulls no punches when he is asked to summarize recent events in Haiti advocacy. As to the 2010 and 2011 elections, "The good news is that we were all over the local and international media, so much so that our opponents thought we had somehow rigged the internet because Google searches kept turning up our reports." Everyone laughs and claps. "The bad news is that Haiti now has a new president [Martelly] elected by only 18 percent of the Haitian people, but with 100% of Secretary Clinton's support. The US selected a president for Haiti who has long-standing ties to right-wing death squads."[122] Concannon also tells the group that Mario Joseph and other BAI and IJDH lawyers were making a presentation to the UN Human Rights Council in Geneva that very day, as part of the Universal Periodic Review of Haiti. Concannon says that the material provided to the council by the collaboration of thirty-seven organizations that BAI and IJDH had brought together "dwarfed" in quality and quantity all else presented, and that a link to a shorter summary of IJDH's report had been retweeted by writers for the Economist and the Miami Herald.

Later in the conference, Concannon joins a more formal panel presentation. There, he chooses to stress that, despite the bleak present, there is hope for Haiti's future. "There really is a fairly simple solution, and I saw it with my own eyes: democracy works in Haiti. The international community and the US just need to allow it to happen," Concannon says. There are plenty of reasons for Americans to want Haiti to succeed, he insists. He points to how the United States has spent billions of dollars in aid to Haiti—money that can halt the perpetual cycle of disaster and rebuild only if the Haitian people are empowered. "And there is always the core concept of Christianity which is shared by other faiths and beliefs—that we have a duty to care for the least of our brothers and sisters."

Since he moved back to the United States from Haiti in 2004, Concannon has persuaded many Americans to agree. The Drexel law students and faculty he addressed will be spending their spring break in Haiti on a fact-finding mission. They are some of the hundreds of US lawyers and law students who have had direct impact in Haiti as part of what one international lawyer calls a Concannon-created volunteer "pipeline" between Haiti and the US legal community. After the earthquake, IJDH enlisted lawyers and law students to help file the complaints with the IACHR challenging camp evictions and exposing the dangerous conditions that led to the rapes of women in the camps. Reports prepared by US volunteers have been submitted to the UN and distributed widely, often forcing the international community and Haitian government to extend additional support to those left homeless and vulnerable.

Ted Oswald has worked on these reports, spent time in Haiti, and helped start Drexel's program while a law student, all with Concannon's encouragement. Oswald says Concannon provides a model of US-Haitian partnership. "There's a humility there with Brian that's really admirable. And I've seen other attorneys who are interested in helping Haiti where that characteristic is lacking—there is often the sense of the American attorney being a savior," Oswald says. "But with Brian, I think he's seasoned enough and humble enough to know that if things are going to change, it's going to have to be in the hands of the Haitians."

Even other Americans with significant experience in Haiti marvel at Concannon's commitment. Dr. Evan Lyon worked in Haiti as a teacher before joining Partners in Health, which has thousands of staff members in the country. As part of PIH, Lyon says, "I was always able to have this fairly quick connection to colleagues and getting things done." He continues:

> I was a cog in a very big machine. Brian has never had that. As I became a doctor, I had a very clear path for how I can work: I connect one-on-one with patients, in a collegial way with doctors and nurses, in a training way with residents and students. Brian has never had that. Not only is he not a Haitian, but the cultural and licensing issues means he is really not able to practice his profession there the way a foreign doctor or nurse can.
>
> So what is most impressive about Brian is his patience and persistence and willingness to accept delayed gratification—or, more accurately, no promise of gratification at all—while pursuing a novel and uncertain path toward reforming a legal system that has never worked for the poor and powerless. And to do so for year after year. I don't think I could do that. I don't think I am made of that. I work hard, and I do plenty, but it takes a unique person to take on the challenge Brian accepts.

As a not-for-profit organization, IJDH is dependent on donations. One of its financial supporters is Karen Ansara of the Ansara Family Fund. Ansara has devoted much of her time to encouraging US groups to support international efforts, and is the founder of a philanthropy consortium called New England International Donors. "IJDH and BAI speak with integrity and authority about the situation in Haiti because they are on the ground in the tent camps and the slums and doing community organizing, yet at the same time advocating at an international level," Ansara says. "The combination is just unbelievably effective. When we visited the BAI offices in Port-au-Prince and heard from one of the women who work with rape survivors—oh my God. It was incredible to hear the stories and know what she sees every day. What can be more convincing than hearing from someone who is living it?"

In an interview, Ansara heaps compliments on everything from IJDH's website to its volunteers to its ability to squeeze every dime out of a shoestring budget. But she saves special praise for the balanced partnership between the Haiti-led and US-led wings of the effort. Before cutting any checks, Ansara studied up on IJDH, and was surprised to learn that Concannon had been a lawyer and working in Haiti at BAI before Joseph joined the effort. Since Concannon seems to be perpetually pushing Joseph into the spotlight, Ansara had just assumed Concannon was the junior partner of the two. Concannon constantly nominates Joseph for human rights awards and recognitions, and steers media inquiries toward Joseph when the language barrier allows. A human rights lawyer tells of calling to invite Concannon to an expenses-paid trip to Paris to address a rights group, and Concannon insisting that Joseph go in his stead. "Who has their ego enough in control to do that?" Ansara asks. She continues:

> But I think Brian can do that because he sees the cause as more important than himself, and he has such respect for Mario—their partnership is really a beautiful thing.
>
> And that in turn gives me such respect for Brian. Despite everything he has seen and lived and committed his life to, he never comes across as self-righteous or shrill. Somehow he maintains a sense of humor and perspective, which of course helps attract people like us to stand with him and Mario in this cause.

In his calls to action for human rights in Haiti, Concannon regularly cites a well-known Haitian proverb: *Men anpil, chay pa lou*—many hands make the load light. Returning to the United States from Haiti recently, I saw some of the hands Concannon would like to enlist in the cause. A large crowd, with a dozen Americans for every Haitian, waited at Toussaint L'Ouverture Airport to board a flight to Miami. Most of the Americans wore cargo pants and baseball caps, along with colorful T-shirts bearing slogans like "Healing Haiti: Northwest Christian Mission" and "Don't Forget Haiti" in English and Creole. An American woman in her thirties speaks to a companion in the security line: "Usually in March, I go on a nice yoga retreat. But this year, I had a calling to make a difference." She is not the only one hearing the call. The Parish Twinning Program of the Americas reports over 340 partnerships between US and Canadian Roman Catholic parishes and "twin" parishes, mostly in Haiti. As in the case of hundreds of other Christian mission programs, the groups provide short-term medical care or assist with safe water, housing, or educational projects in Haiti. The Parish Twinning Program reports that its parishes have sent over $22 million worth of aid to Haiti.[123]

The people of Haiti certainly need this support. Many of these mission efforts focus on remote rural areas where health care and other services are particularly scarce. And the compassion and generosity that animate these efforts is undeniable. Yet it is equally undeniable that Haiti needs a functioning government more than it does a plethora of cabined-off efforts that resemble those already being pursued by thousands of unconnected NGOs on the ground. Concannon went to the Parish

Twinning Program annual conference one year, and was struck by a map of Haiti that included dots representing different projects by the twinning program members. "It was exciting to see how big the program was," Concannon says. "It was also deeply comforting to know that in all the space covered by those dots people were getting some combination of healthcare, education, food, religious education, clean water, etc. But of course, there was lots of space that isn't covered with a dot, where people don't have access to those things. A systemic approach can be seen as filling in the space between the dots, to make sure that everyone's human rights are respected." To a casual observer of Haiti, it seems obvious that no Christian youth group is going to build a countrywide sewage treatment facility. Clearly, no team of doctors and nurses from Nebraska will create a functioning national health-care system.

But Concannon disagrees. He sees the weekly surge of concerned Americans heading to Haiti as an untapped resource for activism to address Haiti's big-picture issues. Concannon is sometimes asked to speak to groups that have sponsored mission trips, and he takes the opportunity to both thank them for their service and urge them to think more broadly:

> These are people who are following what Jesus said: "Whatsoever you do for the least of my brothers . . ." Which is wonderful. But a lot of religious groups kind of take the position of "Give to Caesar what is Caesar's," and they will just do their little part. But a more expansive reading of what Jesus said is that you have to address the underlying social conditions. So my challenge to them is to expand the focus from building schools and hospitals and churches. That is all good, but they are drops in the bucket. These people can use their experiences in Haiti to work on broad systemic changes, too.

Concannon says he has twice seen the evidence of the possibilities inherent in mission-oriented Americans stepping into the advocacy arena. "During the 2004 coup d'état, I was really surprised and disappointed that the media, human rights groups, and development groups failed to step up for the people of Haiti. But two sectors did respond with a real commitment: the National Lawyers Guild [a human rights lawyers group Concannon is active in] and a lot of US Catholic groups who had 'twinning' relationships with Haitian Catholic parishes. These American Catholics were talking to people on the ground and knew what Haitians were saying and feeling."

One of those Catholic groups was the Indiana contingent who successfully lobbied Senator Richard Lugar to press the coup government to release Father Gérard Jean-Juste. The leader of the Indiana coalition was Joe Zelenka. Zelenka began traveling to Haiti in 1990 and founded a twinning relationship between his Indianapolis parish of St. Thomas Aquinas and a small Catholic community in Belle-Rivière, an isolated mountain village in southwest Haiti. The Indiana parish has dug wells in

Belle-Rivière, built a K-12 school where it pays the teacher's salaries and provides school lunches. It has created clean water programs and sent more than a dozen medical missions to the community.[124] Zelenka has served as president of the Parish Twinning Program board and helped raise funds to build Visitation Hospital in Petite-Rivière-de-Nippes.

But Zelenka agrees with Concannon's argument that the relationships between US and Haitian faith communities present an opportunity, and an obligation, to do more:

> Obviously, I think that what the Parish Twinning Program and Visitation Hospital are doing is incredibly important. But will it bring the kind of justice Haiti needs? No. It's just a start. We can send our own money and we can send supplies to our friends in Haiti, but there are still so many people who are homeless or hungry due to underlying issues.
>
> We need to educate ourselves about how the well-being of Haitians continues to be threatened by the US and the rest of the international community, and we need to raise our voices more and more to bring to Haiti the kind of justice they pray for. When folks did just that on behalf of Gerry Jean-Juste, we learned that elected officials like Senator Lugar will listen to us, because we do know a lot about Haiti and the problems there. Americans who go to Haiti care passionately about the people there, and we could have a real impact by bringing the voice of the Haitian people to decision-makers here in the US.

Concannon admits to occasional frustration that even his colleagues in the legal profession often do not envision how they can be a part of the solution in Haiti. Shortly after the earthquake, a group from a Washington, DC-area law school raised an impressive sum of $30,000 to assist Haiti. They decided to give the money to the Red Cross instead of directing it to human rights advocacy. "That would have paid for two years of a Haitian lawyer's salary," Concannon says ruefully. But many other US lawyers and law students have been generous with both time and treasure, and a few have thrown themselves full time into the cause.

One of those lawyers is Meena Jagannath. Jagannath was born in New York City and raised in New Jersey as the younger child of parents who had emigrated from India. Her parents and relatives spoke the southern Indian language of Telugu in the family home, and it became the second of seven languages Jagannath would learn over the years. During one college summer break, Jagannath returned to her parents' home state of Andhra Pradesh to work at a rural development organization, teaching English and researching women's microcredit groups. There, she developed her budding passion for human rights advocacy, nurtured by her parents' examples of how lives can change when poor people are empowered.

"I knew that growing up in the US, I was very distant from the actual reality of life in underdeveloped countries, but until I spent that summer in India, I did not fully appreciate how much of an accomplishment it was for my parents, and my mother in particular, to come from a highly rural, kind of parochial setting to achieve all their success in the US," she says. Jagannath's father is a retired professional mechanical engineer and her mother worked on Wall Street for many years. "They were of rather modest means growing up, and it was amazing that they were able to get their educations and come to the US—especially my mother, who was one of the first women in her village to go to college."

Inspired by her parents' examples, Jagannath volunteered for a variety of international human rights projects while earning her undergraduate degree at Tufts and her master's at Columbia. One of those experiences was in Guatemala, working with Mayan community members who were testifying as witnesses in a genocide trial after their communities were targeted by the country's dictators in the 1980s during the Guatemalan civil war. "The Mayans still don't have much of a voice in Guatemala's politics, but this experience taught me how the law could be used to create a platform for greater political participation for this very marginalized population," Jagannath says. "At the same time, I was excited to discover that I could have a role in the process by being in solidarity with poor persons asserting their rights." Like many advocates, Jagannath stresses the value of human rights campaigns and litigation building off the platform of constitutions, treaties, and statutes. Such campaigns allow long-oppressed people to demand their rights, as opposed to requesting charity or mercy. "Ideally, the law can arm these people with the language they need to assert their own place in the political dialogue and argue for real social change," she says.

Jagannath had just graduated from the University of Washington law school when she heard a presentation by US lawyers who had returned from a fact-finding mission in Haiti. The lawyers described the campaign to stop the epidemic of sexual violence committed against Haitian women in the post-earthquake IDP camps. As it happens, Jagannath had recently picked up a copy of *Mountains beyond Mountains*, and was in the middle of reading Pulitzer Prize–winning author Tracy Kidder's 2003 profile of Paul Farmer's work in Haiti. "It was like an 'Aha' moment, where it became clear to me that Haiti was where I should be," she says now. Jagannath contacted Brian Concannon to volunteer her services to BAI. Soon, she was raising money from family and friends to finance her stay in Haiti, studying to make Haitian Creole her seventh language, and heading to the BAI offices in Port-au-Prince.

There, Jagannath found clear limits on what a young American lawyer can accomplish in a country that is not her own. "I am very aware of the fact that I will not live the consequences of my work, and that it's the Haitian people who will," she says. "So I need to be careful about what my presence is doing in their country. One of the attractive things about BAI is that this is a place where "helping" does not mean you substitute your judgment or your opinions for Haitians.' Instead, you reinforce local capacity and leave it to the folks here in Haiti to do the important work." That philosophy is sometimes easier said than followed, Jagannath learned.

As part of the BAI women's rights advocacy team, Jagannath worked with a Haitian colleague to develop a network of women's grassroots groups advocating for better police and prosecution responses to rape. Eventually, Jagannath realized that both her colleague and some network members were beginning to defer to Jagannath as the leader of the group. "So I decided to take a significant step back and now I am trying to play more of a consultative role," she says. "[My Haitian colleague] is established as the leader now, and that is working much better for everyone."

But Jagannath has also found that US partners on the ground in Haiti can be extremely valuable in providing local advocates and their communities with access to international legal forums and media. From her eyewitness vantage point in Port-au-Prince, Jagannath has drafted reports and contributed to international legal petitions, published several articles in US law journals outlining the human rights challenges in Haiti, and delivered presentations—both live and by Skype from BAI's offices—to audiences in the United States. She says she is privileged to witness the progress in police and court responses to rape victims and her Haitian women colleagues' growing confidence in their ability to make changes in their communities.

Like most BAI and IJDH attorneys who are not from Haiti, Jagannath will return to the United States after a year or two in Port-au-Prince, deliberately leaving the long-term ground-level leadership to Haitians. She says she will continue her human rights career in the US, and take with her the insights gained from working in solidarity with Haitians in their home community. Just as importantly, she will leave with many of her Haitian colleagues and clients a different vision of how Americans can be involved in Haiti. Jagannath would almost certainly reject the term "ambassador," but she and other American lawyers filling similar roles with BAI and IJDH represent the United States in a way that carries significant promise for Haiti-US relations. She says:

People in Haiti do ask, "How is it that you come from a country that has dominated our political situation, and yet you don't have the same view?"

I think that part of our presence here is about letting the people of Haiti know that there are folks in the US who are in solidarity with their struggle, and that we want to help give voice to those who are working to make changes here. There is a lot of criticism to be made about the way the US engages in Haiti, but there are also Americans who are allies with the folks struggling here.

When I compare the experiences that I've had in India and Guatemala and Haiti and all of these places, what strikes me the most is that, empirically, the effects of poverty are similar in all of these settings. The food or the clothes or the language might be different, but people relate to each other in much the same way. I think the struggles of the poor are universal. So it seems to me that it's important to remember that, before we are Americans or Haitians or Indians or whatever we are, we are humans.

8 | Creating Victory for the People

After the visit to Camp Django I described in the opening pages of this book, the group of visiting US lawyers I was with returned to the offices of BAI. By that time, late afternoon was turning into early evening. It was growing dark under the unlit rear shelter where the press conference had taken place earlier that day. We gathered in a circle of folding chairs, along with Mario Joseph and several *finissants*—recent Haitian law school graduates serving an apprenticeship at BAI.

Joseph invited the young *finissants* to introduce themselves to the visitors. In soft-spoken Creole, they shared stories of struggle that mirrored Haiti's recent history. Michel was illegally arrested and held for nine days in prison. Natasha witnessed both her father and brother being shot in the aftermath of the 2004 coup that forced out Jean-Bertrand Aristide. Her family tried in vain to convince the government to pursue justice against the killers. Later, the home of Natasha's family was destroyed in the earthquake. She was living in an IDP camp when she met a BAI attorney and found the opportunity to begin a career advocating for housing rights. Josue tells the group that he left law school to study theology because he did not believe the law could be used to work for justice in Haiti. After he learned about Mario Joseph and BAI, he decided to return to his legal training.

Joseph listens to the stories, and reminds the group that these young Haitian lawyers embody more than the country's problems of poverty and lawlessness. They also represent the opportunity to reclaim the proud legacy of Haiti breaking the chains of enslavement over two hundred years ago. "Haiti is the mother of liberty," Joseph says. "I hope we are now building a new generation of Haitians committed to human rights. Just as we have built a small island of justice here [at BAI] in an ocean of corruption, these attorneys can work together to build an archipelago of justice on this continent."

Their challenge is a considerable one, especially since Haiti's future is inextricably tied to the international community. On one hand, there is a near-global consensus that all humans are entitled to the basic rights BAI and IJDH fight for. Yet thousands of Haitians die of the treatable and preventable disease of cholera, Jean-Claude DuValier walks the streets of Port-au-Prince as a free man, scores of Haitian women were raped with little official response, and millions go without adequate food, water, and shelter. Which leaves the task for Mario Joseph and Brian Concannon to somehow connect the world community's abstract empathy for suffering Haitians into direct and effective action on behalf of their clients and colleagues.

In support of the argument that we all must accept responsibility for alleviating global poverty, the philosopher Peter Singer propounds a famous hypothetical. He asks each member of his audience to imagine a scene where she is wearing her best clothes while walking to an appointment. She passes by a shallow pond where a small child appears to be drowning. It would be very easy to wade into the water and pull the child to safety, although the act would likely soil the rescuer's clothes and make her late for her appointment. Does the passer-by have an obligation to save the child?

Of course, says the audience. Well, Singer replies, don't we have the same obligation to respond to the needs of a struggling child in a foreign land? That child's death from hunger or disease can be prevented by a small donation to a relief effort, he reminds the audience. For most of us, that lifesaving donation poses a similarly minimal inconvenience, such as skipping a movie or dinner out.[1]

Singer concedes that this is a difficult concept for most of us to grasp. Possessing the capacity to save a person halfway across the globe is a very new phenomenon in human history. Before recent advances in transportation and communication, it was usually impossible to get timely information about suffering outside of our immediate surroundings, much less act to provide fast relief. "'Charity begins at home' made sense, because it was only 'at home'—or at least in your town—that you could be confident that your charity would make any difference," Singer writes.[2] But times have changed. Psychologist Steven Pinker, in his 2011 book, *The Better Angels of Our Nature: Why Violence Has Declined*, says that cultural and material development has increased human capacity for sympathy.[3] In her 2007 book, *Inventing Human Rights*, Lynn Hunt argues that the similarly modern notion of universal human rights is a triumph of empathy spreading beyond our immediate clan to others who exist in different social and geographical spheres.[4]

Thanks to several decades of research, we know a bit about how such empathy works. Historians and social scientists have attempted to discover why the majority of ordinary persons, like citizens and soldiers in Nazi Germany, stand by during atrocities while a handful of others are willing to take risks to defy orders and even affirmatively save lives. It turns out that for the minority taking action, the shared characteristic was not some ethical quality or personality trait. The key variable was their personal exposure to injustice.[5]

A study of German soldiers who committed brutal acts in World War II found incidents of soldiers refusing to kill targeted Jews. The resistance occurred when individual victims were observed personally, but virtually no resistance was registered by soldiers herding thousands onto trains for slaughter that would occur out of the soldiers' sight.[6] Psychologist Stanley Milgram's famous experiments in the 1960s at Yale University showed that study subjects who could see the victim of their actions were far less likely to administer what they believed to be withering electric shocks.[7] Three decades later, similar results were obtained by psychologist Joshua Greene, who asked study subjects if they would be willing to divert a trolley on track to kill five people if the diversion would mean that one person would die. Most were willing to take this action. But most of Greene's study subjects also expressed resistance to the notion of pushing a single large man onto the track, again killing one to save five. Proximity to suffering matters, because it spurs feelings of personal responsibility for the other human's well-being.[8]

Joseph and Concannon cite this power of witness in their efforts to encourage delegations, especially lawyers and law students, to travel from the United States to Haiti. While still a law student, Ted Oswald helped organize a still-recurring annual visit to Haiti by Drexel University School of Law students and faculty. He admits to questioning whether his efforts, like those of the many mission-themed visitors to Haiti, represented a wise use of resources. "For the cost of one of our [delegation] trips, you could fund basically a Haitian staff attorney for a year. So you have to look at your goals and motives with some sobriety," Oswald says. "But I'm a fan of these trips, because they radically changed my life and my sense of calling, in that I now want to be a lawyer working for the people of Haiti. I hope the visits have inspired what I would call an integrated life, where your values are matching up with the hardships that you are seeing your Haitian brothers and sisters dealing with."

In essence, Oswald and others return from Haiti with what some may refer to as "a guilty conscience," which ideally can spur them to action. Concannon rejects the notion of guilt being a part of IJDH's recruiting and fundraising process, saying that he and Joseph hope that visits to Haiti provide "a meaningful opportunity [for non-Haitians] to participate, using their privilege, in work that they believe in." But psychologist Robert Lifton, who studied Vietnam War veterans, says that first-hand exposure to suffering can trigger something more obligatory. Lifton identifies that response as the "anxiety of responsibility"—an anxiety that can lead to agitation for change by persons who witness injustice.[9] It is this kind of productive guilt that Singer says should be the comparatively wealthy's default response to global suffering.

For those who never set foot in Haiti, Joseph and Concannon often focus their messages around single clients, even though their organizations' efforts are concentrated on achieving systemic change. A recent IJDH appeal for support on the costs of litigating the cholera claims highlights the story of Nadine, whose father died from cholera. Nadine had to take out loans to retrieve her father's body from a mass grave to provide a proper burial, and Nadine still struggles to repay the debt. Again, social science research supports this strategy. Telling individual stories of suffering and injustice has proven to be the most effective method of inspiring expressions of empathy and acts of support.

For example, Paul Slovic, a psychologist at the University of Oregon, along with colleagues David Vastfjall and Ellen Peters, asked study participants to donate money in response to various appeals to assist in alleviating starvation. When presented with the single case of a seven-year-old girl named Rokia, participants gave more money than they did when presented with statistics portraying the widespread food crisis. Remarkably, the presentation with Rokia alone also out-yielded a presentation with Rokia's same story buttressed by statistical evidence of the breadth of the suffering. A presentation that added a single other child's story to Rokia's also reduced the amount donated.[10] Other studies have shown similar results in favor of the one-on-one connection.[11]

In a paper that derives its title from a statement widely (although apparently erroneously) attributed to Mother Teresa—"If I look at the mass, I will never act. If I look at the one, I will"—Slovic calls the process "psychophysical numbing."[12] He states, "The behavioral theories and data confirm what keen observers of human behavior have long known. Numerical representations of human lives do not necessarily convey the importance of those lives. All too often the numbers represent dry statistics, 'human beings with the tears dried off,' that lack feeling and fail to motivate action."[13] Later, he states, "When it comes to eliciting compassion, the identified individual victim, with a face and a name, has no peer."[14]

To Slovic, this phenomenon is a predictable result of the evolutionary necessity for individuals to focus on protecting their immediate family from the many dangers of primitive life. Yet we are certainly not hardwired to be selfish. Even the legendary economist Adam Smith, who saw such power in the "invisible hand" of self-interest, argued in his book *The Theory of Moral Sentiments* that compassion is as much a part of our nature as egocentricity.[15] But in a global society, there are inevitable limits to our compassion, as essayist Barbara Kingsolver writes:

> Confronted with the knowledge of dozens of apparently random disasters every day, what can a human heart do but slam its doors? No mortal can grieve that much. We didn't evolve to cope with tragedy on global scale. Our defense is to pretend there's no thread of event that connects us, and that those lives are somehow not precious and real like our own. It's a practical strategy, to some ends, but the loss of empathy is also the loss of humanity, and that's no small tradeoff.[16]

The charge for human rights activists, then, is to disturb this self-protecting detachment by visibly connecting the thread from suffering persons to those who can help: hence, the cholera appeal that invokes the plight of Nadine or the press conference that highlights the story of a pregnant woman injured during a camp eviction. As social movement studies have shown, if activists want to move observers from the balcony to the barricades, they have to "frame" injustice around the particular plight of an aggrieved victim.[17]

Haitians see a huge gap between the law on paper, with its promises of justice contained in the Constitution and statutes and international agreements, and the absence of enforceable rights in their daily lives. In confronting this discrepancy, they are not alone. In 2008, the Commission on Legal Empowerment of the Poor, cochaired by economist Hernando de Soto and former US secretary of state Madeleine K. Albright, estimated that four billion people worldwide live outside the protection of the rule of law. That number represents a majority of the world's population—people who have no recourse when they are victimized by assault, have their land or belongings stolen, or are blocked by corrupt officials from accessing the basic necessities of life. For most people on the planet, the shining promise of the Universal Declaration of Human Rights of 1948, and the many international agreements and domestic laws created in its wake, has never been fulfilled. A recent study showed that member states fully complied with orders issued by the Inter-American Court of Human Rights only 5 percent of the time.[18] As Lynn Hunt writes in *Inventing Human Rights*, "The human rights revolution is by definition ongoing."[19]

Gary Haugen, president of the International Justice Mission, and Victor Boutros, a civil rights prosecutor in the US Department of Justice, are among those calling for the human rights movement to shift its attention from creating treaties and laws to enforcing them:

> Suppose that scientists had worked feverishly for two generations to develop and fill warehouses with miracle vaccines that hundreds of millions of vulnerable people desperately needed—but could not access. . . . Similarly, after 60 years of developing and refining human rights law, few of the gains are reaching the people who need them most.
>
> . . . The time has come to move human rights from wholesale to retail—to take the human rights promises stored in the warehouses of national law and deliver them to the poor standing in line for justice.[20]

As academics, development experts, and lawyers before them have concluded, Haugen and Boutros acknowledge that enforceable human rights will occur only when "political will" exists. Certainly, there is no surefire recipe for instantly creating political will. Henry David Thoreau wrote: "Revolutions are never sudden. Not one man, nor many men, in a few years or generations, suffice to regulate events and dispose mankind for the revolutionary moment."[21]

Modern analysts of social movements would agree with Thoreau, but they would also add that there is a tipping point on the question of political will—a time and place and event when energy pent up across generations bursts forth to create lasting reform. Joseph and Concannon and a growing number of supporters believe that the tipping point for Haiti can be the grassroots/transnational movement pushing forward the Haitian cholera claims. The cholera claims could force the world's most influential organization, the UN, to embrace the rule of law in deed as well as in name, and to recognize the poorest of Haitians as individuals with enforceable rights. If successful, the claims could push Haiti toward recovery from all its many natural and unnatural disasters.

Of course, there are skeptics, inside and outside Haiti, as even the cholera victims have discovered. In the summer of 2012, I accompany BAI lawyer Bazelais Thévenot on a drive several kilometers north of the town of St. Marc. As we drive into the countryside toward the Artibonite River, emerald green rice fields surround the road. A rainbow arches over the mountains to the east. The heat had been punishing all day, but as we approach the village of Bocozelle, the temperature starts to cool. Several healthy-looking cows graze on the edges of the fields and a few young people bend over to pull up rice shoots. So much of Haiti is dusty and dry, but these fields are flooded by cool, clear water flowing from a complex series of canals that originate in the Artibonite. The irony, of course, is that this life-giving water turned deadly overnight in October 2010.

We stop at the home of Jacqueline Olonville. A fifty-two-year-old mother of eight, Olonville sells plantains (bananas) and cold drinks out of a battered blue cooler set up by the road that runs through Bocozelle. Olonville was among those who fell ill after drinking from the neighborhood pump that drew from the Artibonite. Her affliction followed cholera's frightening, filthy pattern—severe stomach pain followed by uncontrollable diarrhea and vomiting—but she reached the hospital in time. I ask her if she knew any of those in her community who did not survive the *kolera*, and she nods vigorously. "*Wi. Anpil.*" (Yes. Many.) Especially children and old people, she says.

When Olonville heard that the UN was likely responsible for the devastation all around her, she felt an obligation to take action. She told Thévenot to add her name to the claims filed by BAI. She traveled to the demonstrations against MINUSTAH not only in nearby St. Marc, but also in faraway Mirebalais. Olonville even agreed to speak at the demonstrations on behalf of other victims. "MINUSTAH came here and killed our families and God's children, so I want them to leave and give us back our country," she told the crowd.

Olonville has never taken a stand like this before. She confesses to having doubts about whether she is doing the right thing. As she stands on her porch, she gestures toward the homes of her neighbors, many of whom have mocked her efforts. The neighbors are angry at the UN and frightened of *kolera*, too, she says, but they cite

Haiti's long history of impunity for the powerful. "They say this is a lost cause, and we are wasting our time," Olonville says. "But we are hoping this is not all for nothing and something can come from all this." What would that "something" be, I ask. "*Jistis ak reparasyon!*" she replies—justice and reparation.[22]

The cholera claims face such significant barriers, and also carry so much potential, in part because of the sheer scope of the harm caused. When a reckless act triggers an epidemic that sickens a half-million people and kills more than twice as many people as the 9/11 attacks, proper *reparasyon* is not going to be cheap. Few human rights claims can match the financial magnitude of the requested remedy, likely to total over $30 billion. Historically, the closest analogs have been the claims against Swiss banks for retaining and concealing assets of Holocaust victims and profiting from slave labor (a $1.25 billion payout), the $470 million that Union Carbide was ordered to pay to victims of the 1984 leak of poisonous gas from the Bhopal, India pesticide plant, and claims for reparation for African American slavery (which have met with little legal success to date).[23]

One oft-mentioned potential remedy, the UN assuming the responsibility for creating the desperately needed water and sewage system in Haiti, is remarkably broad. But it also is well tailored to address the problems that led to the tragic epidemic. "Cholera is really a 19th century problem. It's not a modern medical problem," says Dr. Evan Lyon of Partners in Health. Lyon, who has worked in Haiti since 1996, provides one of the most eloquent voices calling for a systemic response to the epidemic. "Medicine can save lives, but to stop the epidemic, there needs to be better infrastructure and better capacity to provide safe clean water to people, and, of course, sanitation."[24]

The cost for building such a system in Haiti is estimated to be about $800 million.[25] It is a huge sum, but it is also not far from the amount the UN spends each year on peacekeeping in Haiti. "I'm not a soldier or a politician," Lyon says. "But without the need for military in Haiti, it seems to me the UN could and should instead invest that money into water systems and get right at the root of the problem."[26]

For advocates, there is a clear benefit to framing the ideal cholera remedy as a fix for the problem that made the UN's negligence so deadly in impact. "The demand that the UN pay for the [water and sewage] infrastructure is a masterstroke," the Haiti Support Group reported in its April 2012 newsletter. "Turning the spotlight on what the UN itself claims, in seeking to deflect blame, is the real cause of the epidemic: lack of access to clean water and the most basic sanitation."[27]

Those water and sanitation problems caused real harm to Haitians well before the cholera outbreak. Haiti has no municipal sewage system and most people live without access to any kind of treated water. A 2002 survey of 147 countries across the world for a Water Poverty Index ranked Haiti dead last.[28] A 2007 study of the water supply in the northern Haiti city of Port-de-Paix showed that most of the water samples taken across the city were bacterially contaminated. Families were living on a fraction of the water suggested for good health, yet still spent 12 percent of their income on water.[29] (By comparison, most US households pay less than 1 percent of income for water and sewage services.) Unsurprisingly, waterborne diseases take the lives of thousands of Haitian children each year. "If we could, as a world community, invest in water and sanitation [in Haiti], we could change the primary dynamic of this epidemic," Lyon says in *Fight the Outbreak*. "There would be side benefits for generations, literally." IJDH estimates that a clean water and sanitation infrastructure would save forty thousand lives in the first decade of its operation.

One of the supporters of the cholera claim is Ruth Wedgwood, a professor of international law and diplomacy at the Paul H. Nitze School of Advanced International Studies at Johns Hopkins. She was formerly a US member of the UN Human Rights Committee, and is still a member of the US State Department's Advisory Committee on International Law. Wedgwood is a firmly entrenched member of the foreign policy establishment, but she does not see the cholera claims as radical:

> I am pretty conservative—even politically incorrect on a number of issues. I am no bleeding heart. But this situation scandalizes me. The major problem is that the claims are for so much money, which is what is causing the UN's paralysis. But what is really needed going forward in Haiti is a new water system, and building that is clearly the right thing to do. If the UN says they don't have the money, that is wrong: they spend $800 million a year in Haiti on peacekeeping. They can reprogram part of it to build a clean water system and pay for prophylaxis supplies to carry the country over while you build the water system.

Wedgwood references the recent mea culpas issued by the UN in the wake of its failure to prevent killings in Rwanda in 1994 and Srebenica in Bosnia and Herzegovina in 1995. "The UN always writes these great reports after the fact, saying we'll do it better next time. It is next time now. All the lamentations from Srebenica, from Rwanda, don't mean anything if there is a new situation with similar mortality that can be fixed."

Another law professor and international human rights expert, NYU Law's Margaret Satterthwaite, agrees with Wedgwood. "Human rights are only going to be successful to the extent that powerful actors themselves recognize them, so it is absolutely necessary that you have to have this institutional acknowledgment," says Satterthwaite, who serves as a consultant to the UN special rapporteur on the human rights to water and sanitation. She continues:

> I really think this case presents a historic moment where the human rights movement has to decide if we are going to hold ourselves to account on the same principles we are applying all over the world.
>
> Human rights law is asking states to limit themselves, it is asking the UN to limit itself, it is asking corporations to limit themselves. If you want to see some

kind of moral leadership, it has to come from the UN. If you have an institution like the UN saying we accept responsibility, we accept that we should be held to the same standards that we ask states to hold themselves to, I think that will be very, very strong precedent. Accountability—acknowledging our mistakes and making it right—is the cornerstone of human rights.

I first spoke with Satterthwaite and Wedgwood in mid-2012, shortly after Wedgwood participated in a Capitol Hill briefing on cholera in Haiti, this one featuring a screening of *Baseball in the Time of Cholera*. "Congress has a role to play here," she said. "The US pays over 25 percent of the UN peacekeeping expenses, and some of the changes we wanted to see in the UN have come about in direct connection to the timing and amount of dues we provide. Or we could give the UN supplementary funding to help with this purpose, which I would support." Wedgwood was encouraged by a recent letter signed by 104 members of Congress urging the UN to take responsibility and action to halt the damage from cholera in Haiti. She thinks the documentary, the media outreach, and the public forums on the crisis are the path to success. "It is like the old LBJ advice [to civil rights activists]: 'If you want the Voting Rights Act, you better make me do it.' You have to create your own political weather."

By December 2012, the congressional petition and the screenings of *Baseball in the Time of Cholera* had been joined by an online petition launched by filmmaker Oliver Stone, demanding UN accountability for cholera in Haiti and garnering twenty-five thousand signatures in its first month.[30] That same month, UN secretary-general Ban Ki-moon restated the outlines of the $2.2 billion initiative to address the cholera epidemic in Haiti. The plan included a variety of measures, most notably the building of desperately-needed water and sanitation infrastructure that cholera victims and their advocates had been calling for. The UN and the international community initially committed to pay only a fraction of the estimated cost of the program.[31] (When asked at the launch who should fund the plan, Médecins Sans Frontières communication officer Yann Libessart was direct: "The people who are responsible for the introduction of the disease into the country.")[32]

Ban and other UN officials still steered away from accepting blame for the cholera epidemic, much less compensating its victims. But the December 2012 announcement did suggest that the UN was feeling the pressure of a full-blown global human rights campaign. Further evidence of the campaign's impact was provided shortly before the cholera class action lawsuit was filed in October of 2013. Navanethem Pillay, the UN high commissioner for human rights, spoke at the same ceremony in Geneva where Mario Joseph was recognized as a finalist for the Martin Ennals Award for Human Rights Defenders. Joseph had used his remarks to issue a strong call for human rights advocates to push the UN to accept responsibility for the suffering cholera has caused in Haiti. Apparently in response to Joseph's speech, Pillay departed from her own prepared remarks to say, "I have used my voice both inside the United Nations and outside to call for the right—for an investigation by the United Nations, by the country concerned, and I still stand by the call that victims of—of those who suffered as a result of that cholera be provided with compensation."[33] It was the first instance of a UN official admitting the need for compensation for Haitian cholera victims, and within hours, news reports about Pillay's statement were crossing the globe. After the lawsuit was filed a few days later, Stephen Lewis, former deputy executive director of UNICEF and Canadian ambassador to the UN, told an interviewer he supported the lawsuit. "I do," Lewis said. "I think it is unequivocal, the responsibility of the United Nations for the cholera outbreak."[34] The UN continued to resist the demands in court, but advocates for cholera victims were heartened by these responses. As the Creole proverb says, *Piti zwazo fè nich li*—little by little, the bird builds her nest.

On a July weekday in 2012, as an unrelenting sun beats down on the streets of downtown Port-au-Prince, sweat pours off three dozen men and a handful of women who sing, dance, and wave homemade signs as they block the entrance to the government social affairs ministry.

This is the latest in a series of demonstrations by the grassroots organization MOLEGHAF (Movement for Liberty and Equality by Haitians for Fraternity), calling on the government to create jobs and increase social support. Some of the signs read, MOLEGHAF *Di Fók Nou Travay*—MOLEGHAF Says We Must Have Work. Most of the protest songs are directed to Haiti's president, Michel Martelly: "Martelly has left us behind!" a young man shouts through a megaphone. Another demonstrator tries to walk through the gates of the ministry, holding an empty bowl and spoon and miming the need to have something to eat.

A police truck filled with five rifle-toting members of the Haitian National Police tries to pass directly through the group. The protesters stop and surround the truck, banging pots and pans within inches of the pointed rifles. It is a tense moment, all the more so because MOLEGHAF members know well the risk they are taking.

It was at a similar demonstration a few weeks ago when Haitian police arrested one of the group's leaders, longtime activist David Oxygene. Days later, four more MOLEGHAF members were arrested in their homes. Two others were arrested at a subsequent protest. Although the charges against the activists were vague, Oxygene remained incarcerated in the National Penitentiary for several weeks. He was transferred to a section of the prison called "Titanic," notorious for its hard-core inmate population and lack of beds and toilet facilities. His court appearances were cancelled.

Until recently, Haiti's inglorious history of its country's leaders imprisoning their political opponents had seemed to be receding into the past. Martelly's predecessor, René Préval, was widely criticized for his administration's response to the January 12, 2010, earthquake, but Préval was also credited with ending politically motivated violence and arrests. Since taking office in 2011, though, Martelly has showed signs of being intolerant of dissent and eager to consolidate power. Martelly has threatened to use force against those who spoke ill of the country, including the press, and members of his staff had roughed up some journalists and destroyed some of their equipment.[35] As of January 2014, Martelly has refused to hold elections to replace the one-third of Haitian senators whose terms have expired, and the president has personally selected 129 of Haiti's 140 mayors. When UN human rights monitor Michel Forst resigned his post in March 2013, he published an open letter and delivered a speech to the UN Human Rights Council, expressing his disappointment over the Martelly government's record of arbitrary and illegal arrests, interference in the justice system, and threats of critical journalists. "I cannot hide from you my concern and my disappointment in the face of how the situation has developed in the fields of the state of law and human rights," Forst said.[36] Bloomberg News echoed those concerns in April 2013 in an editorial: "The drift is toward authoritarianism, of which Haiti has already suffered plenty."[37]

Later in the year, more disturbing events occurred. A Haitian lawyer who had filed a corruption charge against members of President Martelly's family was arrested by government authorities, reportedly for refusing to allow police to search his car.[38] Another lawyer, who was representing the family of a young man who died in police custody, was served with a criminal summons after being threatened by men who came to his office and said, "The people before you were strong and they are now dead. If you don't stop what you are doing, you will have the same."[39] In July 2013, the fifty-eight-year-old judge who was investigating the corruption charges against the Martelly family died suddenly under mysterious circumstances, prompting BAI and IJDH and other advocates to demand an investigation into the judge's death.[40]

Perhaps most worrisome for Haitians looking to put their country's legacy of political repression behind them is Martelly's open embrace of former dictator Jean-Claude Duvalier. (See Chapter 2.) Martelly recruited Duvalier's son and former Duvalier officials to join his administration, and Martelly has argued that Duvalier should receive amnesty for decades of human rights violations, including arresting, torturing, and killing political opponents in the notorious three-prison "Triangle of Death." The comparison is not lost on Mario Joseph, who serves as David Oxygene's attorney. "Oxygene is simply a political prisoner," Joseph said at after Oxygene's arrest. "This is how Duvalier started, too."

Back at the demonstration, the MOLEGHAF members grudgingly allow the police truck to pass. For today, the rifles remain quiet, and no arrests are made. But the activists say that they will not be silenced. Some of their signs include calls for freedom for Oxygene and their other colleagues. The oldest demonstrator is Descuill St. Cyr. "What am I doing here, a fifty-eight-year-old man standing in the road?" he asks. "But I have not had work since 2008, and Martelly needs to be aware of the problems of the poor."

The demonstrators prepare to put away their signs and noisemakers for the day, but close with one last song in Creole. "Martelly, we are asking for work, we are asking for food, and you give us prison," they sing.

Two months later, Mario Joseph finally secures Oxygene's release from prison. The weekly demonstrations continued.

––––––––––

The film *Baseball in the Time of Cholera*, discussed in Chapter 1, was directed by David Darg and Bryn Mooser, who worked in collaboration with Joseph and Concannon, especially in the film's release and promotion. The film represents a best-practices model of persuasion, using the tragic story of Joseph Alvyns's family to illustrate the impact of a countrywide epidemic. As of January 2014, the UN was still denying responsibility for the cholera outbreak, and the case is likely headed for years of litigation. *Baseball in the Time of Cholera* was being shown at film festivals and on college campuses across the country, often accompanied by Concannon or other IJDH representatives issuing calls to action. Joseph Alvyns's family is one of the BAI and IJDH's clients in the cholera case against the UN, and the film closes with Mario Joseph delivering a stirring speech.[41] Joseph is much more comfortable speaking in Creole or French than in English, but his words in the film were in English, and they were strong and clear:

> We will fight for the rights of poor people; fight to change
>   this unjust system.
> I am not afraid. We say in Haiti, *Viktwa se pou pep la*—
>   the victory is for the people. We believe in that.
> All the time, the people of Haiti have the victory. We got the
>   victory in 1803 against the big Napoleonic army from France.
>   We defeated a lot of dictatorships like Duvalier.
> I think the victory is on our side, but we need to keep going
>   and make the struggle and make the fight.
> I'm really confident we'll win this process, not only for Haiti
>   but for the other poor countries.
> It is a fight of the world.

Acknowledgments

Obviously, this book would not exist but for Brian Concannon and Mario Joseph, along with their many brave and dedicated colleagues, Haitian and non-Haitian. Brian and Mario are living examples of compassion and tenacity, and they have inspired me, as they have many others. They also endured my countless questions and many hours of general hanging around that provided the fodder for this book.

Dan Beeton of the Center for Economic Policy and Research, my friends and Indiana University colleagues Florence Roisman and Bob White, Haiti scholar, activist, and teacher Mark Schuller, and the widely admired labor writer and activist Steve Early all gave generously of their time and talents, which are in great demand for all of them. Each provided detailed and enormously helpful comments and suggestions for the book in its draft stages.

Many others expressed their solidarity for the struggle of the people of Haiti by helping in the preparation of this book. Their kindness was expressed in a variety of ways, including reading drafts, guiding me to the "real" stories and issues in Haiti, connecting me to interested audiences, assisting with research and manuscript preparation, or simply offering the support and encouragement every author of a work in progress needs. Those wonderful people include Bill Quigley, Meena Jagannath, Vladimir Laguerre, Nicole Phillips, Don Miller, Joe Zelenka, Karen Ansara, Tracy Kidder, Adam Hochschild, Mike Kinsley, John White, Bobbie Bishop, Frances Dingley Quigley, Dan Carpenter, Gerard Magliocca, Lara Langeneckert, Brigitte Collier, Pooja Bhatia, John Woodcock, the Hon. Patricia Riley, Marjorie Cohn, Eli Bortz, Yasmina Bersbach, Susan deMaine, Bob Healey, and John Hill. The anonymous reviewers for Vanderbilt University Press, along with the Press's copy editor and staff, offered helpful suggestions that led to a better book.

The interviewees and the authors of text sources mentioned in the book, and many others not mentioned, taught me what justice in Haiti is. More importantly, they showed me what it can be. My colleagues and students at the Indiana University Robert H. McKinney School of Law provided encouragement throughout the process, and a John S. Grimes Fellowship provided me very welcome support for the writing of the book.

Special acknowledgment goes to the most special people in my life. This book is dedicated to Ellen White Quigley, who is my role model for all that is kindness and patience and generosity of spirit. And to Sam, Katie, and Jack Quigley, thank you for bringing me more joy and pride than you could ever imagine. I must have been a damn good person in a past life to deserve all the happiness these four have brought to my current one.

Notes

INTRODUCTION

1. Where not otherwise indicated, the quoted material in this book comes from personal conversations and interviews I conducted between 2011 and 2013, and from gatherings and meetings I personally attended during that period.
2. An earlier version of this section was published as Fran Quigley, "Aftershocks: A Report from Haiti," *Commonweal*, March 27, 2012, *www.commonwealmagazine.org*.
3. The survey of IDP camp conditions after the earthquake was conducted by Mark Schuller and colleagues, and reported in "Unstable Foundations: NGOs and Human Rights for Port-au-Prince's Internally Displaced People," in *Tectonic Shifts: Haiti since the Earthquake*, edited by Mark Schuller and Pablo Morales (Boulder, CO: Kumarian Press, 2012), 119–24.
4. For a discussion of the construction practices in Haiti before the earthquake, see Yves Anglandes et al. [members of the Earthquake Engineering Research Institute Reconnaissance Team], "Performance of Buildings in the Haiti Earthquake," *Building Safety Journal Online*, April 2010, *bsj.iccsafe.org*.
5. For an accounting of the dollars pledged and received by Haiti after the earthquake, see UN Office of the Special Envoy to Haiti, *2010–2012 Overall Contributions from Public Sector Donors to Relief and Recovery Efforts in Haiti as of March 2012, in* USD *Millions* (New York: United Nations, 2012); UN Office of the Special Envoy to Haiti, *Analysis Shows 52.3 Percent Disbursement Rate for Haiti Recovery among Public Sector Donors* (New York: United Nations, 2012); and *Haiti: Relief and Reconstruction Watch*, a blog maintained by the Center for Economic and Policy Research at *www.cepr.net*.
6. That 465,996 Haitians were living in "red" buildings was reported in Timothy T. Schwartz with Yves-François Pierre and Eric Calpas, *Barr Survey Final Report* (Washington, DC: USAID, 2011).
7. The survey was reported in Global Justice Clinic/Center for Human Rights and Global Justice, *Yon Je Louvri: Reducing Vulnerability to Sexual Violence in Haiti's* IDP *Camps* (New York: NYU School of Law, 2012), xviii.

CHAPTER 1

1. World Health Organization, "Cholera," Fact Sheet 107, July 2012, *www.who.int*.
2. An earlier version of this section was published as Fran Quigley, "Haitian Cholera Victims to UN: Practice What You Preach," *Truthout*, February 7, 2012, *www.truth-out.org*.
3. Scientific descriptions of the Haitian cholera outbreak are provided in R. Piarroux et al., "Understanding the Cholera Epidemic, Haiti," *Lancet Infectious Diseases*, July 2011, 1161–68; and S. F. Dowell and C. R. Braden, "Implications of the Introduction of Cholera to Haiti," *Lancet Infectious Diseases*, July 2011, 1299–1300.

4. A narrative account of the cholera outbreak in October 2010 in Haiti is contained in Alejandro Craviato et al., *Final Report of the Independent Panel of Experts on the Cholera Outbreak in Haiti* (New York: United Nations, 2011), *www.un.org*.

5. David Darg, "Haiti Cholera Hospital Is a Horror Scene," *AlertNet*, Thomson Reuters Foundation, October 22, 2010, *www.trust.org*.

6. Paul Farmer, *Haiti after the Earthquake* (New York: Public Affairs, 2011), 192.

7. "Cholera in Haiti," *Centers for Disease Control* (October 31, 2013), *wwwn.cdc.gov*.

8. Farmer, *Haiti after the Earthquake*, 3.

9. Cate Oswald, in *Baseball in the Time of Cholera*, directed by David Darg and Bryn Mooser, executive produced by Olivia Wilde and Elon Musk, 2012; available at *www.undeny.org*.

10. For an account of Haiti's efforts to secure the IADB loan and the United States' resistance to the loan's disbursement, see Center for Human Rights and Global Justice (CHRGJ), Partners in Health (PIH), Robert F. Kennedy Memorial Center for Human Rights (RFK Center), and Zanmi Lasante (ZL), *Wòch nan Soley: The Denial of the Right to Water in Haiti* (New York: CHRGJ; Boston: PIH; Washington, DC: RFK Center; Port-au-Prince: ZL, 2008), 10–14, *chrgj.org*, and Paul Farmer, Mary Smith Fawzi, and Patrice Nevil, "Unjust Embargo of Aid for Haiti," 361 *Lancet* 420 (2003).

11. For discussions about cholera becoming endemic in Haiti, see Associated Press, "New Study Shows Cholera Has Evolved," *Fox News*, May 3, 2012, *www.foxnews.com*; and Trenton Daniel, "AP Interview: Expert Says Haiti Has Worst Cholera," *Washington Times*, October 18, 2011, *www.washingtontimes.com*.

12. Mayor Laguerre's accusations against the UN were reported in Mark Doyle, "Haiti's Cholera Row with UN Rumbles On," BBC *News*, December 14, 2011, *www.bbc.co.uk*. (Ironically, Doyle and BBC producer Piers Scholfield received an award for their cholera reporting from the UN Correspondents Association at a December 2012 ceremony presided over by UN secretary-general Ban Ki-moon. See Center for Economic and Policy Research, "UN Gives Journalism Prize to Investigation Exposing UN Responsibility for Cholera—And Still Won't Accept Responsibility," *Haiti: Relief and Reconstruction Watch* [blog], December 19, 2012, *www.cepr.net*.)

13. Jonathan Katz's original account was reported in Associated Press, "UN Testing Base as Source of Cholera Outbreak in Haiti" *Boston Globe*, October 28, 2010, *www.boston.com*. Katz's blog statements were reported in "Truth out, Dying Season in," 70 *Haiti Support Group Briefing* 1–2 (April 2012); available at *www.ijdh.org*. His observations were also reported in Tom Murphy, "Catching Up on Cholera in Haiti," *Humanosphere*, August 16, 2012, *humanosphere.org*, and in Jonathan M. Katz, "In the Time of Cholera: How the UN Created an Epidemic—Then Covered It Up," *Foreign Policy*, January 10, 2013. See also "UN Troops Blamed for Haiti Cholera," *Al Jazeera*, October 30, 2010, *www.aljazeera.com*.

14. Details of the Nepalese troops' exposure to cholera and arrival in Haiti are contained in Bureau des Avocats Internationaux (BAI) and Institute for Justice and Democracy in Haiti (IJDH), "Petition for Relief," November 3, 2011, *www.ijdh.org*.

15. Details of MINUSTAH's history and presence in Haiti can be found at "MINUSTAH Facts and Figures," United Nations website, accessed December 15, 2013, *www.un.org*.

16. Doctors Without Borders, "New Wave of Violence Hits Port-au-Prince, Haiti," news release, August 11, 2006, *www.doctorswithoutborders.org*.

17. For accounts of MINUSTAH's shootings in Cité Soleil in 2005, see Haiti Information Project, "US Embassy in Haiti Acknowledges Excessive Force by UN," *HaitiAction.net*,

January 24, 2007, and Aina Hunter, "U.N. to Investigate Alleged Haiti Massacre," *Village Voice*, August 2, 2005.

18. Mark Schuller, "Is It Time for MINUSTAH to Leave? Popular Perceptions of the UN Stabilization Mission in Port-au-Prince, Haiti," report of an August 2011 survey conducted by a team from the Faculté d'Ethnologie, l'Université d'État d'Haïti, February 14, 2012; available at *www.ijdh.org*.

19. René Préval, quoted in Dan Coughlin, "WikiLeaked US Cables Paint Portrait of Brutal, Ineffectual and Polluting UN Force," *Haïti Liberté*, September 27, 2011, *www.haiti-liberte.com*.

20. Michel Martelly, quoted in "Haiti President Asks That UN Help Rebuild Country with Peacekeeping Funds," *Washington Post*, March 22, 2013.

21. Kim Ives and Ansel Herz, "WikiLeaks Haiti: The Aristide Files," *Nation*, August 5, 2011.

22. Mark Weisbrot, "Is This MINUSTAH's 'Abu Ghraib' Moment in Haiti?" *Guardian*, September 3, 2011, *www.theguardian.com*.

23. HealthRoots, "MINUSTAH: Keeping the Peace, or Conspiring against It? A Review of the Human Rights Record of the United Nations Stabilization Mission in Haiti, 2010–2011," white paper, HealthRoots Student Organization, Harvard School of Public Health, October 2011.

24. Weisbrot, "Is This MINUSTAH's." For other accounts of the sexual misconduct scandals involving MINUSTAH, see US Department of State, "2011 Human Rights Reports: Haiti," May 24, 2012, *www.state.gov*; "Sri Lanka to Probe UN Sex Claims," BBC *News*, November 3, 2007, *news.bbc.co.uk*; and Joseph Guyler Delva, "Pakistani Peacekeepers Sentenced in Haiti Rape Case," Reuters, March 12, 2012, *www.reuters.com*.

25. For an accounting of UN peacekeeper sex scandals globally, see Neil MacFarquhar, "Peacekeepers' Sex Scandals Linger, On Screen and Off," *New York Times*, September 7, 2011, and Colum Lynch, "U.N. Faces More Accusations of Sexual Misconduct," *Washington Post*, March 13, 2005.

26. Marek Nowicki, quoted in Nicolas Lemay-Hébert, "State-Building from the Outside-In: UNMIK and Its Paradox," 20 *Journal of Public and International Affairs* 76 (2009).

27. For an account of the anti-UN protests after the cholera outbreak, see Ansel Herz, "Anger Erupts at U.N. in Haiti as Cholera Toll Nears 1,000," Inter Press Service, November 16, 2010, *www.ipsnews.net*.

28. Evan Lyon, in *Fight the Outbreak: Cholera in Haiti and the United Nations*, produced by the New Media Advocacy Project for IJDH, 2012, *vimeo.com/36517487*.

29. Brian Concannon Jr., in "Exclusive: 5,000 Haitian Cholera Victims Sue U.N. after Deadly Epidemic Kills 6,000, Sickens 450,000," interview by Amy Goodman, *Democracy Now!*, November 8, 2011, *www.democracynow.org*. In August 2013, UN secretary-general Ban Ki-moon recommended a 15 percent reduction in the number of UN troops in Haiti and an examination of the advisability of keeping peacekeepers in the nation. Edith M. Lederer, "UN Chief Proposes Reduction in Force in Haiti," Associated Press, August 20, 2013, *bigstory.ap.org*.

30. Centers for Disease Control and Prevention, "Laboratory Test Results of Cholera Outbreak Strain in Haiti Announced," press release, November 1, 2010, *www.cdc.gov*; and Jonathan M. Katz and Malcolm Ritter, "Study: Haiti Cholera Traced to South Asian Origin," *Boston Haitian Reporter*, December 11, 2010, *www.bostonhaitian.com*.

31. Brigadier General Dr. Kishore Rana's statements were made to BBC News and reported in "Haiti Cholera Outbreak: Nepal Troops Not Tested," BBC *News*, December 8, 2010, *www.bbc.co.uk*.

32. Piarroux et al., "Understanding the Cholera Epidemic." In August 2013, members of the Transnational Development Clinic (part of the Jerome N. Frank Legal Services Organization at Yale Law School), the Global Health Justice Partnership (an initiative of Yale Law School and Yale School of Public Health), and Association Haïtienne de Droit de L'Environnment issued a comprehensive report analyzing both the epidemiological evidence and the legal responsibilities connected to the introduction of cholera to Haiti. The report concluded that "by causing the epidemic and then refusing to provide redress to those affected, the U.N. has breached its commitments to the Government of Haiti, its obligations under international law, and principles of humanitarian relief." Transnational Development Clinic, Global Health Justice Partnership, and Association Haïtienne de Droit de L'Environnment, *Peacekeeping without Accountability: The United Nations' Responsibility for the Haitian Cholera Epidemic* (New Haven, CT: Yale Law School, 2013), 1, *www.law.yale.edu*.

33. Alejandro Craviato et al., *Final Report of the Independent Panel of Experts on the Cholera Outbreak in Haiti* (New York: United Nations, 2011), *www.un.org*.

34. Ibid. One member of the panel, US cholera specialist Dr. Daniele Lantagne, later said new evidence caused her to reconsider the panel's conclusion. "The most likely source of the introduction of cholera into Haiti was someone infected with the Nepal strain of cholera and associated with the United Nations Mirabalais camp," Dr. Lantagne said in October 2012. See Mark Doyle, "Haiti Cholera Epidemic 'Most Likely' Started at UN Camp—Top Scientist," BBC *News*, October 22, 2012, *www.bbc.co.uk*.

35. Quoted in Doyle, "Haiti Cholera Row."

36. Nesirsky's response was reported in Jonathan M. Katz, "Haiti Cholera Likely from U.N., Expert Says," *Washington Times*, December 7, 2010, *www.washingtontimes.com*.

37. Anthony Banbury, quoted in Matthew Mosk, Brian Ross, and Rym Momtaz, "Scientists: UN Soldiers Brought Deadly Superbug to Americas," ABC *News*, January 12, 2012, *abcnews.go.com*.

38. Doyle, "Haiti Cholera Row."

39. Mario Joseph's statements are from an interview conducted by the New Media Advocacy Project in 2012; the unpublished transcript is on file with the author. Long after its October 2010 introduction to Haiti, cholera continues to sicken Haitians and claim lives. The organization Just Foreign Policy has created a "Haiti Cholera Counter," which tracks the latest data at *www.justforeignpolicy.org* (accessed November 16, 2013).

40. Ezili Dantò, "Bill Clinton Admits UN Brought Cholera, Haiti Raped Again," Open Salon blog entry, March 14, 2012, *open.salon.com/blog/ezili_danto*.

41. Ezili Dantò, "Washington Post Cholera Editorial Wants More Haiti Monies: What Happened to $6 Billion?" *Op Ed News*, May 31, 2012, *www.opednews.com*.

42. Concannon's comments are included in the video of the briefing: O'Neill Institute for National and Global Health Law (Georgetown Law Center) and Center for Economic and Policy Research (CEPR), co-sponsors, *Cholera and the Human Right to Health in Post-Earthquake Haiti*, US congressional briefing, April 18, 2012; uploaded to YouTube by CEPR as "Haiti Cholera Hill Briefing," *www.youtube.com/watch?v=naMTR4N8cn0*.

43. "Gross institutional failures": BAI and IJDH, "Petition for Relief," section 1.

44. Ibid., section 57.

45. Ibid., section 93.

46. Ibid., section 6.

47. The terms of the status of forces agreement are discussed in BAI and IJDH, "Petition for Relief"; and in Bri Kouri Nouvèl Gaye et al., "Haiti's Renewal of MINUSTAH's Mandate in Violation of the Human Rights of the Haitian People," Republic of Haiti submission to the UN Universal Periodic Review, Twelfth Working Session of the Working Group on the UPR Human Rights Council, October 3–13, 2011, 2–3 (available at *www.globalpolicy.org*).

48. The UN's failure to create claims commissions was reported in Charanya Krishnaswami and Muneer I. Ahmad, "U.N. Hypocrisy in Haiti," *Washington Post*, March 22, 2013.

49. See World Health Organization, "Revised UN Humanitarian Appeal—Global Health Cluster Plan," February 18, 2010, *www.who.int*, citing the need for careful solid waste disposal because of "structural damage to the already weak water, sanitation and electricity systems," and Centers for Disease Control, "Acute Watery Diarrhea and Cholera: Haiti Pre-decision Brief for Public Health Action," Centers for Disease Control, March 2, 2010, *emergency.cdc .gov*. The CDC report, not anticipating the possibility of introduction of cholera into Haiti from foreign sources, said that the absence of cholera in Haiti made the risk of an outbreak low, but, if it was introduced, "the current water, sanitation, and hygiene infrastructure in Haiti would certainly facilitate transmission of cholera (and many other illnesses)."

50. Deborah Sontag, "In Haiti, Global Failures on a Cholera Epidemic," *New York Times*, March 31, 2012.

51. *Mothers of Srebrenica v. the State of the Netherlands and the United Nations*, Case 200.022.151/01, Appeal Court in the Hague (2010); an unofficial translation of the judgment, provided by the court, is available at *www.haguejusticeportal.net*. The Convention on Privileges and Immunities of the United Nations can be viewed at *www.un.org*.

52. Nicolas LeMay-Hebert, e-mail to Fran Quigley, December 13, 2011.

53. J. P. Shuster, with Ana Ayala, "A Call for U.N. Accountability for Cholera in Post-Earthquake Haiti Part II: The Challenge of U.N. Immunity," O'Neill Institute for National and Global Health Law blog, January 13, 2012, *www.oneillinstituteblog.org*.

54. Ban Ki-moon, "Statement Attributable to the Spokesperson for the Secretary-General on Haiti," February 21, 2013, *www.un.org/sg/statements/?nid=6615*.

55. Brian Concannon Jr., "UN Putting Itself above Own Laws, Principles in Haiti Case," *Boston Globe*, March 5, 2013.

56. "Double Standards: The UN Condemns Baby Doc, Exonerates Itself," *Economist*, March 2, 2013.

57. P. J. Patterson, quoted in Rickey Singh, "Patterson Blasts UN for 'Anti-Haiti' Cholera Stand," *Jamaican Observer*, March 13, 2013.

58. Louise C. Ivers, "A Chance to Right a Wrong in Haiti," *New York Times*, February 22, 2013.

59. Kolektif Mobililizasyon Pou Dedomaje Viktim Kolera Yo, quoted in "Immune. Immoral. Illegal?" 74 *Haiti Support Group Briefing*, 1–4 (June 2013); the article is available under the title "UN Special Envoy on Cholera: 'Silence is the Worst Response'" at *www .haitisupportgroup.org*.

60. A copy of the complaint in *Georges et al. v. United Nations et al.* is available at *www.ijdh.org/ wp-content/uploads/2013/10/Cholera-Complaint.pdf*.

61. The *Times* article was Sontag, "In Haiti, Global Failures on a Cholera Epidemic," March 31, 2012.

62. The statement of the Pakistani and French representatives to the UN Security Council was reported in UN Security Council, "Haiti Mission Head Tells Security Council Progress

Made in Security, Rule of Law, but Recent Resignation of Prime Minister Could Threaten Progress to Democracy," news release (SC/10572), March 8, 2012, *www.un.org*.

63. Matthew Mosk, "Bill Clinton, UN Envoy, Admits Peacekeepers as Source of Haitian Cholera," ABC *News*, March 9, 2012, *abcnews.go.com*.

64. US Department of State, "Remarks by Ambassador Susan E. Rice, US Permanent Representative to the United Nations, on the Security Council Mission to Haiti," statement, February 28, 2012, *www.state.gov*.

65. "Congresswoman Waters Urges United Nations to Commit Resources Eradicate Cholera in Haiti," Office of Congresswoman Maxine Waters, May 30, 2013, *www.waters.house.gov*.

66. UN General Assembly, "Report of the Independent Expert on the Situation of Human Rights in Haiti, Michel Forst" (A/HRC/20/35), April 23, 2012, 18, *www.ohchr.org*.

67. "Truth out, Dying Season in," 70 *Haiti Support Group Briefing* 1–2 (April 2012); available at *www.ijdh.org*.

68. "The UN in Haiti: Damned If You Do," *Economist*, November 10, 2011; and Editorial, "Haiti's Cholera Crisis," *New York Times*, May 12, 2012.

69. Editorial, "Haiti's Cholera Crisis."

70. UNICEF, "Call to Action: A Cholera-Free Hispaniola (Haiti and the Dominican Republic)," media advisory for press briefing held on January 11, 2012, *www.unicef.org*.

71. Ban Ki-moon's statement of cost and unfunded budget was reported in Alexandra Olson, "UN Launches $2.27 Billion Cholera Plan for Haiti, Dominican Republic but Needs Funds," *Huffington Post*, December 11, 2012, *www.huffingtonpost.com*.

72. President Martelly's pledge to revive the Haitian military was reported in Randal C. Archibold, "President Michel Martelly Seeks to Re-create Haiti's Army," *New York Times*, October 26, 2011, *nytimes.com*.

73. *Pote Mak Sonje: The Raboteau Trial*, directed by Harriet Hirshorn, produced by Christine Cynn and Harriet Hirshorn, 2003; DVD on file with author; copies can be obtained by contacting Harriet Hirshorn at harriet6@mac.com.

74. The Haitian resistance to playing its occupiers' preferred game of baseball was referenced in Phillip M. Brown and John S. Shalett, *Cross-Cultural Practice with Couples and Families* (Philadelphia: Haworth Press, 1997), 2:53.

75. David Darg and Bryn Mooser, "What the UN Won't Admit: *Baseball in the Time of Cholera*," *Speakeasy*, *Wall Street Journal*, April 21, 2012, *blogs.wsj.com*.

76. Darg and Mooser, "What the UN Won't Admit"; and Olivia Wilde, "Baseball in the Time of Cholera," *Huffington Post*, April 18, 2012, *www.huffingtonpost.com*.

77. Darg and Mooser, "What the UN Won't Admit."

CHAPTER 2

1. For an accounting of Silvio Claude's arrest and imprisonment, see Inter-American Commission on Human Rights [hereafter IACHR], "Report on the Situation of Human Rights in Haiti," December 13, 1979, chapter 7, section C; available at *www.cidh.oas.org*.

2. Amelie Baron, "Haiti Court Says Human Rights Charges Can Be Brought Against Duvalier," *Reuters*, February 20, 2014, *www.reuters.com*.

3. For a description of Jean-Claude Duvalier's life after his return to Haiti in 2011, see William Booth, "In Haiti, Former Dictator 'Baby Doc' Duvalier Is Thriving," *Washington Post*, January 17, 2012.

4. An earlier version of this section was published as Fran Quigley, "Will Jean-Claude Duvalier Ever Stand Trial for His Crimes against Haiti?" *AlterNet*, January 20, 2012, *www.alternet.org*.

5. For excellent accounts of François Duvalier's 1957 election and subsequent consolidation of power, see Laurent Dubois, *Haiti: The Aftershocks of History* (New York: Metropolitan Books, 2012), 320–42, and Paul Farmer, *The Uses of Haiti* (Monroe, ME: Common Courage Press, 2005), 91–97.

6. Dubois, *Haiti*, 330.

7. Philippe Girard, *Haiti: The Tumultuous History* (New York: Macmillan, 2010), 103.

8. Robert Debs Heinl and Nancy Gordon Heinl, *Written in Blood: The Story of the Haitian People, 1492–1995* (Lanham, MD: University Press of America, 2005), 598.

9. For accounts of Jean-Claude Duvalier's assumption of power and retention of the *tontons makouts*, see Dubois, *Haiti*, 350–59, and Farmer, *Uses of Haiti*, 97–107 and 8–15.

10. Human Rights Watch, *Haiti's Rendezvous with History: The Case of Jean-Claude Duvalier* (New York: Human Rights Watch, 2011), 16–22.

11. The Amnesty International report is *You Cannot Kill the Truth: The Case against Jean-Claude Duvalier* (London: Amnesty International, 2011).

12. Quoted in Human Rights Watch, *Haiti's Rendezvous with History*, 22.

13. Amnesty International, *You Cannot Kill*, 9–10.

14. Alix Fils-Aime, quoted in Evens Sanoh and Trenton Daniel, "Haiti Prisoners Testify in 'Baby Doc' Case," *Miami Herald*, March 7, 2013.

15. Patrick Lemoine, quoted in Human Rights Watch, *Haiti's Rendezvous with History*, 9.

16. Human Rights Watch, *Haiti's Rendezvous with History*, 13.

17. IACHR, *Report on the Situation of Human Rights in Haiti* (Washington, DC: IACHR, 1979).

18. *Le Nouveau Monde*, December 4–5, 1980, quoted in Human Rights Watch, *Haiti's Rendezvous with History*, 21.

19. For an account of the 1980 repression and the visit by the delegation of international journalists, see Americas Watch/Committee to Protect Journalists, *Journalists in Jeopardy: The Haitian Reality* (Washington, DC: Americas Watch; New York: Committee to Protect Journalists, 1984).

20. For details about the Bennett-Duvalier wedding and the expenditures and trips by Michèle Bennett-Duvalier, see Dubois, *Haiti*, 357; Amy Wilentz, *The Rainy Season: Haiti—Then and Now* (New York: Simon and Schuster, 2010), 84–85; and Ralph Pezzullo, *Plunging into Haiti: Clinton, Aristide, and the Defeat of Diplomacy* (Jackson: University Press of Mississippi, 2006), 110.

21. Graham Hancock, *Lords of Poverty: The Power, Prestige, and Corruption of the International Aid Business* (New York: Atlantic Monthly Press, 1992), 180.

22. Paul Lewis, "Haitians Ask French Court for Duvalier Millions," *New York Times*, March 5, 1987. An estimate of $900 million stolen by the Duvaliers was provided in Eric Duhaime, "Haiti: Pourquoi Payer la Dette de Papa Doc?" *Jubilé*, 2000.

23. "Haiti Priest Wins $500 Million Lawsuit," *Catholic Herald*, February 5, 1988.

24. For accounts of Duvalier's departure and the events preceding it, see Wilentz, *Rainy Season*, 48; Dubois, *Haiti*, 356–59; and Farmer, *Uses of Haiti*, 103–6.

25. In late 2013, Duvalier lost his appeal of a Swiss court decision ordering forfeiture of US$5.5 million he had deposited in Swiss banks. In 2011, Switzerland passed legislation that would enable countries like Haiti to more easily obtain funds banked by former rulers.

The legislation was referred to as the "Duvalier Law." Giles Broom, "Swiss Court Denies 'Baby Doc' Dictator's Appeal on Frozen Assets," *Bloomberg News*, September 25, 2013.

26. "Michel Martelly songe à amnistier Duvalier et Aristide" (Michel Martelly considering amnesty for Duvalier and Aristide), *La Presse*, April 18, 2011.

27. Jorge Heine, "Jean-Claude Duvalier Should Be Tried for More Than Corruption," *Toronto Star*, February 5, 2012.

28. Michel Martelly, quoted in Editorial, "The Oxymoron of Haitian Justice," *Washington Post*, February 1, 2012.

29. Wilentz, *Rainy Season*, 35.

30. Edward W. Brooke, *Review of Factors Affecting US Diplomatic and Assistance Relations with Haiti: Submitted by Edward W. Brooke to the Committee on Appropriations, US Senate* (Washington, DC: US Government Printing Office, 1977).

31. Valmé's statement and the Duvalier order for arrest of Rigaud were outlined in Human Rights Watch, *Haiti's Rendezvous with History*, 21 and 28.

32. Duvalier's meeting with Andrew Young was described in ibid., 31.

33. Brooke, Review of Factors, 10.

34. Jean-Claude Duvalier, quoted in Jo Thomas, "Duvalier Defends Arrests, Warns Haiti Won't Tolerate Interference," *New York Times*, December 10, 1980, *nytimes.com*.

35. The theories of Duvalier's legal responsibility for abuse committed under his watch are thoroughly examined in Human Rights Watch, *Haiti's Rendezvous with History*, 24–39.

36. For an account of the post-Duvalier *dechoukaj*, see Wilentz, *Rainy Season*, 50–54, 117–19, 170–71.

37. Haiti's *partie civile* system is described in Brian Concannon Jr., "Haitian Women's Fight for Gender Justice," unpublished chapter, December 2003, 35; available at *www.ijdh.org*.

38. UN Security Council, "Report of the Secretary-General on the United Nations Stabilization Mission in Haiti" (S/2011/183), March 24, 2011, 17, *www.un.org*. The IACHR called for a Duvalier prosecution in "IACHR Urges the Haitian Authorities to Investigate, Try and Punish the Grave Violations to Human Rights," press release, February 1, 2012, *www.oas.org*.

39. For an account of the arguments by Duvalier's lawyers, see Collectif Contre l'Impunité et al., "Open Letter Concerning the Prosecution of Jean-Claude Duvalier," December 14, 2011, published under "Joint Letter: Criminal Proceedings against Jean-Claude Duvalier Should Continue," Open Society Justice Initiative, *www.opensocietyfoundations.org*.

40. "Lettre ouverte au Président de la République, au Premier Ministre et au Ministre de la Justice" (Open letter to the president of the Republic, to the prime minister, and to the minister of justice), *Le Nouvelliste* (Port-au-Prince), February 14, 2011.

41. For a discussion about the statute of limitations question on alleged Duvalier crimes against humanity, see Human Rights Watch, *Haiti's Rendezvous with History*, 34–39.

42. The statement by UN high commissioner of human rights Navi Pillay can be found in Stephanie Nebehay, "Duvalier Must Face Trial for Serious Rights Crimes—UN," Reuters, January 31, 2012. *www.reuters.com*.

43. Michèle Montas, quoted in Human Rights Watch, *Haiti's Rendezvous with History*, 45.

44. Philip J. Crowley, "Daily Press Briefing," US Department of State, January 18, 2011, *www.state.gov*.

45. Merten's statement (the Duvalier case "is a matter for the Haitian courts and for the Haitian people who feel aggrieved") was reported in Booth, "In Haiti." Secretary Clinton's statement

("Ultimately, a decision about what is to be done [about Duvalier] is left to the government and people of Haiti") is in "Interview with Erica Hill of CBS's *The Early Show*," transcript published on the US Department of State website, January 18, 2011, *www.state.gov*.

46. Dubois, *Haiti*, 350.

47. For discussion of the US involvement in Haiti's political and economic affairs throughout Haiti's history, see Chapter 7. For a discussion of the US role in supporting François and Jean-Claude Duvalier's presidencies, see Dubois, *Haiti*, 333–37, 348, 350–56, and Farmer, *Uses of Haiti*, 93–94, 97–107.

48. Tracy Kidder, *Mountains beyond Mountains: The Quest of Dr. Paul Farmer, A Man Who Would Cure the World* (New York: Random House, 2004).

49. Plato, *The Laws*, translated by Trevor J. Saunders (New York: Penguin, 1970), 715d.

50. Magna Carta (1215), clause 39.

51. Mass. Const., part 1, art. XXX.

52. For discussions of the differing traditions of "thick" and "thin" views of the rule of law, see Joseph Raz, "The Rule of Law and Its Virtue," in *Law and Morality: Readings in Legal Philosophy*, edited by David Dyzenhaus and Arthur Ripstein (Toronto: Toronto Studies in Philosophy, 2007), 291; Brian Tamanaha, "The Lessons of Law and Development Studies," 89 *American Journal of International Law* 476 (1995); and Frank Emmert, "Rule of Law in Central and Eastern Europe," 32 *Fordham International Law Journal* 563–68 (2009).

53. For example, article 22 of the Constitution of Haiti reads, "The State recognizes the right of every citizen to decent housing, education, food and social security."

54. UN General Assembly, "Report of the Independent Expert on the Situation of Human Rights in Haiti, Michel Forst" (A/HRC/20/35), April 23, 2012, 11, *www.ohchr.org*.

55. Amartya Sen, *Development as Freedom* (New York: Anchor, 1999), 3–11.

56. Hernando de Soto, *The Mystery of Capital* (New York: Basic Books, 2000), 64–66.

CHAPTER 3

1. Accounts of Jimmy Charles's arrest, incarceration, and his family's efforts to find him are contained in BAI and IJDH, "Petition to the Inter-American Commission on Human Rights on Behalf of Jimmy Charles against the Republic of Haiti," January 18, 2006, *www.ijdh. org*; and Haitian Press Agency, "Jimmy Charles and Journalist Summarily Executed in Haiti for Witnessing Police Crimes," January 17, 2005 (available at *williambowles.info*).

2. For an account of Yvon Neptune's arrest and incarceration, see Jens Iverson, *Eight Perspectives on Yvonne Neptune v. Haiti*, 32 *Hastings International and Comparative Law Review* 611 (2009).

3. Jean-Charles Deus Charles, quoted in Haitian Press Agency, "Jimmy Charles."

4. Accounts of the violence after the 2004 coup are contained in "International Advocates File Lawsuit against Haiti's Pick for Prime Minister," *Caribbean Life*, July 20, 2011; and Darren Eli, "Mario Joseph: Fighting for the Rule of Law in Haiti," *Haiti Action Network*, April 25, 2007.

5. Mario Joseph, quoted in Eli, "Mario Joseph."

6. The 1987 Constitution of Haiti can be viewed at Georgetown University's Political Database of the Americas, *pdba.georgetown.edu/constitutions/haiti/haiti1987.html*. The Haitian penal code (in French), the American Convention on Human Rights, the American Declaration of

the Rights and Duties of Man, and the Haitian police code of conduct (*Loi relative à la Police nationale*) can be viewed at the website of the OAS, *www.oas.org*. The Universal Declaration of Human Rights can be viewed at the UN website, *www.un.org*.

7. The 1989 Inter-American Court of Human Rights *Velásquez Rodríguez* decision can be found at the University of Minnesota Human Rights Library, *www1.umn.edu/humanrts/iachr/Annuals/app27-96.html*.

8. The UN Basic Principles on the Independence of the Judiciary can be found at the website of the UN Office of the High Commissioner for Human Rights, *www2.0hchr.org*.

9. Amnesty International, *Haiti: Disarmament Delayed, Justice Denied* (London: Amnesty International, 2005), 13.

10. IACHR, *Haiti: Failed Justice or the Rule of Law? Challenges ahead for Haiti and the International Community* (Washington, DC: OAS, 2006), 47, *cidh.org*.

11. The looting was reported in BAI and IJDH, "Petition."

12. For an account of the firing of five Supreme Court justices by the interim Haiti government, see IACHR, *Haiti*, 15.

13. James Foley, quoted in Ansel Herz and Kim Ives, "WikiLeaked Cables Testify to PM Nominee's Repressive Past," *Haïti Liberté*, July 19, 2011. For an account of Bernard Gousse's role in the removal of Judge Jean Sénat Fleury and his pursuit of charges against Father Gérard Jean-Juste, see BAI and IJDH, "Human Rights Lawyers File Petition against President Martelly's Pick for Prime Minister," press release, July 13, 2011, *www.commondreams.org*.

14. Mayard-Paul's citation of Gousse's experience was reported in Herz and Ives, "WikiLeaked Cables."

15. Franklin D. Roosevelt, quoted in Karl E. Meyer, "Editorial Notebook: The Perils of 'Nation Building,'" *New York Times*, October 17, 1993, *nytimes.com*.

16. Vivienne O'Connor, "The Rule of Law in Haiti after the Earthquake," *Peace Brief* 18, US Institute of Peace, April 15, 2010, *www.usip.org*.

17. The government of Haiti's estimate was reported in UN General Assembly, "Report of the Independent Expert on the Situation of Human Rights in Haiti, Michel Forst" (A/HRC/20/35), April 23, 2012, 6, *www.ohchr.org*.

18. Approximately 8 percent of the five thousand prisoners who escaped after the earthquake were recaptured, per International Crisis Group, "Keeping Haiti Safe: Police Reform," *Latin America/Caribbean Briefing* 26, September 8, 2011, *www.crisisgroup.org*.

19. National Center for State Courts, *Haiti: Rule of Law Assessment* (Washington, DC: National Center for State Courts, 2004).

20. Jamal Benomar, *Rule of Law Assistance in Haiti: Lessons Learned* (Washington, DC: World Bank, 2001); and Hans Joerg Albrecht, Louis Aucoin, and Vivienne O'Connor, *Building the Rule of Law in Haiti: New Laws for a New Era* (Washington, DC: US Institute for Peace, 2009).

21. The April 2005 visit by the IACHR to Haitian prisons was reported in IACHR, *Haiti*, 68.

22. Ibid., 21.

23. Ibid., 36.

24. Accounts of post-earthquake violence perpetrated by Haitian police come from US Department of State, *2010 Human Rights Report: Haiti* (Washington, DC: US Department of State, 2011); and US Department of State, *2011 Human Rights Report: Haiti* (Washington, DC: US Department of State, 2011).

25. UN News Service, "Enhancing Rule of Law Vital for Peace and Security in Haiti, UN Report Says," UN News Centre, March 31, 2011, *www.un.org*.

26. American Bar Association, "Cross-Institutional Training Encourages Coordination between Haiti's Magistrate School and the National Police Academy," Haiti News page, ABA Rule of Law Initiative, October 2011, *www.americanbar.org*.

27. UN News Service, "UN Official: Despite Progress, Haiti Facing Challenges on Justice Reform and Poverty," UN News Centre, September 17, 2012, *www.un.org*.

28. US Department of State, *2011 Human Rights Report: Haiti*, 5–7.

29. For reports of corruption in the justice system, see ibid., 11, 13.

30. For accounts of vigilante justice post-earthquake, see ibid., 31; and US Department of State, *2010 Human Rights Report: Haiti*, 2–3.

31. "MINUSTAH Facts and Figures," UN website, accessed December 15, 2013, *www.un.org*.

32. Ansel Herz, "The Death of Gérard Jean-Gilles: How the UN Stonewalled Haitian Justice," *Haïti Liberté*, September 27, 2011.

33. Deborah Sontag and Walt Bogdanich, "Eight Guilty for Prison Massacre in Rare Trial of Haiti's Police," *New York Times*, January 19, 2012.

34. The Préval administration's success at reducing state-sponsored political violence was noted in UN News Service, "Enhancing Rule of Law."

35. The reference to "emasculating" Lavalas comes from statements of the European Union and Canadian ambassadors to Haiti, as reported in one of the US diplomatic cables obtained by WikiLeaks and quoted in Dan Coughlin and Kim Ives, "WikiLeaks Haiti: Cable Depicts Fraudulent Election," *Nation*, June 8, 2011.

36. Jake Johnston and Mark Weisbrot, *Haiti's Fatally Flawed Election* (Washington, DC: Center for Economic and Policy Research, 2011).

37. Mario Joseph, quoted in Eli, "Mario Joseph."

38. Benomar, "Rule of Law Assistance," 14.

39. John Locke, *The Works of John Locke* (London: Tegg, 1823), 2:174.

40. Winston Churchill, *Blood, Sweat, and Tears* (Bloomsburg, PA: Haddon Craftsmen, 1941), 45; and E. P. Thompson, *Whigs and Hunters* (New York: Pantheon, 1975), 266.

41. Niall Ferguson, *Civilization: The West and the Rest* (New York: Penguin, 2011), 12.

42. Ibid., 13.

43. Amartya Sen, "What Is the Role of Legal and Judicial Reform in the Development Process," lecture delivered at the World Bank Global Conference on Comprehensive Legal and Judicial Development, Washington, DC, June 5, 2000, 10; transcript available at *siteresources.worldbank.org/INTLAWJUSTINST/Resources/legalandjudicial.pdf*.

44. Hernando de Soto, *The Mystery of Capital: Why Capitalism Triumphs in the West and Fails Everywhere Else* (New York: Basic Books, 2000), 64–66.

45. De Soto's estimate of $5 billion in unused Haitian capital appeared in Matthew Miller, "The Poor Man's Capitalist: Hernando de Soto," *New York Times Magazine*, July 1, 2001, *nytimes.com*.

46. The discussion of the projects abandoned or delayed because of land title problems was contained in Susana Ferreira, "Haiti's Road to Reconstruction Blocked by Land Tenure Disputes," Reuters, January 26, 2013, *www.reuters.com*.

47. *Haiti: Where Did the Money Go?*, written and produced by Michele Mitchell and Ivan Weiss, 2011; accessed December 15, 2013, at *www.youtube.com*.

48. Daron Acemoglu and James A. Robinson, *Why Nations Fail: The Origins of Power, Prosperity, and Poverty* (New York: Crown Business, 2012).

49. Adam Davidson, "Why Some Countries Go Bust," *New York Times Magazine*, March 13, 2012.

50. For a review of such studies, see Jonathan Isham et al., "Civil Liberties, Democracy and the Performance of Government Projects," 11 *World Bank Economic Review* 219 (1997).

51. Ferguson, *Civilization*, 127–28.

52. De Soto, *Mystery of Capital*, 105–51.

53. Gunnar Myrdal, *An American Dilemma: The Negro Problem and Modern Democracy* (New York: Harper, 1944), 998–1004; and Thomas H. Marshall, *Citizenship and Social Class and Other Essays* (Cambridge: Cambridge University Press, 1950), 10–14.

54. Robert Danino, "The Legal Aspects of the World Bank's Work on Human Rights," address at "Human Rights and Development: Towards Mutual Reinforcement," a conference co-sponsored by the Ethical Globalization Initiative and the Center for Human Rights, New York University School of Law, March 1, 2004), 15, *www.worldbank.org*.

55. World Bank spending estimates were reported in David Trubek, "The Rule of Law in Development Assistance: Past, Present and Future," in *The New Law and Economic Development: A Critical Appraisal*, edited by David M. Trubek and Alvaro Santos (Cambridge: Cambridge University Press, 2006), 74; and *The World Bank Annual Report 2008* (New York: World Bank, 2008), 57.

56. Jess Ford et al., *Foreign Assistance: Rule of Law Funding Worldwide for Fiscal Years 1993–98*, report to congressional requesters (Washington, DC: US General Accounting Office, 1999), 3.

57. USAID, *Fiscal Year 2008 Agency Financial Report* (Washington, DC: USAID, 2008), 16.

58. Maria Dakolias, David Freestone, and Peter Kyle, *Legal and Judicial Reform: Observations, Experiences and Approach of the Legal Vice Presidency* (Washington, DC: World Bank, 2002), 5, *documents.worldbank.org*.

59. For discussions of the phenomenon of equating "law reform" with "judicial reform," see Thomas Carothers, "Promoting the Rule of Law Abroad: The Problem of Knowledge," working paper, Carnegie Endowment for International Peace Rule of Law Series, January 28, 2003, 8, *carnegieendowment.org*, and Erik G. Jensen, "The Rule of Law and Judicial Reform: The Political Economy of Diverse Institutional Patterns and Reformers' Responses," in *Beyond Common Knowledge: Empirical Approaches to the Rule of Law*, edited by Erik G. Jensen and Thomas C. Heller (Stanford, CA: Stanford University Press, 2003), 345.

60. Linn Hammergren, "International Assistance to Latin American Justice Programs: Toward an Agenda for Reforming the Reformers," in Jensen and Heller, *Beyond Common Knowledge*, 314. See also Jensen, "Rule of Law," 350–51.

61. World Bank, *Implementation Completion and Results Report (IBRD-44010) on a Loan of US$33.00 Million Equivalent to the Republic of Guatemala for a Judicial Reform Project* (ICR0000623) (Washington, DC: World Bank, 2008).

62. Ibid., 42.

63. Jensen, "Rule of Law," 350.

64. The 1999 labor rights grant to Haiti was described in *Unequal Equation: The Labor Code and Worker Rights in Haiti* (Washington DC: American Center for International Labor Solidarity/AFL-CIO, 2003), 50.

65. Kirsti Samuels, "Rule of Law Reform in Post-Conflict Countries: Operational Initiatives and Lessons Learnt," Conflict Prevention and Reconstruction Paper No. 37, World Bank Social Development Papers, October 2006, 17–18, *siteresources.worldbank.org*.

66. Frank Upham, "Mythmaking in the Rule of Law Orthodoxy," working paper, Carnegie Endowment for Peace Rule of Law Series, September 10, 2002, 7, *carnegieendowment.org*.

67. See William C. Prillaman, *The Judiciary and Democratic Decay in Latin America: Declining Confidence in the Rule of Law* (Santa Barbara, CA: Praeger, 2000), 163–65; Stephen Lord et al., *Former Soviet Union: US Rule of Law Assistance Has Had Limited Impact and Sustainability* (Washington, DC: US General Accounting Office, 2001); and Rosa Ehrenreich Brooks, "The New Imperialism: Violence, Norms and the 'Rule of Law,'" 101 *Michigan Law Review* 2280 (2003).

68. The $11.4 billion estimate for total international aid to Haiti is derived from data reported by the Organisation for Economic Co-operation and Development, "OECD.Stat Extracts," accessed December 15, 2013, *stats.oecd.org*. The $97 million figure for USAID-supported justice programming for Haiti in the late 1990s was reported in Jess Ford, *Foreign Assistance: Lack of Haitian Commitment Limited Success of US Aid to Justice System*, testimony before the Committee on International Relations, House of Representatives, September 19, 2000 (Washington, DC: US General Accounting Office, 2000). The UNDP and Government of Canada's $11.6 million project was reported in UNDP, "Canada Steps Up Support for Planned Reform of Haiti's Justice System," news release, March 7, 2006.

69. National Center for State Courts, *Haiti*, 7.

70. Benomar, "Rule of Law Assistance," 10.

71. National Center for State Courts, *Haiti*, 39.

72. Ibid., 72.

73. An account of the IFES's role in overthrowing the Aristide government in 2004 is contained in Thomas M. Griffin, *Haiti Human Rights Investigation: November 11–21, 2004* (Miami: Center for the Study of Human Rights, University of Miami School of Law, 2004).

74. "Political will" references are included in National Center for State Courts, Haiti," 6, 7, 8, and 13; Benomar, "Rule of Law Assistance," 4; IACHR, *Haiti*, 73; Jean Sénat Fleury, *The Challenges of Judicial Reform in Haiti* (Littleton, MA: ISCS Press, 2009), 85; and Gary Haugen and Victor Boutros, "And Justice for All: Enforcing Human Rights for the World's Poor," *Foreign Affairs*, May/June 2010, *www.foreignaffairs.com*. Other references to "political will" being the missing ingredient for law reform are included in "Commission on Legal Empowerment of the Poor, and United Nations Development Programme, *Making the Law Work for Everyone* (New York: United Nations, 2008), 5–6; Gary Goodpaster, "Law Reform in Developing Countries," 13 *Transnational Law and Contemporary Problems* 661 (2003); Hammergren, "International Assistance," 297; and Gordon Barron, "The World Bank and Rule of Law Reforms," working paper, Development Studies Institute, London School of Economics and Political Science, December 2005, *www.lse.ac.uk*.

75. Carothers, "Promoting," 3.

76. Ibid., 8.

77. Ibid., 10.

78. This discussion of the role of political will in law reform, and the lessons to be learned from the study of social movements, was initially presented in Fran Quigley, "Growing Political Will from the Grassroots: How Social Movement Principles Can Reverse the Dismal Legacy of Rule of Law Interventions," 41.1 *Columbia Human Rights Law Review* 13–66 (2009).

79. Some of the studies of social movements referred to: Lewis M. Killian, "Organization, Rationality and Spontaneity in the Civil Rights Movement," 49 *American Sociological Review* 782 (1984); Charles Tilly, *Social Movements, 1768–2004* (Boulder, CO: Paradigm, 2004), 90–92; Håkan Thörn, *Anti-Apartheid and the Emergence of a Global Civil Society* (Basingstoke, UK: Palgrave Macmillan, 2006); Elena Zdravomyslova, "Opportunities and Framing in the Transition to Democracy: The Case for Russia," in *Comparative Perspectives in Social Movements: Opportunities, Mobilizing Structures and Framing*, edited by Doug McAdam, John D. McCarthy, and Mayer N. Zald (Cambridge: Cambridge University Press, 1996), 122–37; John K. Glenn III, *Framing Democracy: Civil Society and Civic Movements in Eastern Europe* (Stanford, CA: Stanford University Press, 2001), and Rita K. Noonan, "Women against the State: Political Opportunities and Collective Action Forces in Chile's Transition to Democracy," 10 *Sociological Forum* 81 (1995).

80. For descriptions of classical collective behavior theory, see Ted Gurr, *Why Men Rebel* (Princeton, NJ: Princeton University Press, 1970), and Ralph Turner and Lewis Killian, *Collective Behavior* (Englewood Cliffs, NJ: Prentice-Hall, 1972).

81. For descriptions of resource mobilization theory, see John McCarthy and Mayer Zald, "Resource Mobilization and Social Movements: A Partial Theory," 82 *American Journal of Sociology* 1213 (1977). See also Jo Freeman, "Resource Mobilization and Strategy: A Model for Analyzing Social Movement Organizations Actions," in *The Dynamics of Social Movements*, edited by John McCarthy and Mayer Zald (New York: Winthrop, 1979), 167–89. For a description of political process theory, see Doug McAdam, "Tactical Innovation and the Pace of Insurgency," 48 *American Sociological Review* 736–37 (1983).

82. Killian, "Organization, Rationality and Spontaneity."

83. Haugen and Boutros, "And Justice for All."

84. Aldon Morris, "Black Southern Student Sit-In Movement: An Analysis of Internal Organization," 46 *American Sociological Review* 744 (1981).

85. Saul Alinsky, *Reveille for Radicals* (New York: Vintage, 1969), 85–88.

86. Samuels, "Rule of Law Reform," 21.

87. Discussion of the elite financial supporters of these movements is contained at Peter Drier, *The 100 Greatest Americans in the 20th Century: A Social Justice Hall of Fame* (New York: Nation Books, 2012), 121–22 (early twentieth-century US women's labor and suffrage movements); David Arnold, *Gandhi* (London: Longman, 2001), 92 ("One cannot but be struck by the extent to which India's saintly Mahatma and foremost peasant leader was bankrolled by the capitalist class"); J. D. McCarthy and M. N. Zald, *The Trend of Social Movements in America: Professionalization and Resource Mobilization* (Morristown, NJ: General Learning Press, 1973), 13 (US civil rights movement); Thörn, *Anti-Apartheid*, 32–33, 67 (antiapartheid movement); and J. Craig Jenkins and Charles Perrow, "Insurgency of the Powerless: Farm Worker Movements (1946–1972)," 42 *American Sociological Review* 266 (1977) (US farmworker movement).

88. Jenkins and Perrow, "Insurgency of the Powerless," 251.

89. Hugo Fruhling, "From Dictatorship to Democracy: Law and Social Change in the Andean Cone of South America," in *Many Roads to Justice: The Law-Related Work of the Ford Foundation Grantees around the World*, edited by Mary McClymont and Stephen Golub (New York: Ford Foundation, 2000), 61–81.

90. Erving Goffman, *Frame Analysis: An Essay on the Organization of Experience* (Holliston, MA: Northeastern, 1974), 7.

91. Robert Benford and David A. Snow, "Framing Process and Social Movements: An Overview and Assessment," 26 *Annual Review of Sociology* 615 (2000).

92. Gary Blasi and John T. Jost, "System Justification Theory and Research: Implications for Law, Legal Advocacy and Social Justice," 94 *California Law Review* 1119 (2006).

93. See Benford and Snow, "Framing Process," 615, for citations of several studies that show how movements identify "victims" of injustice and amplify their victimization into "injustice frames" created in advance of collective protest.

94. Richard Kluger, *Simple Justice* (New York: Vintage, 2004), 753–54.

95. A discussion of the effect of the 1971 International Court of Justice ruling is contained in Gene Sharp, ed., *Waging Nonviolent Struggle: 20th Century Practice and 21st Century Potential* (Boston: Porter Sargent, 2005), 205–16.

96. Jane Perlez and David Rhode, "Pakistan Attempts to Crush Protests by Lawyers," *New York Times*, November 6, 2007.

97. Lucie E. White, "To Learn and Teach: Lessons from Driefontein on Lawyering and Power," 1988 *Wisconsin Law Review* 699 (1988).

98. Joshua Paulson, "Ousting a Guatemalan Dictator—1944," in Sharp, *Waging Nonviolent Struggle*, 149–155.

99. Fleury, *Challenges of Judicial Reform*, 85.

CHAPTER 4

1. Marie Denise Fleury, in *Pote Mak Sonje: The Raboteau Trial*, directed by Harriet Hirshorn, produced by Christine Cynn and Harriet Hirshorn, 2003; DVD on file with author; copies can be obtained by contacting Harriet Hirshorn, harriet6@mac.com.

2. Colin Granderson, in ibid.

3. For an account of Emmanuel "Toto" Constant's career as a paramilitary leader and relationship with the CIA, see Sewell Chan, "The Saga of 'Toto' Constant," *New York Times*, May 23, 2007.

4. For an account of the human rights violations committed after the 1991 coup, see Human Rights Watch/Americas and National Coalition for Haitian Refugees, *Terror Prevails in Haiti: Human Rights Violations and Failed Diplomacy* (Washington, DC: Human Rights Watch/Americas; New York: National Coalition for Haitian Refugees, 1994), *www.hrw.org*.

5. Camille LeBlanc, in *Pote Mak Sonje*.

6. Daniel Roussière, in ibid.

7. Michèle Pierre-Louis, in ibid.

8. Marie Denise Fleur, in ibid.

9. For an account of the diaspora activism pushing for the United States to ensure Aristide's return, see Beverly Bell, *Walking on Fire* (Ithaca, NY: Cornell University Press, 2001), 15–16.

10. For an account of the conditions imposed by the US on Aristide's return, see Peter Hallward, *Damming the Flood: Haiti and The Politics of Containment* (London: Verso, 2010), 50–51, 56–58.

11. Human Rights Watch, "US Urged to Return Seized Haitian Documents," Human Rights Watch News, November 4, 1999, *www.hrw.org*.

12. Center for Economic and Policy Research, "A Corps Revived? Both Presidential Candidates Want to Bring Back the Haitian Army," *Haiti: Relief and Reconstruction Watch* (blog), March 9, 2011, *www.cepr.net*.

13. For an account of BAI's founding and original mission, see Ken Bresler, "If You Are Not Corrupt, Arrest the Criminals: Prosecuting Human Rights Violators in Haiti," case study, Harvard University Project on Justice in Times of Transition, Spring 2003.

14. Florence Elie, in *Pote Mak Sonje.*

15. Bresler, "If You Are Not Corrupt," 7–8.

16. Ibid., 7.

17. Brian Concannon Jr., quoted in ibid., 6.

18. Bresler, "If You Are Not Corrupt," 2.

19. Reed Brody, in *Pote Mak Sonje.*

20. For an account of the trial for Malary's murder, see Bresler, "If You Are Not Corrupt," 9.

21. Mario Joseph, interview by New Media Advocacy Project, 2012; transcript on file with author.

22. Bresler, "If You Are Not Corrupt," 4–9.

23. The reference to Mario Joseph in the *New York Times* was made in "World Briefing: Americas: Haiti: Aristide's Prime Minister Freed," *New York Times*, July 28, 2006.

24. Martin Ennals Award for Human Rights Defenders, "Mario Joseph—Haiti—Final Nominee for Martin Ennals Award, 2013," accessed December 11, 2013, *www.martinennalsaward .org.* The reference to "Nobel Prize for human rights" was made in Martin Ennals Award for Human Rights Defenders, "African Gay Human Rights Defender Honored with Human Rights Award in Geneva," press release, October 11, 2011, *www.martinennalsaward.org.*

25. Paul Farmer, "Letter of Nomination of Mario Joseph for Bishop Oscar Romero Award," March 1, 2011, copy on file with author.

26. Amnesty International Legal Network, "Haiti—Human Rights Defenders at Risk: Rénan Hédouville and Other Members of CARLI, and lawyer Mario Joseph," action alert (AMR 36/058/2004), November 2004, *www.amnesty.org.*

27. Amnesty International, "Haiti: Lawyers in Haiti Threatened and Intimidated," action alert (AMR 36/009/2012), October 4, 2012, *www.amnesty.org.*

28. Center for Economic and Policy Research, "Three Years Later, We Still Don't Know: Where Is Lovinsky Pierre-Antoine?" *Haiti: Relief and Reconstruction Watch* (blog), August 12, 2010, *www.cepr.net.*

29. Mario Joseph's speech outside the MINUSTAH base in St. Marc can be viewed in *Haitian Cholera* Victims Demonstrate in front of MINUSTAH Base for 2011 Human Rights Day, filmed and edited by Nick Stratton, at *www.youtube.com* (uploaded January 17, 2012).

30. Concannon, in *Pote Mak Sonje.*

31. Bresler, "If You Are Not Corrupt," 13.

32. Concannon, quoted in ibid., 15.

33. For an account of the Raboteau victims' advocacy pretrial, see Bresler, "If You Are Not Corrupt," 17.

34. Ibid., 12.

35. Deborah Charles, in *Pote Mak Sonje.*

36. The estimate of a 48.7 percent literacy rate in Haiti comes from "Haiti," in *The World Factbook*, 2012–2013 (Washington, DC: US Central Intelligence Agency, 2012), *www.cia.gov.*

37. An account of Joseph's and Concannon's efforts to supplement the Raboteau jury pool is included in Bresler, "If You Are Not Corrupt," 16, 20.

38. Joseph, in *Pote Mak Sonje.*

39. Deborah Charles, Rosiane Profil, and Marie Claudette Senatus, in ibid.

40. Pierre Michel, in ibid.

41. Marc-Antoine Thebault, in ibid.

42. Profil, in ibid.

43. Adama Dieng, quoted in Amnesty International, "Haiti: Obliterating Justice, Overturning of Sentences for Raboteau Massacre Is a Huge Step Backwards," public statement (AMR 36/006/2005), May 26, 2005, *www.amnesty.org*.

44. Joseph, in *Pote Mak Sonje*.

45. Alfonso Chardy, "INS Arrests Ex-Colonel Given Life in Haiti for His Role in Massacre," *Miami Herald*, June 22, 2001.

46. For accounts of the Raboteau defendants' whereabouts, see Trenton Daniel and Susannah A. Nesmith, "Freed Rights Abusers back on Streets," *Miami Herald*, March 15, 2004; Human Rights Watch, "Panama Urged to Prosecute Haitian Coup Leaders," *Human Rights Watch News*, November 11, 1999, *www.hrw.org*; and John Kifner, "Not Looking Back, Cedras Flies to Panama Exile," *New York Times*, October 14, 1994.

47. Amnesty International, "Haiti: Obliterating Justice."

CHAPTER 5

1. For a recitation of the death toll, numbers displaced and other data regarding the 2010 earthquake, see "Haiti," *New York Times*, April 12, 2012, and *Haiti: Human Security in Danger* (Paris: International Federation for Human Rights, 2012), 7.

2. An overview of the destruction caused by the 2008 storms is contained at Rory Carroll, "We Are Going to Disappear One Day," *Guardian*, November 7, 2008.

3. A useful perspective on the roles of NGOs in Haiti is provided by Justin Podur, "Help That Hurts: An Interview with Tim Schwartz about Haiti," *ZNet*, March 18, 2012, *www.zcommunications.org*. See also Deepa Panchang, "'Waiting for Helicopters'? Perceptions, Misperceptions, and the Right to Water in Haiti," in *Tectonic Shifts: Haiti since the Earthquake*, edited by Mark Schuller and Pablo Morales (Boulder, CO: Kumarian Press, 2012), 183–92.

4. The 80 percent figure is provided by Kevin Edmonds, "NGOs and the Business of Poverty in Haiti," in Schuller and Morales, *Tectonic Shifts*, 63–64. Mark Schuller reports in *Killing with Kindness: Haiti, International Aid, and NGOs* (New Brunswick, NJ: Rutgers University Press, 2012), 6, that more than 80 percent of the health clinics and 90 percent of Haiti's schools are run by private organizations.

5. The comparison between external relief dollars and Haitian government revenue was made in Katie Klarreich and Linda Polman, "The NGO Republic of Haiti," *Nation*, November 19, 2012.

6. Pooja Bhatia, "Invest in America before It Is Too Late," *Daily Beast*, October 3, 2011, *dailybeast.com*.

7. Earl Kessler, quoted in Janet Reitman, "Beyond Relief: How the World Failed Haiti," *Rolling Stone*, August 18, 2011.

8. IDB, "Third Conference on Haiti's Economic and Social Development, Washington, DC, April 14, 2009," news release, April 14, 2009, *www.iadb.org*.

9. Quoted in Schuller, *Killing with Kindness*, 158–59.

10. "The Help That Haiti Needs" forum was hosted on the *Room for Debate* blog of the *New York Times*, January 14, 2010, *roomfordebate.blogs.nytimes.com*.

11. Brian Concannon Jr., "Work with the Haitian Government," in "Help That Haiti Needs."

12. Robert Fatton Jr., "Repair the Government," in "Help That Haiti Needs."

13. Amy Wilentz, "A WPA Rather Than an NGO," in "Help That Haiti Needs."

14. Robert Maguire, "Aid for the Countryside," in "Help That Haiti Needs."

15. The outcomes of direct budget assistance to the African countries were reported in Enzo Caputo, Antonie de Kemp, and Andrew Lawson, "Assessing the Impacts of Budget Support: Case Studies in Mali, Tunisia and Zambia," working paper, Network on Development Evaluation of the OECD (Organisation for Economic Co-operation and Development) Development Assistance Committee, October 2011, *www.oecd.org*.

16. Elizabeth Sepper et al., "The Human Rights Obligations of OAS Member States Providing International Assistance in the Region: A Brief to the Inter-American Commission on Human Rights for a Hearing on the Economic and Social Rights Situation in Haiti following the Earthquake and the Human Rights Obligations of OAS Member States," March 9, 2010 (available at *www.ijdh.org*). The themes of the brief are described in Brian Concannon Jr. and Bea Lindstrom, "Cheaper, Better, Longer-Lasting: A Rights-Based Approach to Disaster Response in Haiti," 25 *Emory International Law Review* 1148–49 (2011).

17. A listing of all government humanitarian pledges, commitments, and contributions to Haiti is compiled and regularly updated by the UN Office of Coordination of Humanitarian Affairs at *Financial Tracking Service: Tracking Global Humanitarian Aid Flows*, *fts.unocha.org*. The amount donated and how it has been spent was analyzed in Bill Quigley and Amber Ramanauskas, "Haiti: Where Is the Money?—Researcher Version," *HaitiAction.Net*, January 4, 2012.

18. William Easterly, *White Man's Burden: Why the West's Efforts to Aid the Rest Have Done So Much Ill and So Little Good* (New York: Penguin, 2006); and Dambisa Moyo, *Dead Aid: Why Aid Is Not Working and How There Is a Better Way for Africa* (New York: Penguin, 2010).

19. The US military response was reported in Peter Hallward, *Damming the Flood: Haiti and the Politics of Containment* (London: Verso, 2010), 321–27.

20. Ibid., 326.

21. The denunciation of the US military response in Haiti by Nicaragua and the other countries was reported in Charles Vorbe, "Earthquake, Humanitarianism, and Intervention in Haiti," in Schuller and Morales, *Tectonic Shifts*, 59–62.

22. James M. Roberts and Ray Walser, American Leadership Necessary to Assist Haiti after Devastating Earthquake," WebMemo 2754, Heritage Foundation, January 13, 2010.

23. Frei's commentary was reported in Hallward, *Damming the Flood*, 325.

24. For accounts of Haitians responding to emergency needs after the earthquake, see Yolette Etienne, "Haiti and Catastrophe: Lessons Not Learned" in Schuller and Morales, 29–30; and Chenet Jean-Baptiste, "Haiti's Earthquake: A Further Insult to Peasants' Lives," in Schuller and Morales, *Tectonic Shifts*, 99. Mark Schuller wrote about the grassroots responses to community needs in the post-2004 coup era in *Killing with Kindness*, 189.

25. For an account of the suffering resulting from the US prioritization of military flights, see Hallward, *Damming the Flood*, 321–27; the accusations of a focus on rescues at buildings frequented by foreigners were reported in ibid., 324.

26. Jonathan M. Katz, *The Big Truck That Went By: How the World Came to Save Haiti and Left Behind a Disaster* (New York: Palgrave Macmillan, 2013), 72.

27. Quoted in Colin Dayan, "The Secret History of the Haitian Earthquake: A Conversation with Jonathan M. Katz," *Boston Review*, June 25, 2013, *www.bostonreview.net*.

28. Hallward, *Damming the Flood*, 322.

29. Jarry Emmanuel, quoted in Ginger Thompson and Damien Cave, "Officials Strain to Distribute Aid as Violence Rises," *New York Times*, January 17, 2010.

30. Evan Lyon, in "With Foreign Aid Still at a Trickle, Devastated General Hospital in Port-au-Prince Struggles to Meet Overwhelming Need," interview by Amy Goodman, *Democracy Now!*, January 20, 2010, *www.democracynow.org*.

31. Reports of large aid agencies refusing to distribute aid without military escorts were discussed in Melinda Miles, "Assumptions and Exclusion: Coordination Failures during the Emergency Phase," in Schuller and Morales, *Tectonic Shifts*, 48.

32. Kenneth H. Merten, "Situation in Haiti," on-the-record briefing, US Department of State, February 12, 2010, *www.state.gov*.

33. UN Office of the Secretary-General's Special Adviser on Community-Based Medicine and Lessons from Haiti, "Assistance Tracker," last updated December 2012, *www .lessonsfromhaiti.org/assistance-tracker*.

34. Josef Leitmann, quoted in Center for Economic and Policy Research, "Haiti Reconstruction Fund: Building Back . . . When?" *Haiti: Relief and Reconstruction Watch* (blog), April 12, 2012, *www.cepr.net*.

35. David Gootnick et al, *Haiti Reconstruction:* USAID *Infrastructure Projects Have Had Mixed Results and Face Sustainability Challenges*, report to congressional requesters (Washington, DC: US Government Accountability Office, 2013).

36. Julie Walz and Vijaya Ramachandran, "Haiti: Three Years after the Quake and Not Much Has Changed," *Global Development: Views from the Center* (blog), Center for Global Development, December 11, 2012, *www.cgdev.org*. See also Ramachandran and Walz, "US Spending in Haiti: The Need for Greater Transparency and Accountability," brief, Center for Global Development, February 2013.

37. Jake Johnston and Alexander Main, "Breaking Open the Black Box: Increasing Aid Transparency and Accountability in Haiti," issue brief, Center for Economic and Policy Research, April 2013, *www.cepr.net*.

38. Office of the Haiti Special Coordinator, "Fast Facts on US Government's Work in Haiti: Interim Haiti Recovery Commission," fact sheet, US Department of State, January 8, 2011, *www.state.gov*.

39. An account of the IHRC and its relations with the Haitian people is contained in Joris Willems, "Deconstructing the Reconstruction: The IHRC," in Schuller and Morales, *Tectonic Shifts*, 41–45. The full text of the letter from Haitian members of the IHRC can be found at "HAITI—Haitian Members of the Reconstruction Commission Say They Are Being Marginalised," *Caricom News Network*, January 1, 2011. Further reporting of the events at that meeting can be found in Deborah Sontag, "Rebuilding in Haiti Lags after Billions in Post-Quake Aid," *New York Times*, December 23, 2012.

40. Quoted in Reitman, "Beyond Relief."

41. The criticisms of the IHRC are outlined in Willems, "Deconstructing the Reconstruction."

42. The website of the Haiti Reconstruction Fund is *www.haitireconstructionfund.org*. The HRF operations are analyzed by the Center for Economic and Policy Research in "Inside the Haiti Reconstruction Fund Annual Report," *Haiti: Relief and Reconstruction Watch* (blog), July 26, 2011, *www.cepr.net*.

43. These disbursement figures were obtained from the Office of the Special Envoy for Haiti, "International Assistance," data last updated December 2012*www.haitispecialenvoy.org*. A critique of the disbursement practices of aid post-earthquake is included in Center for Economic and Policy Research, "Evaluation of Donor Response to Haiti Earthquake Shows 'Building Back Better' Nothing but A Slogan," *Haiti: Relief and Reconstruction Watch* (blog), March 2, 2012, *www.cepr.net*.

44. Joia Mukherjee, quoted in "Partners in Health Medical Director and Director of Advocacy and Policy Urge Donor Countries to Support the Haitian Government," press release, Partners in Health, March 27, 2010. Ironically, the chief reason donors give for bypassing direct aid to the Haitian government—a fear of corruption—is fueled by the low salaries paid to Haitian government officials. As Jonathan Katz points out in *The Big Truck That Went By*, 129, aid supporting Haitian traffic cops and customs bureau employees to earn better than their current sub-poverty salaries of less than $400 per month would likely work to lessen corruption in those sectors.

45. Jake Johnston, "Haiti's Fight for Transparency," *Caribbean Journal*, May 3, 2012, *www.caribjournal.com*. Johnston penned the op-ed as a Center for Economic Policy and Research staff member.

46. DARA, "Focus on Haiti: Building Back Better?" research paper for the Humanitarian Response Index, 2011, 12, *daraint.org*.

47. Mark Schuller, "*Rat Mode, Soufle*: Foreign Domination," in Schuller and Morales, *Tectonic Shifts*, 35.

48. Jacob Kushner, "US Spent $140 Million of Haiti Earthquake Aid on Controversial Food Exports," *Pulitzer Center on Crisis Reporting*, January 11, 2012, *pulitzercenter.org*.

49. Concannon, "Work with the Haitian Government."

50. Chavannes Jean-Baptiste, quoted in Kushner, "US Spent $140 Million."

51. Mark Weisbrot, Jake Johnston, and Rebecca Ray, "Using Food Aid to Support, Not Harm, Haitian Agriculture," issue brief, Center for Economic and Policy Research, April 2010.

52. For a brief discussion of the role US agribusiness plays in US food aid, see Claire Provost and Felicity Lawrence, "US Food Aid Programme Criticised as 'Corporate Welfare' for Grain Giants," *Guardian*, July 18, 2012.

53. President Préval's remarks were reported in Matthew Bigg, "Long-Term Food Aid Risk to Haitian Economy—Preval," Reuters, March 8, 2010, *www.reuters.com*.

54. For a discussion of the US policy of "tied aid," see Bread for the World Institute, "Untie Aid: Tied Aid Is Not Cost-Effective and Undermines Capacity-Building," in *Our Common Interest: Ending Hunger and Nutrition; 2011 Hunger Report* (Washington, DC: Bread for the World), 86–88, *www.hungerreport.org*. USAID reported a change in policy in 2012, but that change does not affect food aid. See Claire Provost, "USAID Now Free to Buy Goods From Companies in Poor Countries," *Guardian*, February 6, 2012.

55. "USAID Development Efforts Benefit US Economy," USAID *FrontLines*, March/April 2001, 21.

56. Organisation for Economic Co-operation and Development, *2006 Survey on Monitoring the Paris Declaration: Overview of the Results*, (Paris: OECD, 2007), 85, 120.

57. The centralization of Haiti's population in Port-au-Prince is discussed in Chenet Jean-Baptiste, "Haiti's Earthquake," 98–100, and in Kathleen A. Tobin, "Population Density and Housing in Port-au-Prince: Historical Construction of Vulnerability," 39 *Journal of Urban History* 1045–61 (2013).

58. Etienne, "Haiti and Catastrophe," 29.

59. Jeffrey Sachs, "Haiti's Road to Recovery," *Guardian*, January 31, 2010.

60. Chenet Jean-Baptiste, "Haiti's Earthquake," 97–100.

61. DARA, "Focus on Haiti," 13.

62. Johnston, "Haiti's Fight for Transparency."

63. An account of the recruiting of Haitian government workers by NGOs was included in Madeline Kristoff and Liz Panarelli, "Haiti: A Republic of NGOs?" *Peace Brief* 23, US Institute for Peace, April 26, 2010, *www.usip.org*; and Evelyne Trouillot, "*Abse Sou Klou*: Reconstructing Exclusion," in Schuller and Morales, *Tectonic Shifts*, 106.

64. Préval, quoted in Jacqueline Charles, "Groups Jockey for Role in Haiti Revival," *Miami Herald*, March 9, 2010.

65. François Grünewald and Andrea Binder, with Yvio Georges, *Inter-Agency Real-Time Evaluation in Haiti: 3 Months after the Earthquake* (Berlin: Global Public Policy Institute and Groupe URD, 2010), 54, *www.gppi.net*.

66. USAID Office of Inspector General, "Audit of USAID's Efforts to Provide Shelter in Haiti," Audit Report 1-521-11-003-P, April 19, 2011, *oig.usaid.gov*.

67. USAID Office of Inspector General, "Audit of USAID's Cash-for-Work Programs in Haiti," Audit Report 1-521-10-009-P, September 24, 2010, *oig.usaid.gov*.

68. Jake Johnston, "Blacklisted Contractor Continues Receiving Government Money through Haiti Contracts," *Hill Congress Blog*, December 2, 2011, *thehill.com*.

69. Bill Vastine, quoted in Reitman, "Beyond Relief."

70. "The Shelters That Clinton Built," *Nation*, July 12, 2011.

71. See Trenton Daniel, "New Hotels Arise amid Ruins in Haitian Capital," *Yahoo News*, April 30, 2012, *www.yahoo.com*. ("'It's nice to build hotels to bring tourists but first you need to think of your citizens,' said Ben Etienne, a 36-year-old resident of a hilly encampment in Peguyville that fills with mud during Haiti's rainy season.")

72. An account of the problems of Yéle is found in Deborah Sontag, "In Haiti, Little Can Be Found of a Hip-Hop Artist's Charity," *New York Times*, October 11, 2012.

73. An account of the protests against the Red Cross was included in Marjorie Valbrun, "After The Quake, Praise Becomes Resentment in Haiti," *iWatch News*, Center for Public Integrity, January 12, 2012, *www.publicintegrity.org*.

74. Thomas Tighe, quoted in Stephanie Strom, "Haiti Crisis Prompts Fresh Talk of Pooling Relief Money," *New York Times*, February 1, 2010. The discrepancy between the Red Cross and PIH presence in Haiti pre-earthquake was reported in this same article.

75. "THE GOLD RUSH IS ON!" and private company efforts to profit from the earthquake response were reported in Ansel Herz and Kim Ives, "After the Quake, a 'Gold Rush' for Haitian Contracts," in Schuller and Morales, *Tectonic Shifts*, 77–78.

76. Lewis Lucke, quoted in Ansel Herz and Kim Ives, "WikiLeaks Cables Reveal: After the Quake, a 'Gold Rush' for Haitian Contracts," *Haïti Liberté*, June 21, 2011.

77. Quoted in Panchang, "Waiting for Helicopters," 185, 186.

78. An account of the Clinton Foundation videos was included in Isabeau Doucet and Isabel MacDonald, "Building Illusions: A Case Study of Bill Clinton's Photo-Op Philanthropy," in Schuller and Morales, *Tectonic Shifts*, 79.

79. Jean Cene, in *Haiti: Where Did the Money Go?* written and produced by Michele Mitchell and Ivan Weiss, 2011; accessed December 15, 2013, at *www.youtube.com*.

80. Jacky Lumarque, in Valbrun, "After the Quake."

81. The Oxfam report is described in Amber Hildebrandt, "Haiti Suffers after 'Year of Indecision': Oxfam," CBC *News*, January 5, 2011, *www.cbc.ca*.

82. Ricardo Seitenfus, quoted in Arnaud Robert, "OAS Representative in Haiti Sharply Critical of Foreign Aid and Occupation," translated by David Holmes Morris, *Lo de allá . . . : News and Views from Latin America*, December 20, 2010, *lo-de-alla.org*.

83. Tim Schwartz, quoted in Hallward, *Damming the Flood*, 333.

84. Deborah Sontag, "Rebuilding in Haiti Lags after Billions in Post-Quake Aid," *New York Times*, December 23, 2012.

85. Schuller, *Killing with Kindness*, 176.

86. Nigel Fisher, quoted in Frances Roble, "Critics Question Funds Raised for Haiti," *Miami Herald*, January 9, 2011.

87. Schuller, *Killing with Kindness*, 176.

88. International Organization for Migration, "IOM Steps Up Efforts to Contain Cholera in Haiti's Camps and Provinces," press briefing note, December 11, 2010, *www.iom.int*.

89. Mark Schuller, "Unstable Foundations: NGOs and Human Rights for Port-au-Prince's Internally Displaced People," in Schuller and Morales, *Tectonic Shifts*, 119–24; and Nicole Phillips et al., "'We've Been Forgotten': Haiti's IDP Camps Eight Months after the Earthquake," in Schuller and Morales, *Tectonic Shifts*, 179–82. LAMP stands for *Libète Ak Medesin Pou Ayiti*—liberty and health for Haiti.

90. Schuller, "Unstable Foundations,"120.

91. Phillips et al., "We've Been Forgotten," 180; and Schuller, "Unstable Foundations," 122.

92. Schuller, "Unstable Foundations," 121.

93. Phillips et al., "We've Been Forgotten," 180.

94. Ibid., 182.

95. Panchang, "Waiting for Helicopters," 183–91.

96. Schuller, *Killing with Kindness*, 6, 174.

97. Center for Economic and Policy Research, "Donor Disbursements Slowing According to Latest Data from Special Envoy," *Haiti: Relief and Reconstruction Watch* (blog), April 25, 2012, *www.cepr.net*.

98. Melinda Miles, "Assumptions and Exclusion: Coordination Failures during the Emergency Phase," in Schuller and Morales, *Tectonic Shifts*, 49.

99. Paul E. Farmer, "Message from the Deputy Special Envoy," in *Summary Report on Activities, June 2009–December 2010* (New York: Office of the Special Envoy for Haiti, 2011), *www.lessonsfromhaiti.org*.

100. The survey of humanitarian workers was reported in Amanda M. Klasing, P. Scott Moses, and Margaret L. Satterthwaite, "Measuring the Way Forward in Haiti: Grounding Disaster Relief in the Legal Framework of Human Rights," 13 *Health and Human Rights: An International Journal* 1–21 (July 2011).

101. For a discussion of international agencies' adoption of a human rights-based approach to aid and development, see Brian Concannon Jr. and Bea Lindstrom, "Cheaper, Better, Longer-Lasting: A Rights-Based Approach to Disaster Response in Haiti," 25 *Emory International Law Review* 1157 (2011). Concannon and Lindstrom reference several UN documents reiterating its commitment to a human rights-based approach to development and aid, including *Documenting Lessons Learned for Human Rights–Based Programming: An Asia-Pacific Perspective* (Bangkok: UNESCO, 2008), 3. UN agencies—including United Nations International Children's Emergency Fund (UNICEF), United Nations Development Fund for Women (UNIFEM), United Nations Development Programme (UNDP), World Health Organization (WHO), and the Joint United Nations Programme on HIV and AIDS (UNAIDS)—have also expressly adopted the rights-based approach. See Dzodzi Tsikata, "The Rights-Based Approach to Development: Potential for Change or More of the Same?" IDS *Bulletin*, October 2004, 130.

102. The briefings to the IACHR are included in Elizabeth Sepper et al., "The Human Rights Obligations of OAS Member States Providing International Assistance in the Region: A Brief to the Inter-American Commission on Human Rights for a Hearing on the Economic and Social Rights Situation in Haiti following the Earthquake and the Human Rights Obligations of OAS Member States," March 9, 2010 (available at *www.ijdh.org*) and summarized in IJDH, "Rights Groups Testify about Haiti and Human Rights before Inter-American Commission: Testimony Details Haiti Aid Challenges, Presses for Commission Investigation," March 23, 2010, *www.ijdh.org*.

103. An explanation of Partners in Health's "accompaniment" approach is found at Joia Mukherjee, Sarah Roberto, Alex Lassegue, and Lauren Spahn, "Human Rights through Accompaniment," *Harvard International Review*, August 23, 2010.

104. A discussion of the human rights-based approach to development's grounding in international law is provided in Concannon and Lindstrom, "Cheaper, Better, Longer-Lasting," 1148–59.

105. For a more thorough discussion of the international community's agricultural policies and their effects on Haiti, see Chapter 7.

106. See Center for Human Rights and Global Justice (CHRGJ), Partners in Health (PIH), Robert F. Kennedy Memorial Center for Human Rights (RFK Center), and Zanmi Lasante (ZL), *Wòch nan Soley: The Denial of the Right to Water in Haiti* (New York: CHRGJ; Boston: PIH; Washington, DC: RFK Center; Port-au-Prince: ZL, 2008), 10–14, *chrgj.org*.

107. IACHR, "IACHR Stresses Duty to Respect Human Rights during the Emergency in Haiti," press release, February 2, 2010, *www.cidh.oas.org*.

108. Deepa Panchang, "Withholding Water: Cholera, Prejudice, and the Right to Water in Haiti," *Women's International Perspective*, May 31, 2012, *thewip.net*.

109. UN General Assembly, "Report of the Independent Expert on the Situation of Human Rights in Haiti, Michel Forst" (A/HRC/20/35), April 23, 2012, 3, *www.ohchr.org*.

110. The mid-2010 survey of organizations working in Haiti was reported in Klasing, Moses, and Satterthwaite, "Measuring the Way Forward."

111. UN Office of the High Commissioner for Human Rights, *Claiming the Millennium Development Goals: A Human Rights Approach*, (New York: United Nations, 2008), 15.

112. Edmond Mulet, in "Battle for Haiti," produced and directed by Dan Reed, *Frontline*, January 11, 2011, *www.pbs.org*.

113. An earlier version of this section was first published as Fran Quigley, "Things Are Difficult: A Post-Earthquake Disaster in Haiti," *Common Dreams*, April 12, 2013, *www.commondreams.org*.

114. Mario Joseph, Patrice Florvilus, and Nicole Phillips, "Request for Precautionary Measures for Petitioner Marcel Germain and Petitioners B, C, and D from Camp Grace Village, on Behalf of Their Respective Communities," petition to the IACHR, February 19, 2013; available at *www.ijdh.org*.

115. The IACHR's "Mesures conservatoires MC-52-13" (Precautionary measures MC-52-13) were listed in a letter (in French) from Elizabeth Abi-Mershed, assistant executive secretary of the IACHR, to Mario Joseph and Patrice Florvilus, March 26, 2013; a copy of the letter is available at *www.ijdh.org*.

CHAPTER 6

1. International Women's Human Rights Clinic at the City University of New York School of Law [hereafter IWHRC] et al., "Request by the International Women's Human Rights Clinic at the City University of New York School of Law, MADRE, the Institute for Justice and Democracy in Haiti, Bureau des Avocats Internationaux, Morrison and Foerster LLP, the Center for Constitutional Rights, and Women's Link Worldwide for Precautionary Measures under Article 25 of the Commission's Rules of Procedure," petition submitted to the IACHR, October 19, 2010, appendix A; available at *www.madre.org*.

2. Ibid.

3. Global Justice Clinic/Center for Human Rights and Global Justice, *Yon Je Louvri: Reducing Vulnerability to Sexual Violence in Haiti's IDP Camps* (New York: NYU School of Law, 2012), xviii.

4. Athena R. Kolbe et al. *Assessing Needs after the Quake: Preliminary Findings from a Randomized Survey of Port-au-Prince Households* (Ann Arbor: University of Michigan, 2010), 23.

5. Global Justice Clinic/Center for Human Rights and Global Justice, *Yon Je Louvri*, 36.

6. The UN/Government of Haiti study was reported in Daraine Luton, "Haiti's Rate of Fertility Tripled—Report," *Jamaica Gleaner*, October 22, 2010. The estimate of two-thirds of those pregnancies being unwanted was reported in MADRE et al., *Our Bodies Are Still Trembling: Haitian Women Continue to Fight against Rape* (New York: MADRE; Flushing, NY: International Women's Human Rights Clinic, City University of New York School of Law; Port-au-Prince: IJDH; and Boston: BAI, 2011), 15; available at *www.madre.org*.

7. The prevalence of HIV among Haitians was reported in "Caribbean HIV & AIDS Statistics," *Avert*, December 1, 2012, *www.avert.org*. Fears of STDs were reported in Luton, "Haiti's Rate of Fertility."

8. Human Rights Watch, *"Nobody Remembers Us": Failure to Protect Women's and Girls' Rights to Health and Security in Post-Earthquake Haiti* (New York: Human Rights Watch, 2011). This report is the source for the mortality rates mentioned (14).

9. Ibid., 32–33.

10. The reports on Haitian women's and girls' limited access to health care and education, historic victimization by rape, and comparatively limited access to political power and economic self-sufficiency are provided in IACHR, *The Right of Women in Haiti to Be Free from*

Violence and Discrimination (Washington, DC: IACHR, 2009). The 60 percent in extreme poverty figure is provided in International Monetary Fund, "Haiti: Poverty Reduction Strategy Paper, 2008–2010," IMF Country Report No. 08/115, March 2008, 24, *www .imf.org*. The report on current distribution of political leadership by sex was included in Meena Jagannath, "Barriers to Women's Access to Justice in Haiti," 15 CUNY *Law Journal* 1 (2012).

11. An account of the loss of Myriam Merlet, Magalie Marcelin, and Anne Marie Coriolon was included in Jessica Ravitz, "Women's Movement Mourns Death of 3 Haitian Leaders," CNN, January 25, 2010, *www.cnn.com*.

12. For a discussion of women's vulnerability post-disaster, see Jane M. Henrici, Allison Suppan Helmuth, and Jackie Braun, *Women, Disasters, and Hurricane Katrina* (Washington, DC: Institute for Women's Policy Research, 2010).

13. MADRE et al., *Our Bodies*, 8.

14. Global Justice Clinic/Center for Human Rights and Global Justice, *Yon Je Louvri*.

15. Quoted in Human Rights Watch, *Nobody Remembers Us*, 51.

16. IWHRC et al., "Request," appendix A.

17. MADRE et al., *Our Bodies*, 18.

18. A discussion of Haitian law as applied to incidents of sexual violence, along with accounts of the police not responding to complaints, is included in Jagannath, "Barriers."

19. "Battle for Haiti," produced and directed by Dan Reed, *Frontline*, January 11, 2011, *www.pbs.org*.

20. Global Justice Clinic/Center for Human Rights and Global Justice, *Yon Je Louvri*, 74.

21. Mario Joseph, quoted in Anastasia Moloney, "What Justice for Haiti's Rape Survivors?" *TruthLaw*, February 16, 2012.

22. Trenton Daniel, "UN Report on Haiti Shows Few Prosecutions," Associated Press, June 27, 2012, *www.bigstory.ap.org*.

23. IACHR, *Right of Women*, 3.

24. Meena Jagannath, "Women's Global Health Update: Fighting the Epidemic of Sexual Violence in Post-Earthquake Haiti," presentation at Indiana University School of Medicine, Indianapolis, February 15, 2012.

25. Quoted in Jagannath, "Barriers."

26. MADRE et al., "Statement Submitted to the UN Commission on the Status of Women for the 56th Session (February 29–March 9, 2012) Concerning the Empowerment of Rural Women and Their Role in Poverty and Hunger Eradication, Development and Current Challenges in Haiti," November 21, 2011; available at *ijdh.org*.

27. Quoted in Meena Jagannath, "Interview with Marie Esther Felix," August 13, 2011.

28. Ibid.

29. Ibid.

30. IWHRC et al., "Request," appendix A.

31. Jayne Fleming's affidavit was included in ibid.

32. Quoted in Global Justice Clinic/Center for Human Rights and Global Justice, *Yon Je Louvri*, 73.

33. The International Covenant on Civil and Political Rights and the Convention on the Rights of the Child can be viewed at the website of the UN Office of the High Commissioner of Human Rights, *www2.0hchr.org/english*. The American Convention

on Human Rights, the Inter-American Convention on the Prevention, Punishment and Eradication of Violence against Women (also known as the Convention of Belém Do Pará), and the Haitian penal code (in French) can be found at the website of the OAS, *www.oas .org*. The 1987 Constitution of Haiti can be viewed at Georgetown University's Political Database of the Americas, *pdba.georgetown.edu/constitutions/haiti/haiti1987.html*.

34. Fritz Deshommes, "The 1987 Constitution: A Lever for the True 'Re-Foundation' of a Nation," in *Tectonic Shifts: Haiti since the Earthquake*, edited by Mark Schuller and Pablo Morales (Boulder, CO: Kumarian Press, 2012), 251.

35. Mesita Attis, quoted in Beverly Bell, "'We Bend, but We Don't Break': Fighting for a Just Reconstruction in Haiti," in Schuller and Morales, *Tectonic Shifts*, 216.

36. Bell, "We Bend," 215–16.

37. Haitian author Edwidge Danticat wrote a novel about the queen: *Anacaona: Golden Flower, Haiti, 1490* (New York: Scholastic, 2005).

38. For an account of Haitian women's groups' activism historically, see "'We Need to Stay Vigilant': An Interview with Lise-Marie Dejean," in Schuller and Morales, *Tectonic Shifts*, 227–31.

39. MADRE et al., *Our Bodies*, 23.

40. Beverly Bell, *Walking on Fire: Haitian Women's Stories of Survival and Resistance* (Ithaca, NY: Cornell University Press, 2001).

41. "Expressing the Sense of the House of Representatives that the United States Should Work with the Government of Haiti to Address Gender-Based Violence against Women and Children," H. R. 521, 112th Cong., 2nd Sess. (2012).

42. "Database of UPR Recommendations—Haiti," Universal Periodic Review Info, accessed December 16, 2013, *www.upr-info.org*

43. The groups' submission to the UN Human Rights Council was MADRE et al., "Gender-Based Violence against Haitian Women and Girls in Internal Displacement Camps," Republic of Haiti submission to the UN Universal Periodic Review, 12th Session of the Working Group on the UPR, UN Human Rights Council, October 3–14, 2011; available at *ijdh.org*.

44. IACHR, "Women and Girls Residing in 22 Camps for Internally Displaced Persons in Port-au-Prince, Haiti," precautionary measure (PM 340/10), in IACHR *Annual Report 2010* (Washington, DC: IACHR, 2010), 52 (III.C.1), *www.cidh.oas.org*.

45. IJDH memorandum to the UN Human Rights Committee, July 9, 2012, on file with author.

46. UN General Assembly, "Report of the Independent Expert on the Situation of Human Rights in Haiti, Michel Forst" (A/HRC/20/35), April 23, 2012, 15.

47. Delra, quoted in Angela Robson, "Haiti: Men Supporting Women's Rights," *Guardian*, November 20, 2011.

48. Jagannath, "Barriers."

49. Mario Joseph and Jeena Shah, "Combating Forced Evictions in Haiti's IDP Camps," in Schuller and Morales, *Tectonic Shifts*, 139.

50. Center for Economic and Policy Research, "Beyond the Headlines: Is the Reduction of the IDP Population a Sign of Success?" *Haiti: Relief and Reconstruction* (blog), January 10, 2012, *www.cepr.net*.

51. International Organization for Migration, "Displacement Tracking Matrix: V2.0 Update," March 16, 2011, 11, *www.eshelter-cccmhaiti.info/jl/pdf/*

DTM_*V2_Report_15_March_2011_English.pdf*. The most recent report on displaced persons and forced evictions is found in Amnesty International, *"Nowhere to Go": Forced Evictions in Haiti's Displacement Camps* (London: Amnesty International, 2013).

52. Haiti E-Shelter and CCCM Cluster, "December 2012—Fact Sheet," *From Camps to Communities: Haiti Emergency Shelter and Camp Coordination Camp Management*, Inter-Agency Standing Committee, UCLBP (L'Unité de Construction de Logements et de Bâtiments Publics), *www.eshelter-cccmhaiti.info*.

53. International Federation for Human Rights, *Haiti: Human Security in Danger* (Paris: International Federation for Human Rights, 2012), 11.

54. Joseph and Shah, "Combating Forced Evictions," 141.

55. For an account of one of the housing protests, see Trenton Daniel, "Protest over Evictions in Haiti Blocks Traffic," *Miami Herald*, August 2, 2011.

56. For an account of the mid-2012 campaign, see Roger Annis, "Haiti's Quake Victims Step Up," *Haïti Liberté*, July 4, 2012. A core allegation of the campaign was that the Martelly government had used a combination of pressure and small stipends to remove displaced Haitians from the IDP camps in the most visible public areas of Port-au-Prince near the palace and the airport, without any comprehensive plan for relocating Haitians who had lost their homes in the earthquake. See, for example, Trenton Daniel, "Haiti Park Standoff Highlights Conflict over Land," Associated Press, August 30, 2012, *www.bigstory.ap.org*.

57. "Truth out, Dying Season in," 70 *Haiti Support Group Briefing* 1–2 (April 2012); available at *www.ijdh.org*.

58. "Remarks by Ambassador Susan E. Rice, US Permanent Representative to the United Nations, on the Security Council Mission to Haiti," statement, US Department of State, February 28, 2012, *www.state.gov*.

59. Matthew Mosk, "Bill Clinton, UN Envoy, Admits Peacekeepers as Source of Haitian Cholera," ABC *News*, March 9, 2012, *abcnews.go.com*.

60. Amnesty International, "Haiti—Arbitrary Arrest/Prisoner of Conscience: Gérard Jean-Juste," Urgent Action alert (AMR 36/008/2005), July 25, 2005, *www.amnesty.org*.

61. Ashoka, "What Is a Social Entrepreneur?," accessed November 11, 2013, *www.ashoka.org*.

62. David Brooks, "Sam Spade at Starbucks," *New York Times*, April 12, 2012.

63. J. Gregory Dees, "David Brooks, Politics and Social Entrepreneurs," *Dowser*, April 23, 2012, *dowser.org*.

64. Sally Osberg, "Social Entrepreneurs 'Refreshingly Uncynical'—But Not at All Delusional," *Huffington Post*, April 20, 2012, *huffingtonpost.com*.

65. Ashoka, "What Is a Social Entrepreneur?"

66. Amy Kapczynski and Jonathan M. Berger, "The Story of the TAC Case: The Potential and Limits of Socio-Economic Rights Litigation in South Africa," in *Human Rights Advocacy Stories*, edited by Deena R. Hurwitz, Margaret L. Satterthwaite, and Douglas B. Ford (Eagan, MN: Foundation Press, 2009), 47.

67. Ibid., 4.

68. The Indian and Nigerian examples are discussed in Alice Donald and Elizabeth Mottershaw, "Evaluating the Impact of Human Rights Litigation on Policy and Practice: A Case Study of the UK," 1 *Journal of Human Rights Practice* 340 (2009).

69. The approach is outlined in Brian Concannon Jr., "The Bureau des Avocats Internationaux, a Victim-Centered Approach," in *Effective Strategies for Protecting Human Rights*, edited by

David Barnhizer (London: Ashgate Press, 2001). A more recent description of the same philosophy is contained in Meena Jagannath, Nicole Phillips, and Jeena Shah, "A Rights-Based Approach to Lawyering: Legal Empowerment as an Alternative to Legal Aid in Post-Disaster Haiti," 10 *Northwestern Journal of International Human Rights* 7 (2011).

70. Jagannath, Phillips, and Shah, "Rights-Based Approach to Lawyering," 10.

CHAPTER 7

1. For a comparison of the Chile and Haiti earthquakes' impact, see Frank Bajak, "Chile-Haiti Earthquake Comparison: Chile Was More Prepared," *Huffington Post*, February 27, 2010, *www.huffingtonpost.com*.
2. Brian Concannon Jr., quoted in Greg O'Brien, "Concannon, Haiti: A 'Visceral' Connection," *Boston Irish Reporter*, August 31, 2011, *www.bostonirish.com*.
3. Paul Farmer, *The Uses of Haiti* (Monroe, ME: Common Courage Press, 2005), 212.
4. For accounts of Haiti's prerevolutionary history, see Laurent Dubois, *Haiti: The Aftershocks of History* (New York: Metropolitan Books, 2012), 17–23, and Farmer, *Uses of Haiti*, 53–59.
5. Boukman's speech was reported in Dubois, *Haiti*, 91–92.
6. The classic account of Haiti's revolution is C. L. R. James, *The Black Jacobins: Toussaint L'Ouverture and the San Domingo Revolution* (New York: Vintage, 1989). See also Laurent Dubois, *Avengers of the New World: The Story of the Haitian Revolution* (Cambridge, MA: Harvard University Press, 2004); Dubois, *Haiti*, 23–42; and Farmer, *Uses of Haiti*, 59–63.
7. Toussaint L'Ouverture, quoted in Dubois, *Haiti*, 38.
8. George Washington, quoted in Randall Robinson, *An Unbroken Agony: Haiti, from Revolution to the Kidnapping of a President* (New York: Basic Civitas, 2007), 8. For a discussion of how the US response to the Haitian revolution shaped an expanded model of executive power in the United States, see Robert J. Reinstein, "Slavery, Executive Power and International Law: The Haitian Revolution and American Constitutionalism," 53 *American Journal of Legal History* 142–237 (2013); available at *papers.ssrn.com*.
9. Thomas Jefferson, quoted in Robinson, *Unbroken Agony*, 8.
10. Robert Hayne, quoted in Rayford Whittingham Logan, *The Diplomatic Relations of the United States with Haiti, 1776–1891* (Chapel Hill: University of North Carolina Press, 1941), 227.
11. The possible impact of the Haitian Revolution on Gabriel Prosser and Nat Turner is discussed in Minkah Makalani, "Pan-Africanism," in *Africana Age: African and African Diasporan Transformations in the 20th Century* (online exhibition curated by the Schomburg-Mellon Humanities Summer Institute), 2011, *www.exhibitions.nypl.org*.
12. Accounts of Haiti's influence on John Brown and Haiti's subsequent memorializing of the US abolitionist are included in Robinson, *Unbroken Agony*, 65; and Dubois, *Haiti*, 135–36.
13. Dubois, *Haiti*, 97–105.
14. The nineteenth-century pattern of "gunboat diplomacy" in Haiti's relationships with the United States and other nations is described in Farmer, *Uses of Haiti*, 74–78; and Dubois, *Haiti*: 204–11.
15. For an extensive account of the US occupation of Haiti from 1915 to 1934, see Dubois, *Haiti*, 211–64.

16. Logan, *Diplomatic Relations*, 125–27.

17. Dubois, *Haiti*, 212.

18. "Haiti and Its Regeneration by the United States," 38 *National Geographic Magazine* 497 (1920).

19. Dubois, *Haiti*, 244.

20. Smedley Darlington Butler, quoted in ibid., 228.

21. Butler, quoted in Howard Zinn and Anthony Arnove, *Voices of A People's History of the United States*, 2nd ed. (New York: Seven Stories Press, 2009), 251–52.

22. An account of the referendum on the new constitution is contained in Dubois, *Haiti*, 244–48.

23. *Financial America*, quoted in Paul Farmer, *Aids and Accusation: Haiti and the Geography of Blame* (Berkeley: University of California Press, 1993), 180.

24. Quoted in Dubois, *Haiti*, 275.

25. Dubois, *Haiti*, 259–64.

26. Ibid., 266.

27. An account of François Duvalier's prepresidential political activity and his initial election is included in Matthew J. Smith, *Red and Black in Haiti: Radicalism, Conflict and Political Change, 1934–1957* (Chapel Hill: University of North Carolina Press, 2009), 161–85.

28. Heinl and Heinl, *Written in Blood*, 602.

29. Accounts of the money and military support the US provided to François Duvalier's regime are included in Farmer, *Uses of Haiti*, 92–94, and Dubois, *Haiti*, 333–37.

30. An account of the money and military support the United States provided to Jean-Claude Duvalier's regime is included in Dubois, *Haiti*, 350–54, 355.

31. An account of the end of Jean-Claude Duvalier's rule of Haiti is provided in Amy Wilentz, *The Rainy Season: Haiti—Then and Now* (New York: Simon and Schuster, 1989), 19–49. See also Farmer, *Uses of Haiti*, 102–7.

32. Alex Dupuy, "The Neoliberal Legacy in Haiti," in Schuller and Morales, *Tectonic Shifts*, 24.

33. Mark Danner, "To Heal Haiti, Look to History, Not Nature," *New York Times*, January 21, 2010.

34. The government of Haiti's estimate that its debt to France cost $21 billion was reported in Jacqueline Charles, "Aristide Pushes for Restitution from France," *Miami Herald*, December 18, 2003.

35. The report that 80 percent of Haitian government revenue was spent on debt service before the US invasion was provided in Patrick Bellegarde-Smith, *Race, Class and Ideology: Haitian Ideologies for Underdevelopment, 1806–1934* (New York: American Institute for Marxist Studies, 1982), 15.

36. Deepa Panchang, "'Waiting for Helicopters': Perceptions, Misperceptions, and the Right to Water in Haiti," in *Tectonic Shifts: Haiti since the Earthquake*, edited by Mark Schuller and Pablo Morales (Boulder, CO: Kumarian Press, 2012), 186.

37. Robert Maguire, *Haiti after the Donors' Conference: A Way Forward* (Washington, DC: US Institute for Peace, 2009), 5.

38. American Center for International Labor Solidarity/AFL-CIO, *Unequal Equation: The Labor Code and Worker Rights in Haiti* (Washington, DC: American Center for International Labor Solidarity, 2003), 5.

39. Farmer, *Uses of Haiti*, 99.

40. Quoted in ibid., 45.

41. The IMF and World Bank "structural adjustment" programming and philosophy is discussed in William Easterly, "IMF and World Bank Structural Adjustment Programs and Poverty," in *Managing Currency Crises in Emerging Markets*, edited by Michael P. Dooley and Jeffrey A. Frankel (Chicago: University of Chicago Press, 2003), 361–82.

42. Peter Hallward, *Damming the Flood: Haiti and the Politics of Containment* (London: Verso, 2007), 15.

43. Dupuy, "Neoliberal Legacy in Haiti."

44. The 1978 World Bank admission and Duvalier admission were reported in ibid., 26.

45. Paul Collier, "Haiti: From Natural Catastrophe to Economic Security," report for the secretary-general of the UN, January 2009, 6; available at *www.focal.ca*.

46. J. F. Hornbeck, *The Haitian Economy and the* HOPE *Act* (Washington, DC: Congressional Research Service, 2010).

47. The 2011 survey of Haitian garment factories was reported in Katz, *Big Truck*, 142–43.

48. Deborah Sontag, "Earthquake Relief Where Haiti Wasn't Broken," *New York Times*, July 5, 2012. See also Haiti Grassroots Watch, "The Case of Caracol," article 6 of "Haiti—Open for Business," *Haiti Grassroots Watch*, November 29, 2011, *haitigrassrootswatch.squarespace.com*.

49. Haiti Grassroots Watch, "The Caracol Industrial Park: Worth the Risk?" *Haiti Grassroots Watch*, March 7, 2013, *haitigrassrootswatch.squarespace.com*.

50. "José Agustín Aguerre, quoted in Sontag, "Earthquake Relief." For further discussion of the park, see Haiti Grassroots Watch, "Case of Caracol."

51. Haitian garment assembly workers report being fired if they are identified as supporting a union or criticizing work conditions. Center for Economic Policy and Research, "Investigation Finds Evidence of Violations of Union Rights in Garment Industry," *Haiti: Relief and Reconstruction Watch* (blog), November 30, 2011, *www.cepr.net*; and Ian Trupin, "Tell Gildan and Hanes: Re-hire SOTA Union Leaders Immediately!," United Students Against Sweatshops, November 11, 2011, *www.usas.org*.

52. Solidarity Center, "A Post-Earthquake Living Wage Estimate for Apparel Workers in the Sonapi Export Processing Zone," March 3, 2011, *www.solidaritycenter.org*.

53. International Labour Organization and International Finance Corporation, *Better Work Haiti: Garment Industry 5th Biannual Synthesis Report under the* HOPE *II Legislation* (Geneva: International Labour Organization and International Finance Corporation, 2012), *betterwork.com*.

54. Worker Rights Consortium, *Stealing From the Poor: Wage Theft in the Haitian Apparel Industry* (Washington, DC: Worker Rights Consortium, 2013), *www.workersrights.org*. Spokespersons for some of the factories named in the report told the *New York Times* that the allegations of wage theft are not true. Randal C. Archibold and Steven Greenhouse, "Group Says Haitian Garment Workers Are Shortchanged on Pay," *New York Times*, October 15, 2013.

55. Center for Economic Policy and Research, "Investigation Finds Evidence."

56. International Finance Corporation, *Integrated Economic Zones in Haiti: Market Analysis* (Washington, DC: International Finance Corporation, 2011).

57. An earlier version of this section was published as Fran Quigley, "Haitian Sweatshops: Made in the USA," *Working in These Times*, March 21, 2013, *www.inthesetimes.com*.

58. Former Associated Press correspondent in Haiti Jonathan Katz says, "The goal for years had clearly been to build up garment factories, rebuild the assembly sector and get as many Haitians as possible into those places, to sew as much as possible for as little money as possible. There's really no doubt that this was the US government's strategy and the major US investment strategy. Decentralization was very clearly an obstacle." In Colin Dayan, "The Secret History of the Haitian Earthquake: A Conversation with Jonathan M. Katz," *Boston Review*, June 25, 2013, *www.bostonreview.net*.

59. The "counter-plantation" system, also known as the *métayage* system, is described in Alex Dupuy, *Haiti in the World Economy: Class, Race, and Underdevelopment since 1700* (Boulder, CO: Westview Press, 1989), 91, 98.

60. The 20 percent Caribbean rice tariff average was referenced in Mark Schuller, *Killing with Kindness* (New Brunswick, NJ: Rutgers University Press, 2012), 21.

61. Yolette Etienne, "Jumping over the Fire," in *Walking on Fire*, ed. Beverly Bell (Ithaca, NY: Cornell University Press, 2001), 120.

62. For discussions of the effects of the international community's agricultural policies on Haiti, see Center for Human Rights and Global Justice et al., "Right to Food, Water and Sanitation," Republic of Haiti submission to the UN Universal Periodic Review, 12th Session of the Working Group on the UPR, UN Human Rights Council, October 3–14, 2011), 71, 76–77 (available at *ijdh.org*), and Brian Concannon Jr. and Bea Lindstrom, "Cheaper, Better, Longer-Lasting: A Rights-Based Approach to Disaster Response in Haiti," 25 *Emory International Law Review* 1163–64 (2011).

63. Marc Cohen, quoted in Maura R. O'Connor, "Subsidizing Starvation: How American Tax Dollars Are Keeping Arkansas Rice Growers Fat on the Farm and Starving Millions of Haitians," *Foreign Policy*, January 11, 2013, *www.foreignpolicy.com*.

64. O'Connor, "Subsidizing Starvation."

65. For a discussion of the causes and effects of deforestation, see Concannon and Lindstrom, "Cheaper, Better, Longer-Lasting," 1161–62.

66. Death tolls from tropical storm Jeanne were compiled by USAID and reported in Mark Weisbrot and Luis Sandoval, *Update: Debt Cancellation for Haiti: No Reason for Further Delays* (Washington, DC: Center for Economic and Policy Reform, 2008), 14.

67. Brian Concannon Jr. "Another Unnatural Disaster," *Boston Haitian Reporter*, October 2004.

68. For a discussion of the causes and effects of the overpopulation of Port-au-Prince, see Dupuy, "Neoliberal Legacy of Haiti," 26.

69. For accounts of the popular movement for democracy and election of Jean-Bertrand Aristide in 1990, see Farmer, *Uses of Haiti*, 107–36, and Hallward, *Damming the Flood*, 29–33.

70. The USAID-funded study was described in Lisa McGowan, *Democracy Undermined, Economic Justice Denied: Structural Adjustment and the Aid Juggernaut in Haiti*, (Washington, DC: Development Group for Alternative Policies, 1997), 96.

71. Quoted in Paul Quinn-Judge, "US Reported to Intercept Aristide Calls," *Boston Globe*, September 8, 1994.

72. Latell quoted in William Blum, *Killing Hope: US Military and* CIA *Interventions since World War II* (London: Zed Books, 2003), 374. For an account of the CIA support of 1991 coup leaders, see 375–77.

73. An account of the US response to Haitian refugees from the coup government is included in Maurice Weaver, "'Killing the Dream': Chilling Documentary Raises Provocative Questions," *Chicago Tribune*, September 27, 1992.

74. The demonstration in support of Aristide was described in Seth Faison Jr., "Thousands of Haitians Protest Coup," *New York Times*, October 12, 1991. Randall Robinson discussed his hunger strike in "Haiti at Brink Again—US Owes Help," *Final Call*, February 16, 2004.

75. For discussion of the concessions by Aristide in return for US support of his return to Haiti, see Hallward, *Damming the Flood*, 46–61, and Dubois, *Haiti*, 363.

76. "Testimony of Former President William J. Clinton," in *Building on Success: New Directions in Global Health*, hearing, US Senate Committee on Foreign Relations, March 10, 2010.

77. Christopher Dodd, quoted in Walt Bogdanich and Jenny Nordberg, "Mixed US Signals Helped Tilt Haiti toward Chaos," *New York Times*, January 29, 2006.

78. For a discussion of the US and international community limiting aid to Haiti by virtue of the Dole Amendment and politically-motivated embargoes, see Vijaya Ramachandran and Julie Walz, *Haiti: Where Has All the Money Gone?* (Washington, DC: Center for Global Development, 2012), 3.

79. A detailed account of the disputed 2000 legislative elections is contained in Hallward, *Damming the Flood*, 78–80.

80. Amy Wilentz (in a 1992 piece for *Reconstruction*), quoted in Noam Chomsky, "Democracy Enhancement," *Z Magazine*, May 1994; available at *www.chomsky.info*.

81. For an account of the blocked IADB loan, see Center for Human Rights and Global Justice (CHRGJ), Partners in Health (PIH), Robert F. Kennedy Memorial Center for Human Rights (RFK Center), and Zanmi Lasante (ZL), *Wòch nan Soley: The Denial of the Right to Water in Haiti* (New York: CHRGJ; Boston: PIH; Washington, DC: RFK Center; Port-au-Prince: ZL, 2008), 10–14, *chrgj.org*.

82. Evan Lyon, in "Partners in Health Physician on Haiti: 'Cholera Will Not Go Away until Underlying Situations That Make People Vulnerable Change,'" interview by Amy Goodman, *Democracy Now!*, October 26, 2010, *www.democracynow.org*.

83. Jean Paul Jacklin, "Chute d'Aristide: Les révélations de Guy Philippe à Signal FM," *Le Matin*, May 27, 2007. English paraphrase in Schuller, *Killing with Kindness*, 159.

84. For an account of the 2004 coup of Jean-Bertrand Aristide, see Robinson, *Unbroken Agony*.

85. Deb Riechmann, "Bush Sends US Marines to Haiti," *Washington Post*, March 1, 2004, *www.washingtonpost.com*.

86. Richard Boucher, quoted in ibid.

87. For further accounts of the actions of the 2004 coup government, see Chapters 3 and 4.

88. Paul Farmer, *Haiti after the Earthquake* (New York: Public Affairs, 2011), 39.

89. For discussions on the disparity of wealth in Haiti, including reporting of the millionaires per capita and 1 percent wealth figures, see Mark Schuller, "Uncertain Ground: Haiti's Earthquake and Its Aftermath," *Huffington Post*, February 15, 2010, *huffingtonpost.com*; Arnaud Robert, "Haiti's 1 Percent: A Look at The Lives of Plenty in the Land of the Poor," *Foreign Policy*, January 12, 2012; and Simon Romero, "Quake Accelerated Chasm That Has Defined Haiti," *New York Times*, March 27, 2010.

90. Hallward, *Damming the Flood*, 3.

91. Mario Joseph discusses the Haitian pattern of coups d'état in Eli, "Mario Joseph."

92. For a discussion of the US interest in supporting the Duvaliers as a hedge against Central American and Caribbean Communism, see Dubois, *Haiti*, 335–37.

93. Carolyn Leitch, "Analysts Upsize Gildan's Targets," *Toronto Globe and Mail*, April 12, 2005.

94. Farmer, *Uses of Haiti*, 348.

95. For a contemporaneous criticism of Human Rights Watch's failure to respond vigorously to the 2004 Haitian coup, see Miguel Tinker Salas, Gregory Wilpert, and Greg Grandin, *Critics Respond to Human Rights Watch's Defense of Venezuela Report*, (New York: North American Congress on Latin America, 2009). ("The atrocities in Haiti did not prompt Human Rights Watch to hold major press conferences, publish op-eds in the Washington Post, or undertake any of the other high profile media or lobbying campaigns that it has taken against the government of Venezuela. This was true even while prominent members and supporters of Haiti's constitutional government were being held in jail as political prisoners.")

96. Maxine Waters, quoted in allie123, "The Earthquake Didn't Kill Him the System Did, Loresca's Story: 9 Months after EQ," *Daily Kos* (blog), October 12, 2010, *www.dailykos.com*.

97. "WikiLeaks Haiti: *The Nation* Partners with *Haïti Liberté* on Release of Secret Haiti Cables," *Nation*, June 1, 2011.

98. Ives and Herz, "WikiLeaks Haiti: The Aristide Files."

99. Ibid.

100. Dan Coughlin and Kim Ives, "WikiLeaks Haiti: The PetroCaribe Files," *Nation*, June 1, 2011.

101. David E. Lindwall, quoted in Dan Coughlin and Kim Ives, "Let Them Live on $3 a Day," *Nation*, June 1, 2011.

102. Nicholas Casey, "US Senator Warns Aid to Haiti is at Risk," *Wall Street Journal*, July 22, 2010; and Reuters, "Lawmakers Urge Clinton to Ensure Haiti Elections are Inclusive," *New York Times*, October 8, 2010.

103. Quoted in Dan Coughlin and Kim Ives, "WikiLeaks Haiti: Cable Depicts Fraudulent Election," *Nation*, June 8, 2011.

104. Ibid.

105. The Center for Economic and Policy Research findings on the 2010–2011 elections were reported in Mark Weisbrot and Jake Johnston, "Haiti's Fatally Flawed Election," in Schuller and Morales, *Tectonic Shifts*, 199–204.

106. Transparency International, *Corruption Perceptions Index 2012*, December 5, 2012, *cpi.transparency.org*.

107. Jacqueline Charles and Jay Weaver, "Miami Bribery Probe Zeroes In on Haiti's Ex-Leader Aristide," *Miami Herald*, March 3, 2012.

108. Quoted in Gina Athena Ulysse, "Why Haiti Needs New Narratives Now More Than Ever," in Schuller and Morales, *Tectonic Shifts*, 241.

109. Ibid.

110. David Brooks, "The Underlying Tragedy," *New York Times*, January 14, 2010.

111. "Pat Robertson Says Haiti Paying for 'Pact to the Devil,'" CNN, January 13, 2010, *www.cnn.com*.

112. Abe Sauer, "Our Government-Funded Mission to Make Haiti Christian: Your Tax Dollars, Billy Graham's Son, Monsanto and Sarah Palin," *Awl*, January 20, 2011. Some commentators see widespread hostility toward Vodou as being a motivator for many international interventions that have been particularly harmful to Haiti: "The attacks on Vodou practice,

desecration of temples and killing of priests can't be separated from the vision of a new sani-
tized culture that the United States, Canada, and other places have for Haiti. . . . There is
something about Haiti that cannot be ignored: it is the most black, the most African-based
peasantry in the Caribbean. There's a strong element of racism here, and a much larger
attempt to destroy a unique, vibrant, and radical culture." Dayan, "Secret History."

113. Ivan W. Miller, quoted in Dubois, *Haiti*, 237.
114. John Russell, quoted in Dubois, *Haiti*, 237.
115. Lawrence Harrison, "Voodoo Politics," *Atlantic Monthly*, June 1993, 101–2.
116. Jared Diamond, *Collapse: How Societies Choose to Fail* (New York: Viking, 2005), 333.
117. Jared Diamond, "Romney Hasn't Done His Homework," *New York Times*, August 1, 2012.
118. Diamond, *Collapse*, 336.
119. Ulysse, "Why Haiti Needs New Narratives," 242.
120. Farmer, *Uses of Haiti*, 293.
121. Robinson, *Unbroken Agony*, 26.
122. For another critique of the US involvement in the Haitian elections of 2010 and 2011,
see IJDH et al., "Haitian and International Organizations Call on US Administration
to Support Genuinely 'Free, Fair and Credible' Elections in Haiti," statement, February
1, 2011; available at *www.lawg.org/storage/documents/Haiti/Statement_on_Haiti_
Elections_020111_FINAL-1.pdf.*
123. "Twin Parish Relationships," Parish Twinning Program of the Americas, accessed November
25, 2013, *www.parishprogram.org.*
124. "Haiti," St. Thomas Aquinas Church and School, April 4, 2012, *staindy.org.*

CHAPTER 8

1.   Peter Singer explains this hypothetical in "The Drowning Child and the Expanding Circle,"
New Internationalist, April 1997.
2.   Ibid.
3.   Steven Pinker, *The Better Angels of Our Nature: Why Violence Has Declined* (New York:
Viking, 2011).
4.   Lynn Hunt, *Inventing Human Rights: A History* (New York: Norton, 2007), 28–29.
5.   Eyal Press discussed many of these studies on empathy in *Beautiful Souls* (New York: Farrar,
Straus and Giroux, 2012).
6.   Christopher Browning, *Ordinary Men* (New York: HarperCollins, 1992).
7.   Stanley Milgram, *Obedience to Authority* (New York: Harper and Row, 1974).
8.   Joshua Greene et al., "An fMRI Investigation of Emotional Management in Moral
Judgment," *Science*, September 24, 2001, 2105–8.
9.   Robert Jay Lifton, *The Broken Connection: On Death and the Continuity of Life* (Arlington,
VA: American Psychiatric Publishers, 1983), 144.
10. Paul Slovic, "'If I Look at the Mass I Will Never Act': Psychic Numbing and Genocide," 2
Judgment and Decision Making 79–95 (April 2007), *journal.sjdm.org.*
11. Some of the studies showing understanding and empathy negatively influenced by the
number of impacted persons cited include Tehila Kogut and Ilana Ritov, "The Singularity
of Identified Victims in Separate and Joint Evaluations," 97 *Organizational Behavior and
Human Decision Processes* 106–16 (2005), and Joshua Susskind, Kristin Maurer, Vinita

Thakkar, David L. Hamilton, and Jeffrey W. Sherman, "Perceiving Individuals and Groups: Expectancies, Dispositional Inferences, and Causal Attributions," 76 *Journal of Personality and Social Psychology* 181–91 (1999).

12. "Quotes Falsely Attributed to Mother Teresa and Significantly Paraphrased Versions or Personal Interpretations of Statements That Are Not Her Authentic Words," *Mother Teresa of Calcutta Center*, last updated July 19, 2010, *www.motherteresa.org.*

13. Ibid. "Human beings with the tears dried off" is from S. Slovic and P. Slovic, "Numbers and Nerves: Toward an Affective Apprehension of Environmental Risk," 13 *Whole Terrain* 14–18 (2004).

14. Slovic, "If I Look."

15. Adam Smith, *The Theory of Moral Sentiments* (London: A. Millar, 1759).

16. Barbara Kingsolver, *High Tide in Tucson: Essays from Now or Never* (New York: Harper, 1996), 231–32.

17. For the social movement theory of framing, see Chapter 3 generally, and Robert Benford and David A. Snow, "Framing Process and Social Movements: An Overview and Assessment," 26 *Annual Review of Sociology* 615 (2000).

18. Darren Hawkins and Wade Jacoby, "Partial Compliance: A Comparison of the European and Inter-American American Courts for Human Rights," 25 *American Political Science Association* (August 18, 2008).

19. Hunt, *Inventing Human Rights*, 29.

20. Gary Haugen and Victor Boutros, "And Justice for All: Enforcing Human Rights for the World's Poor," *Foreign Affairs*, May/June 2010, *www.foreignaffairs.com.*

21. Henry David Thoreau, *The Journal of Henry David Thoreau* (Layton, UT: Gibbs Smith 1984), 22.

22. An earlier version of this section was published as Fran Quigley, "Will the UN Finally Take Responsibility for the Cholera Outbreak in Haiti?" *Indianapolis Star*, October 22, 2013, *www.indystar.com.*

23. An overview of the Swiss Banks settlement with Holocaust survivors is contained on the official website for the US District Court for the Eastern District of New York case, *Swiss Banks Settlement: In re Holocaust Victim Assets Litigation*, last updated November 6, 2013, *www.swissbankclaims.com.* On the Union Carbide decision, see "*Bano v. Union Carbide* Case History," Earth Rights International, accessed December 15, 2013, *www.earthrights.org.* On the claims regarding African American slavery, see Christina Lutz, "The Death Knell Tolls for African American Reparations in In re African American Slave Descendants Litigation," 3 *Seventh Circuit Review* 532 (2008).

24. Evan Lyon, quoted in Kim Ives, "Lawyers for Haiti Cholera Victims Tell UN: 'Immunity Cannot Mean Impunity,'" *Haïti Liberté*, April 11, 2012, *www.haiti-liberte.com.*

25. The estimate was attributed to the Centers for Disease Control in Editorial, "Haiti's Cholera Crisis," *New York Times*, May 12, 2012.

26. Evan Lyon, in *Fight the Outbreak: Cholera in Haiti and the United Nations*, produced by the New Media Advocacy Project for IJDH, 2012, *vimeo.com/36517487.*

27. "Truth out, Dying Season in," 70 *Haiti Support Group Briefing* 1–2 (April 2012); available at *www.ijdh.org.*

28. The 2002 study was reported in D. C. Esty and P.K. Cornelius, eds., *Environmental Performance Measurement: Global Report 2001–2002* (New York: United Nations, 2002).

29. The 2007 study was cited in Center for Human Rights and Global Justice (CHRGJ), Partners in Health (PIH), Robert F. Kennedy Memorial Center for Human Rights (RFK Center), and Zanmi Lasante (ZL), *Wòch nan Soley: The Denial of the Right to Water in Haiti* (New York: CHRGJ; Boston: PIH; Washington, DC: RFK Center; Port-au-Prince: ZL, 2008), 19–39, *chrgj.org*.

30. Oliver Stone, "End Haiti's Killer Cholera Epidemic—UN Action Now!," petition (posted by Robert Naiman), Avaaz, December 5, 2012, *avaaz.org*.

31. UN News Service, "UN Launches New Initiative to Eliminate Cholera in Haiti and Dominican Republic," UN News Centre, December 11, 2012, *www.un.org*.

32. Yann Libessart, quoted in Isabeau Doucet, "Haiti's Cholera Crisis," *Nation*, March 20, 2013.

33. Trenton Daniel, "UN Official Makes Rare Case for Compensation for Haiti Cholera Victims," *Huffington Post*, October 8, 2013, *www.huffingtonpost.com*.

34. Roger Annis, "Stephen Lewis, Canada's Former UN Ambassador, Says the World Body Must be Accountable for Cholera in Haiti," Canada Haiti Action Network, October 14, 2013, *canadahaitiaction.ca*.

35. Center for Law and Global Justice, *Freedom of the Press in Haiti: The Chilling Effects on Journalists Critical of the Government* (San Francisco: University of San Francisco School of Law, 2012), *www.usfca.edu*.

36. Michel Forst, quoted in Jonathan Katz, "Haiti's Inconvenient Truth: Was a U.N. Diplomat Pushed Out of His Position for Airing Port-au-Prince's Dirty Laundry in Public?," *Foreign Policy*, April 4, 2013, *www.foreignpolicy.com*. Forst's statement was read by a translator in "Interactive Dialogue with Independent Expert on the Situation of Human Rights in Haiti" (webcast), United Nations, March 19, 2013, *webtv.un.org*.

37. Editorial, "To Rebuild Haiti, Restoring Democracy Is a Must," *Bloomberg View*, April 7, 2013.

38. Jacqueline Charles, "Arrest of Haiti Government Critic Triggers Protests," *Miami Herald*, October 23, 2013.

39. Other Worlds, "Human Rights Groups Petition Inter-American Commission to Protect Threatened Haitian Lawyer," September 15, 2013, *www.otherworldsarepossible.org*.

40. Francklyn B. Geffrard, "Haiti: Political Assassination? Suspicious Death of Judge Who Called for Prosecution of Presidential Family," Center for Research on Globalization, July 19, 2013, *www.globalresearch.ca*. IJDH and BAI's request that the Inter-American Commission on Human Rights investigate Judge Jean Serge Joseph's death and recent attorney arrests is available at *www.ijdh.org*.

41. *Baseball in the Time of Cholera*, directed by David Darg and Bryn Mooser, executive produced by Olivia Wilde and Elon Musk, 2012; available at *www.undeny.org*.

Index

Photographs are in an unpaginated gallery following page 110.
Entries refer to photographs by the figure number in bold (e.g., **fig. 1**).